GRASSROOTS INNOVATION MOVEMENTS

Innovation is increasingly invoked by policy elites and business leaders as vital for tackling global challenges like sustainable development. Often overlooked, however, is the fact that networks of community groups, activists and researchers have been innovating grassroots solutions for social justice and environmental sustainability for decades. Unencumbered by disciplinary boundaries, policy silos or institutional logics, these 'grassroots innovation movements' identify issues and questions neglected by formal science, technology and innovation organizations. Grassroots solutions arise in unconventional settings through unusual combinations of people, ideas and tools.

This book examines six diverse grassroots innovation movements in India, South America and Europe, situating them in their particular dynamic historical contexts. Analysis explains why each movement frames innovation and development differently, resulting in a variety of strategies. The book explores the spaces where each of these movements has grown, or attempted to do so. It critically examines the pathways they have developed for grassroots innovation and the challenges and limitations confronting their approaches.

With mounting pressure for social justice in an increasingly unequal world, policy makers are exploring how to foster more inclusive innovation. In this context grassroots experiences take on added significance. This book provides timely and relevant ideas, analysis and recommendations for activists, policy makers, students and scholars interested in encounters between innovation, development and social movements.

Adrian Smith is Professor of Technology and Society at the Science Policy Research Unit, and a researcher with the STEPS Centre (Social, Technological and Environmental Pathways to Sustainability), University of Sussex, UK.

Mariano Fressoli is assistant researcher at the National Scientific and Technical Research Council (CONICET, Argentina) and researcher at CENIT (Centro de Investigaciones para la Transformación) and STEPS Latin America.

Dinesh Abrol is Professor at the Institute for Studies in Industrial Development (ISID), New Delhi, India, and a Visiting Faculty with the Transdisciplinary Research Cluster on Sustainability Studies at Jawarhalal Nehru University. He was previously a Chief Scientist at the Council for Scientific and Industrial Research's National Institute of Science, Technology and Development Studies, India.

Elisa Arond is a PhD candidate at the Graduate School of Geography, Clark University, USA, and is also affiliated with the STEPS Centre, University of Sussex, UK.

Adrian Ely is Senior Lecturer at the Science Policy Research Unit and Deputy Director of the STEPS Centre (Social, Technological and Environmental Pathways to Sustainability), University of Sussex, UK.

Pathways to Sustainability Series

This book series addresses core challenges around linking science and technology and environmental sustainability with poverty reduction and social justice. It is based on the work of the Social, Technological and Environmental Pathways to Sustainability (STEPS) Centre, a major investment of the UK Economic and Social Research Council (ESRC). The STEPS Centre brings together researchers at the Institute of Development Studies (IDS) and SPRU (Science and Technology Policy Research) at the University of Sussex with a set of partner institutions in Africa, Asia and Latin America.

Series Editors:

Ian Scoones and Andy Stirling
STEPS Centre at the University of Sussex

Editorial Advisory Board:

Steve Bass, Wiebe E. Bijker, Victor Galaz, Wenzel Geissler, Katherine Homewood, Sheila Jasanoff, Melissa Leach, Colin McInnes, Suman Sahai, Andrew Scott

Titles in this series include:

Dynamic Sustainabilities
Technology, environment, social justice
Melissa Leach, Ian Scoones and Andy Stirling

Avian Influenza
Science, policy and politics
Edited by Ian Scoones

Rice Biofortification
Lessons for global science and development
Sally Brooks

Epidemics
Science, governance and social justice
Edited by Sarah Dry and Melissa Leach

Regulating Technology
International harmonization and local realities
By Patrick van Zwanenberg, Adrian Ely, Adrian Smith

The Politics of Asbestos
Understandings of risk, disease and protest
By Linda Waldman

Contested Agronomy
Agricultural research in a changing world
James Sumberg and John Thompson

Transforming Health Markets in Asia and Africa
Improving quality and access for the poor
Edited by Gerald Bloom, Barun Kanjilal, Henry Lucas and David H. Peters

Pastoralism and Development in Africa
Dynamic change at the margins
Edited by Ian Scoones, Andy Catley and Jeremy Lind

The Politics of Green Transformations
Ian Scoones, Melissa Leach and Peter Newell

Carbon Conflicts and Forest Landscapes in Africa
Edited by Melissa Leach and Ian Scoones

Governing Agricultural Sustainability
Global lessons from GM crops
Phil Macnaghten and Susana Carro-Ripalda

Gender Equality and Sustainable Development
Edited by Melissa Leach

Adapting to Climate Uncertainty in African Agriculture
Narratives and knowledge politics
Stephen Whitfield

One Health
Science, politics and zoonotic disease in Africa
Edited by Kevin Bardosh

Grassroots Innovation Movements
Adrian Smith, Mariano Fressoli, Dinesh Abrol, Elisa Arond and Adrian Ely

GRASSROOTS INNOVATION MOVEMENTS

Adrian Smith, Mariano Fressoli, Dinesh Abrol, Elisa Arond and Adrian Ely

Routledge
Taylor & Francis Group
LONDON AND NEW YORK

earthscan
from Routledge

First published 2017
by Routledge
2 Park Square, Milton Park, Abingdon, Oxon OX14 4RN

and by Routledge
711 Third Avenue, New York, NY 10017

Routledge is an imprint of the Taylor & Francis Group, an informa business

© 2017 Adrian Smith, Mariano Fressoli, Dinesh Abrol, Elisa Arond and Adrian Ely

The right of Adrian Smith, Mariano Fressoli, Dinesh Abrol, Elisa Arond and Adrian Ely to be identified as authors of this work has been asserted by them in accordance with sections 77 and 78 of the Copyright, Designs and Patents Act 1988.

All rights reserved. No part of this book may be reprinted or reproduced or utilised in any form or by any electronic, mechanical, or other means, now known or hereafter invented, including photocopying and recording, or in any information storage or retrieval system, without permission in writing from the publishers.

Trademark notice: Product or corporate names may be trademarks or registered trademarks, and are used only for identification and explanation without intent to infringe.

British Library Cataloguing-in-Publication Data
A catalogue record for this book is available from the British Library

Library of Congress Cataloging-in-Publication Data
Names: Smith, Adrian, 1948- author.
Title: Grassroots innovation movements / Adrian Smith, Mariano Fressoli, Dinesh Abrol, Elisa Arond and Adrian Ely.
Description: Abingdon, Oxon; New York, NY: Routledge, 2017. | Includes bibliographical references.
Identifiers: LCCN 2016011363 | ISBN 9781138901216 (hb) | ISBN 9781138901223 (pb) | ISBN 9781315697888 (ebk)
Subjects: LCSH: Technological innovations—Social aspects—Case studies. | Social movements—Case studies. | Environmentalism—Case studies.
Classification: LCC HM846.S57 2017 | DDC 303.48/4—dc23
LC record available at https://lccn.loc.gov/2016011363

ISBN: 978-1-138-90121-6 (hbk)
ISBN: 978-1-138-90122-3 (pbk)
ISBN: 978-1-315-69788-8 (ebk)

Typeset in Bembo Std
by Swales & Willis Ltd, Exeter, Devon, UK

Printed and bound in Great Britain by
TJ International Ltd, Padstow, Cornwall

"The book gives a fresh look at the fundamentals of grassroots innovation, re-visiting old and recent themes with novel and challenging approaches through a rich and diverse collection of stories that explore initiatives to build pathways for grassroots innovation, their achievements and limitations."

(Dr Hebe Vessuri, Senior Researcher, UNAM-CENPAT/CONICET-IVIC, Mexico, Argentina and Venezuela)

"Innovation can often appear remote: something that others do, and present it to us as the latest, must-have technology. This book suggests a different reality. We are all innovators: individuals and communities, rich and poor, north and south. We must recognise, nurture and harness this wealth of innovation potential, and help ensure all people can access, adapt and use the technologies they need to live a healthy, meaningful and sustainable life."

(Amber Meikle, Technology Justice campaign, Practical Action)

"This book brings a unique and valuable comparative perspective to the study of technology and social movements. From India to South America and Europe, Grassroots Innovation takes us on a global tour of design, innovation, and democracy. The book's detailed case studies will appeal to a wide range of readers, from first-time students to seasoned experts and designers."

(David Hess, Professor of Sociology, Vanderbilt University and author of *Alternative Pathways in Science and Industry*)

"The value of this book lies in its laying out for us the not so visible world of grassroots innovations, where peoples' innovations, not the big industrial innovations, are treated as mainstream technologies. There is another important insight. That the social movements linked to the promotion of such innovations, apart from solving real problems, are addressing broader societal dichotomies and developing an alternative political paradigm. The grassroots innovation movement empowers communities by inviting their participation in the creation of increasingly relevant social technologies."

(Dr Suman Sahai, founder Chairperson, Gene Campaign, Delhi)

CONTENTS

List of tables x
Acknowledgements xi
List of abbreviations and acronyms xiii

1 Introducing grassroots innovation movements 1

2 An analytical framework for studying grassroots innovation movements 16

3 Socially useful production 32

4 The appropriate technology movement in South America 56

5 People's Science Movements 80

6 Hackerspaces, fablabs and makerspaces 100

7 The Social Technology Network 123

8 The Honey Bee Network 145

9 Grassroots innovation movements: lessons for theory and practice 165

10 Conclusions 191

References *199*
Index *215*

TABLES

1.1	The worlds of grassroots innovation movements and institutions for science, technology and innovation	7
4.1	AT organizations/centres in South America	61
5.1	Challenges addressed by People's Science Movements	81
9.1	A summary of the context and framings for grassroots innovation in each case study movement	167
9.2	Spaces and strategies for grassroots innovation	179
9.3	Insertion and mobilization strategies for grassroots innovation movements	183
9.4	Framings, spaces and strategies, and pathways for grassroots innovation movements	186
9.5	Contributions to development pathways coming from grassroots innovation movements	187

ACKNOWLEDGEMENTS

Many individuals gave freely of their time and experience during the course of the research project that informed this book, either via interviews, focus groups, workshops, meetings or other forums, as well as reviewing and commenting on earlier drafts of chapters. All were tremendously kind and open, despite their demanding work and other calls on their time. Librarians, archivists and others provided important materials, as well as space to think and write. Naming people specifically opens the dilemma of knowing where to stop. And since the list is far too long for a just place to stop, we thank you all collectively for your wonderful contributions, and acknowledge how completely dependent we were upon you, and stress how grateful we are for allowing the research to happen. We hope the results prove mutually helpful, especially to the grassroots innovation movements themselves, without whose trust and cooperation the research would have been impossible.

The book is the product of an international research project led by the STEPS Centre co-hosted by the Science Policy Research Unit and the Institute of Development Studies at the University of Sussex. STEPS stands for Social, Technological and Environmental Pathways to Sustainability, and the Centre acts as a hub for a wide range of international research and engagement collaborations, thanks to core funding from the Economic and Social Research Council. We are very grateful to our STEPS colleagues and collaborators for their support and inputs to this project. More information about STEPS can be found at www.steps-centre.org.

Harriet Dudley at the STEPS Centre deserves particular mention for her support throughout, and for keeping us and the project going by organizing meetings, travel, visits and contracts, and generally being brilliant. Nathan Oxley has also been an inspired and inspiring contributor to the work. He has helped with our communications and public engagement in the project, and in so doing contributed important reflections upon what we were doing. In a similar vein, we are grateful to colleagues at our home institutions, the Science Policy Research Unit, Fundación Cenit, Centre for Studies in Science Policy and Clark University, for providing such a convivial community in which to work.

Some of the research reported in this book benefits from associated projects with colleagues who were not part of the book writing. In particular, we thank Hernán Thomas and his team at the Universidad Nacional de Quilmes, Rafael Dias at Universidade Estadual de Campinas in Brazil and Sabine Hielscher and Georgina Voss at the Science Policy Research Unit. These associated projects were supported by the International Development Research Centre, the Economic and Social Research Council's Centre for Innovation and Energy Demand, and the TRANSIT project (Transformative Social Innovation Theory) under the European Union's Framework Seven Programme.

The book has been written collectively. It is not an edited volume. We have learnt a lot together during this project and have had the privilege to be able to organize many face-to-face discussions and side-by-side research activities. Reflecting case study responsibilities, however, the analysis for the chapters about each movement was led by one of the team, but sometimes written in partnership with another team member, and then commented upon by the whole team. Dinesh Abrol led the Honey Bee Network and People's Science Movement chapters, with help from Adrian Ely. Mariano Fressoli and Elisa Arond led jointly the appropriate technology chapter. Mariano Fressoli led the Social Technology Network chapter. Adrian Smith led the socially useful production and hackerspace, fablabs and makerspaces chapters. All other chapters were written jointly. They were then brought into publishable shape thanks to the copy-editing of Monica Allen, and the patient support of Helen Bell and Margaret Farrelly at Routledge.

It has been a great experience. We hope the results prove worthwhile and helpful for others, just as many people were so helpful to us.

Adrian Smith, Mariano Fressoli,
Dinesh Abrol, Elisa Arond, Adrian Ely
Brighton, Buenos Aires, Delhi, Bogotá
January 2016

ABBREVIATIONS AND ACRONYMS

Abong	Brazilian Association of Non-governmental Organizations
AIPSN	All India Peoples Science Network
AT	appropriate technology
BBF	Bank of Brazil Foundation
BoP	bottom of the pyramid
CAITS	Centre for Alternative Industrial and Technological Systems
CECITEB	Centro Científico Tecnológico Barrancas
CERD	Centre for Ecology and Rural Development
CET	Centro de Educación Tecnológica
CETAAR	Centro de Estudios sobre Tecnologías Apropiadas de Argentina
CETAL	Centro de Estudios sobre Tecnología Apropiada para América Latina
CETEC	Fundação Centro Tecnológico de Minas Gerais
CEUTA	Centro Uruguayo de Tecnología Apropiada
CIAL	Corporación de Investigación en Agricultura Alternativa
CIAT	Centro Internacional para la Agricultura Tropical
CLADE	Latin America Consortium of Agroecology and Development
CNPq	National Council of Science and Technology Development
COP	Conference of the Parties to the UN Framework Convention on Climate Change
COSTFORD	Centre of Science and Technology of Rural Development
CSIR	Council of Scientific and Industrial Research
CSSTD	Centre for Studies in Science, Technology and Development
CTA	Centro de Tecnología Apropiada, Catholic University
CTD	Centre for Technology and Development
DARPA	Defense Advance Research Projects Agency
DIY	do-it-yourself
DSF	Delhi Science Forum

DST	Department of Science and Technology (India)
ENDA	Environmental Development Action in the Third World
ESPRIT	European Strategic Programme on Research in Information Technology
FEDETA	Fundación Ecuatoriana de Tecnología Apropiada
FINEP	Financiadora de Estudos e Projetos
GIAN	Grassroots Innovation Augmentation Network
GLC	Greater London Council
GLEB	Greater London Enterprise Board
HBN	Honey Bee Network
IAAC	Institute of Advanced Architecture Catalunya
ICTs	information and communications technologies
IIM-A	Indian Institute of Management Ahmedabad
IIT	Indian Institute of Technology
IPRs	intellectual property rights
IRTC	Integrated Rural Technology Centre
ITDG	Intermediate Technology Development Group
ITS	Institute of Social Technology
KSSP	Kerala Sasthra Sahithya Parishad, Kerala Science Literature Movement
KVIC	Khadhi and Village Industries Commission
LEEN	London Energy and Employment Network
LIN	London Innovation Network
LNTN	London New Technology Network
MIT	Massachusetts Institute of Technology
MPVS	Madhya Pradesh Vigyan Sabha
MVIF	Micro Venture Innovation Fund
NELP	North East London Polytechnic
NGO	non-governmental organization
NIF	National Innovation Foundation
NWGPL	National Working Group on Patent Laws
OECD	Organisation for Economic Co-operation and Development
P1MC	One Million Cisterns Programme
PAIS	Sustainable and Integrated Agro-Ecological Production
PIC	prior informed consent
PPST	Patriotic and People-oriented Science and Technology Group
PSM	People's Science Movement
PT	Workers' Party (Brazil)
PTTA	Appropriate Technologies Transfer Programme Brazil
R&D	research and development
RTS	Rede de Tecnologia Social
S&T	science and technology
SEBRAE	Serviço Brasileiro de Apoio às Micro e Pequenas Empresas
SEMTA	Servicios Múltiples de Tecnologías Apropiadas
SENAES	Solidarity Economy Secretariat
SIDBI	Small Industries Development Bank of India

SOPPECOM	Society for Promoting Participatory Ecosystem Management
SRISTI	Society for Research and Initiatives for Sustainable Technologies and Institutions
SSD	Science and Society Division
ST	social technology
STD	Society for Technology and Development
STEPS	Social, Technological and Environmental Pathways to Sustainability
STN	Social Technology Network
TRIPS	Trade-Related Aspects of Intellectual Property Rights
UDAP	Unit for the Development of Alternative Products
UMIST	University of Manchester Institute of Science and Technology
UN	United Nations
UNDP	United Nations Development Programme
UNEP	United Nations Environment Programme
WIPO	World Intellectual Property Organization

1
INTRODUCING GRASSROOTS INNOVATION MOVEMENTS

In August 2015, while we were writing this book, a group of sustainability activists were gathering in the grounds of a borrowed château on the outskirts of Paris. They were intent upon 'eco-hacking' the future. What this meant was turning the château into a temporary innovation camp, equipped with the tools for developing a variety of technologies of practical and symbolic value for low-carbon living. These prototypes made use of open source designs and instructions in order that others can access, adapt and make use of these developments. The activity of the camp was publicized widely through social media and drew the attention of many commentators and even senior politicians (see www.poc21.cc for examples).

The camp was called POC21. Its location and timing were significant. Paris was gearing up to host in December 2015: the 21st Conference of the Parties to the United Nations Framework Convention on Climate Change (COP21), and the latest meeting of governments and global elites figuring out how to address climate change. Meanwhile, POC21 stands for, and seeks, a 'proof of concept' for an alternative approach. POC21 brought together on site over a hundred makers, designers, engineers, scientists and geeks, drawn from various international activist networks, and many more who joined in virtually over social media, or visited, and committed to prototyping for a fossil-free, zero-waste society. The designs and hacks they developed collaboratively ranged from low-cost wind turbines, to facilities for urban farming, to a 3D-printed bottle-top water filtration device; from easy-build cargo bikes, to open source energy monitors, to permaculture; and from low-consumption recirculating showers, to portable solar power packs. Their alternative approach is based on the premise that people at the grassroots level already have the ideas, knowledge, tools and capabilities required to create their own innovative solutions to climate change and sustainable development. Drawing upon practical initiatives connected to a variety of open source, collaborative peer production networks globally, the aim at POC21 is to mobilize a mainstreaming of these ready-made solutions. Immediately after their five-week camp, the organizers of POC21 set out the follow-up challenge as 'how can we turn this momentum into a sustainable movement' (email correspondence, 30 September 2015).

This book argues that a movement already exists. POC21 taps into increasing interest among growing groups and networks of people for directly hacking, making and modifying the world they find around them, and refashioning it towards more inclusive, fairer and sustainable goals. Furthermore, POC21 connects unconsciously to a longer tradition of subverting high-level summitry in order to raise awareness of grassroots solutions. These subversions go right back to the first United Nations (UN) Summit on the Human Environment in Stockholm in 1972. At the Stockholm summit, a group called Powwow convened activists who emphasized their argument, for radically different development alternatives to the political and economic interests of the industrialists and policymakers orchestrating the main summit, with the organization of a demonstration of alternative technologies emblematic of the futures Powwow wanted (Boyle and Harper, 1976; Faramelli, 1972). Although largely forgotten now, the legacy of Powwow, as with POC21, can be seen as one of a multitude of demonstrations of grassroots innovation arising around the world over decades, and whose associated social movements have bequeathed practices as varied as wind energy and participatory design, agroecology and eco-housing, as well as an insistent idea that alternative forms of innovation and sustainable developments are necessary and possible. POC21 was another moment galvanizing grassroots innovation for sustainable developments.

Opening this book with examples such as POC21 and Powwow might give the impression that grassroots innovation for sustainable developments is predominantly a Northern environmentalist concern. Far from it! In the same year that Rachel Carson's *Silent Spring* (1962) highlighted alarming industrial contamination and environmental decline, and became catalytic for Northern environmentalism, activists in Kerala launched Kerala Sasthra Sahithya Parishad (KSSP, lit. Kerala Science Literature Forum), a programme for making science and technology work for the needs and priorities of local communities. Initially, KSSP involved a group of science writers and teachers who published textbooks in their local language, aiming to make science and technology more widely available and socially relevant to grassroots communities, rather than to the plans of elite industrial modernizers. Similar groups formed across India and joined together into the People's Science Movement. Their vision was to re-imagine and reorientate science and technology towards the lived experiences and knowledges of local communities. Over the years, the movement has dedicated itself to grassroots activism and improvements in people's lives that work towards different kinds of sustainable developments compared both to the high modernist ambitions of the Indian state and to Gandhian village self-sufficiency.

High-level summitry provides arenas for grassroots innovators from the global South too (Letty et al., 2012). Examples in agroecology, housing, energy and recycling, developed through initiatives such as the Social Technology Network in Brazil, were displayed at the People's Summit in Flamengo Park at the Rio+20

Summit. Activists in these networks consciously draw upon lessons from experiences from appropriate technology in South America two decades earlier; and they connect with wider social movements today to press for a different kind of development. A thorough critique of industrialization models offered by elites was an important part of the Powwow agenda in Stockholm. Like POC21, the Social Technology Network and many others since, Powwow recognized that solutions had to work in diverse circumstances. But what all these grassroots innovation movements share is a commitment to helping people access tools for building alternatives.

The aim in this book is to make grassroots innovation movements more visible, and to learn from their experiences, in order that people can better understand, appreciate and engage with them in the pursuit of sustainable developments. We do this by analysing six case studies from different places and different times:

- the movement for socially useful production (UK, 1976–1986)
- the appropriate technology movement (South America, 1970s and 1980s)
- the People's Science Movement (India, 1960s to present)
- hackerspaces, fablabs and makerspaces (international, 2000s to present)
- the Social Technology Network (Brazil, 2000s to present)
- the Honey Bee Network (India, 1990s to present).

Across these cases, we attempt to identify within their diverse situations some common causes and deep-seated challenges that other grassroots innovation movements might recognize and connect with. Such possibilities will inevitably play out differently in different contexts, but perhaps with greater facility thanks to learning with others from elsewhere. We will explain the choice of these cases and our approach later in this chapter. For now, we wish to elaborate a little more upon what we mean by grassroots innovation movements and upon some of the challenges of studying their pathways to sustainable developments.

Radical roots and alternative routes

Throughout the history of social movements for both environmentalism and development, there has existed an associated undercurrent of practical grassroots innovation committed to values of social justice and environmentally sustainable developments (Hess, 2007; Rist, 2011; Schumacher, 1973; Smith, 2005; Thackara, 2015). In North and South, in cities and rural settings, networks of activists, development workers, community groups and neighbours have been working with people to generate bottom-up solutions for sustainable developments; solutions that respond to the local situation and the interests and values of the communities involved; and where those communities have control over the processes involved and the outcomes. Initiatives have flourished, and struggled, in sectors as diverse as water and sanitation, housing and habitats, food and agriculture, energy, mobility, manufacturing, health, education, communications and many other spheres of activity. Whether born of material and economic necessity, or motivated by social issues marginalized by the conventional innovation systems of states and markets, networks of people promote and coordinate alternative activity attentive to these needs and issues. They develop discourse and mobilize supportive resources among wider publics. It is this activity that constitutes what we mean by grassroots innovation movements and gives us our working definition (see also Gupta et al., 2003; Seyfang and Smith, 2007).

Grassroots innovation proceeds through groups and activities different from mainstream innovation processes in institutions such as universities, public research and development (R&D) labs and innovation departments at companies; and which have traditionally networked around formally organized research institutions. Innovation policy aims are generally expressed as an imperative to catch up with or keep up with an apparently universal techno-economic frontier, typically based in information technology, biotechnology and nanotechnology (Freeman, 1992; Perez, 1983). Furthermore, mainstream institutions for science, technology and innovation are generally aimed at nurturing partnerships between firms and science and technology institutes, fostering entrepreneurship and incentivizing returns on investment in innovation activities whose outputs boost competitiveness and economic growth.

In contrast, our interest in grassroots innovation movements involves studying how grassroots groups understand and mobilize around questions of local development. What are alluring about grassroots innovation movements are claims that they involve a base of local actors and therefore different forms of knowledge, including community-based and indigenous knowledge and the knowledge of the lay public in the process of innovation. Unconcerned and unconstrained by disciplinary boundaries or institutional constraints, movements can identify issues and questions that are not usually regarded by science, technology and innovation institutions, and they can search for solutions differently too. However, none of this is automatic or assured. Grassroots innovation is hard work; participation requires patience and stamina, and practical dilemmas challenge cherished values, as do structural disadvantages presented by prevailing political economies and institutions. The extent to which the grassroots innovation movements enable creativity, inclusion and the agency of local actors in the complexities of innovation is something that will be explored in this book.

Importantly, among the openings that grassroots innovation movements help cultivate are plural ideas about what constitutes sustainable developments. The global consultation process of the World Commission on Environment and Development in the mid-1980s brought together some of the issues at stake in sustainable developments, and eventually reported with this widely cited definition in 1987:

> Sustainable development is development that meets the needs of the present without compromising the ability of future generations to meet their own needs. It contains within it two key concepts:

- the concept of 'needs', in particular the essential needs of the world's poor, to which overriding priority should be given;
- the idea of limitations imposed by the state of technology and social organization on the environment's ability to meet present and future needs.

(World Commission on Environment and Development, 1987, p. 43)

There is much to debate in this definition. What are essential needs? What is meant by environmental limitations? What is a state of technology? What kinds of developments, and for whom, and why? Who gets to decide these things? Any application of these principles has to grapple with questions of development purposes, directions of innovation and issues of social justice. Looked at dynamically and constructively, calls for sustainable developments simply raise defining questions, without being definitive on the answers. Sustainable development is thus valuable as an essentially contested concept overflowing with normative content (Jacobs, 1999). It is a matter for principled debate and democratic action to figure out how to construct development pathways that express values of environmental integrity and social justice. The pathways to sustainable developments need to be plural (Leach et al., 2010).

To take one illustrative contrast, large solar electricity farms operated by multinational utility companies create quite a different sustainability compared to smaller community cooperatives installing panels in their neighbourhoods (Smith et al., 2015). Questions of distributive and procedural social justice look quite different under each arrangement: who benefits from a hitherto marginally interesting resource such as daylight, made newly valuable by shifting social priorities and technological advances? Why are the benefits of this widely shared resource distributed in particular ways, and why should historically determined access to capital and markets privilege access to this local resource? Pluralist sustainable developments also involve questions of cognitive justice in terms of what kinds of knowledge and experience count in deliberating upon the relative prominence of different criteria for shaping and choosing between solutions. Knowledge about local histories and culture can affect the relative legitimacy and consequences of different developments, compared to, say, the more abstracted cost–benefit knowledge that may count as more legitimate for distant investors and with different interests.

In studying grassroots innovation movements, we are interested in how groups and networks address questions of development, how they seek to express their values in their innovation activities and what shapes the pathways they build through that activity. We do not wish to impose our own definitions of sustainable development, and nor do we intend our comparative study to test who performs best to externally derived criteria. For us, questions of the broader social visions and implications of specific sustainable developments are made richer by attending to grassroots innovation movements working under different conditions and for various purposes in different places. Here are groups of people who are trying to create solutions to challenges as they see them, working to criteria that can differ from mainstream institutions and using novel forms for producing knowledge, appropriating technology and coordinating social organization. It is a matter for politics to arbitrate between whose solutions are 'best', for whom, or in what combination under the circumstances. It is a matter for analysis to understand how grassroots innovation movements provide a source of reflexivity in society, by pointing to the contention and plurality involved in sustainable developments and opening up more spaces for doing the politics of alternative sustainabilities. It is this analysis that we attempt in this book.

Of course, hard-nosed summit negotiators and seasoned observers may well dismiss grassroots initiatives such as POC21 as politically naïve or idealistic. We think such dismissals are too hasty. It is our contention that it is important to recall the grassroots origins of many contemporary sustainability solutions and to take seriously initiatives in that tradition today. Global summitry, intergovernmental agreements and the greening of capital involve institutional representatives locked within a development logic tied to conventional economic growth, deciding what to concede to principles for sustainable development. Frameworks and programmes are developed, and commitments made and funds released, as evident most recently in the Sustainable Development Goals launched in September 2015. But are these declarations and programmes really addressing root causes of problematic development pathways or ameliorating the consequences while continuing along the same pathways? Meanwhile, coming from the grassroots, and evident around the fringes of these big events, are groups of people improvising practical possibilities for sustainable livelihoods as they see them, and informed by values and visions for social futures quite different from top-down measures of economic growth. Who really has the freedom to be innovative here? What happens if we look more widely and more carefully? Grassroots pathways will inevitably have their own drawbacks and shortcomings, but they nevertheless open up debate and ideas about innovation for sustainable developments.

Institutional encounters

Modern science, technology and innovation institutions have historically struggled to recognize other modes of knowledge production, including indigenous and community-based knowledge and non-codified forms of knowledge. Table 1.1 contrasts the worlds of grassroots innovation movements with conventional institutions for developing science, technology and innovation (adapted from Fressoli et al., 2014). We have to be careful here. It is not our intention to create a top-down/bottom-up dichotomy. Indeed moves to more open science and inclusive innovation are blurring the boundaries and making things more porous. As such, what become interesting are the encounters, relationships and possibilities that emerge when grassroots initiative opens up different possible pathways for developments, and how these might interact, challenge and prompt responses in more conventional and institutionalized pathways of development. And, given our focus in grassroots innovation, how the practices developed among grassroots networks

TABLE 1.1 The worlds of grassroots innovation movements and institutions for science, technology and innovation

	Grassroots innovation movements	Science, technology and innovation institutions
Protagonists	Local communities, grassroots activists, civil society organizations, social entrepreneurs, worker cooperatives, NGOs, social movements	Universities, research centres, venture capital, firms, science ministries, entrepreneurs
Priorities	Social values, convivial communities, livelihoods, sustainable developments	Codified knowledge, economic growth, competitiveness
Incentives and drivers	Social need, voluntarism, cooperation	Expert authority, reputation, market demand
Resources	Development assistance, social capital, public finance, grassroots ingenuity, local knowledge, activist organization	Public finance, corporate investment, venture capital, scientific expertise and training
Locations of activity	Villages, factories, neighbourhoods, community projects, social movements	Laboratories, R&D centres, boardrooms, ministries, markets
Typical knowledge forms	Situated knowledge, tacit	Scientific and technical knowledge
Appropriation	Knowledge commons, freely shared practices, activist guidebooks and media	Intellectual property, scientific journals, licensed technologies
Emblematic fields of activity	Agroecology, community health, small-scale renewable energy, housing	Biotechnology, medicine, nanotechnology, geo-engineering

Source: Adapted from Fressoli et al., 2014.

interact with more conventional institutions for science and technology. It is the encounters, intersections and hybrid arrangements between the two worlds in Table 1.1 that interest us as much as any resistance, contestation and countering.

While a strict definition of grassroots innovation sees innovations coming from within local communities (see later), in practice it can also involve actions with and by people working in more conventional science, technology and innovation institutions. As we will see, public programmes can develop to connect the two. At times, grassroots initiatives benefit from the programmes and resources moved by global summits and agreements. Periodically, international programmes such as those for appropriate technology, Local Agenda 21 and inclusive innovation have lifted grassroots innovation up as an object of interest to policymakers (see, e.g. OECD, 2015). Policy and business are again taking notice of this bottom-up innovative activity. Agendas for inclusive innovation, open innovation and social innovation are drawing grassroots innovation to the attention of elite national and international agencies (OECD, 2015; World Bank, 2012). Most recently, fourteen grassroots examples were highlighted by UN Headquarters on 27 September 2015 at its Solutions Summit to accompany the launch of the Sustainable Development Goals and as 'part of a longer-term grassroots effort to lift-up exceptional innovators . . . who are addressing one or more of the seventeen sustainable development goals' (www.solutions-summit.org).

However, precisely because grassroots innovation develops so often as an undercurrent in society, it is usually invisible to elite policymakers, business leaders and professional non-governmental organizations (NGOs). Thus when support does arise, it can be an awkward encounter, orchestrated by elites' assumptions and norms that miss the point motivating the original grassroots innovation movement. It is typical, for example, for policy initiatives to seek solutions from grassroots activity that can 'scale up' and be 'rolled out'. Measures are taken, for example, to make it easier for grassroots innovators to access and work with research institutions and economic development agencies in the pursuit of new products, processes and business models.

Here the presumption is that grassroots innovation is simply the generation of ingenious products, requiring some professional design and marketing help and the protection of intellectual property; when in practice such 'prototypes' are actually the most visible aspects of much more complex and rooted local development activities. The isolation, bounding, enclosure and marketing of these visible objects of grassroots innovation activity, such as an agricultural technique, is much harder than imagined because it loses sight of the intangible features and local development gains motivating the original small-scale effort. Rather than figuring out how to scale up apparently innovative objects, policy might think about how to scale down its institutions for further cultivating grassroots innovative capabilities. In this book we want to draw attention to the possibilities and difficulties arising in such encounters between grassroots innovation and institutions for science and technology.

The reality on the ground is one of countless initiatives involving a shifting kaleidoscope of diverse groups working at grassroots level over decades, finding ways to manifest environmental integrity and social justice through practical activity, and sometimes engaging with policy, science and technology institutions in the hope of advancing their aims. Grassroots innovation might be diverse, messy and difficult to commercialize or support bureaucratically precisely because groups are drawing upon their distinct histories, cultures and priorities in their communities when addressing universal challenges of feeding, housing, water, sanitation, health, providing energy, livelihoods and having fun. Some initiatives might spread widely, but all ultimately need to be rooted locally.

Others have done remarkable jobs in documenting and illustrating grassroots activity in areas as varied as food, shelter, water and sanitation, energy, clothing, transport, manufacturing or recreation; whether Fritz Schumacher in *Small Is*

Beautiful (1973), through most recently to John Thackara in *How to Thrive in the Next Economy* (2015); and in the continuing work of the Honey Bee Network founded by Anil Gupta (Gupta et al., 2003). While we will come across examples in this book also, we do so in the pursuit of seeing how grassroots innovations connect as a *movement* that encounters institutions of science, technology and development, as these movements try collectively to advance broader visions of social change and build alternative pathways. As such, we look beyond specific grassroots initiatives in themselves, and examine the networks that try to promote, galvanize and support grassroots innovation as a generic activity for producing knowledge, technology and social organization in which community action is at the centre.

Grassroots innovation movements

In *Alternative Pathways in Science and Industry* (2007), David Hess takes as his point of departure the observation that social movement activities and consequences are not limited to protest and the securing of rights, but that social movements can also be generative of an alternative material culture. Andrew Jamison makes a similar point in relation to knowledge production in *The Making of Green Knowledge* (2001). Our work in this book follows their lead. It is important to avoid thinking about such innovations only as spin-offs of environmentalism, say, or freedom movements in (post-)colonial struggles. We need to think about grassroots innovation as a movement in itself; generating innovative activity that aims for practical expressions of core social values that contribute to alternative pathways, as David Hess puts it. As such, grassroots innovation is something worth promoting and supporting because it is an activity open to experimentation for social change. Grassroots innovation movements seek to prototype social change and act upon social change. We explain this further in Chapter 2.

There is always innovative activity at grassroots level operating beneath the radar of economic and scientific institutions. Those institutions conventionally set research and development agendas, and provide support and resources, and market and capitalize upon innovation in society. However, innovative grassroots activity attains movement characteristics only when motivated by an explicit normative desire for social change committed to values of social justice and environmental sustainability. Many people in the maker movement, for example, voluntarily develop new devices and objects and share them online. There are thousands of designs freely available. Often these activities are motivated for purposes of fun, recreation, personal challenge and displaying virtuosity. Indeed, the maker movement may be committed to values of conviviality and sharing that appear quite striking, compared to the marketized innovation imperatives under dominant economic institutions. Yet when makers seek to develop a business from their crowd-sourced designs they tend to reproduce practices not so different from business as usual. They celebrate and follow Silicon Valley models for start-up entrepreneurship and disruptive innovation that is actually quite conformist in terms of economic development. And when the maker movement becomes a market for making, in which countless suppliers of materials and appropriators of designs find new sources of profit, coupled with little concern for who is included or excluded in this scene, nor with much concern for the social and economic structures being reproduced, then makers look less of a social movement (Ratto and Boler, 2014). Many in the maker movement accept as given the existing order of things and seek only to be innovative within it. When commitments to social change do come to the fore, and begin to direct the kind of innovation undertaken, then the activity becomes part of a grassroots innovation movement. We see this occurring in some of the hackerspaces, fablabs and makerspaces that are the focus of study in Chapter 6.

In practice, hard and fast distinctions can be difficult to pin down. For example, developing open hardware instructions for building a remote-controlled drone collaboratively through online social media networks is often motivated for reasons of fun and recreation in maker networks. But when drone instructions are adopted within networks that also build in sensors and link to data platforms to monitor environmental change remotely, do drone hobbyists become enrolled in a grassroots innovation movement? International networks such as Public Laboratory exist precisely for that reason. They develop and share cheap, open source monitoring technologies, drawing in knowledge and ideas from wide varieties of sources through their community of developers, in order to empower people who use the devices to demand healthier local environments from public institutions. Here is grassroots innovation that helps people demonstrate more effectively.

Examples like this point to the increasingly proliferating intersections and hybrids between different forms of grassroots innovations and conventional institutions. Grassroots innovative activities can make use of technologies developed in industrial innovation systems and sold by global high-tech corporations; while global firms appropriate ideas and practices developed originally by alternative technologists and activists. Corporations now make use of ideas about open innovation pioneered among hackers in free software and free culture movements; while hackerspaces creatively appropriate laser cutters and other digital fabrication tools developed originally by industrial capital seeking to deskill labour and automate production (Noble, 1984; Söderberg, 2013). It is important to note and understand these flows and interdependencies between the grassroots and institutions; and to expect, as we follow grassroots innovation movements, that we are likely to confront considerable complexity in the relations between initiatives, tools, networks, movements and institutions.

But is taking science and technology to the grassroots really grassroots innovation? We think it is when these processes lead to new forms of producing knowledge and new ways of improving livelihoods, and with the grassroots having control over those processes and a stake in the outcomes. The Social Technology Network, for instance, involved groups from across South America collaborating in the generation, dissemination and reapplication of innovations for sustainable development. An important aspect of the networks was recognition of the need for local learning and empowering communities to make innovative adaptations when applying social technologies in different places (Miranda, Lopez and Couto Soares, 2011) – a focus on active grassroots empowerment, rather than simply diffusing ready-made solutions in which the communities in question remain relatively passive recipients.

Others adopt a more circumscribed notion of grassroots innovation movements. Under this view, grassroots innovation arises from the ingenuity and capability within local communities, or even of individual informal inventors (Gupta et al., 2003). Grassroots innovation is a purely indigenous phenomenon. Given the encounters noted above, however, and the global proliferation of knowledge, ideas, tools and practices, we see such tight definitional restriction as a limitation. We think grassroots innovators improvise and make use of whatever tools, resources and knowledge lie to hand and are less concerned about their provenance – the important point is that the innovators have power in the processes and a stake in the outcomes of the innovation (Smith et al., 2014).

It can be argued, and we recognize, that our more expansive view weakens the notion of grassroots innovation movements by opening it up to the kinds of consultancy-driven, participatory development already prevalent in the development industry and whose good intentions are confounded at times through unreflexive application of external 'solutions' that disempowers communities, or empowers them selectively in ways not welcomed by the recipients. Anil K. Gupta founded the Honey Bee Network precisely because he was frustrated with his experience in professional development consultancy that ended up extracting and undermining knowledge and innovation in local communities. Honey Bee's development of scouting techniques, working in the languages of the communities concerned, and careful recognition of individual inventors by name (Gupta et al., 2003) reflect this concern to focus and build grassroots ingenuity, rather than expropriate it.

Certainly, the risks exist. Grassroots innovation can be co-opted as a term for continued local engagements that see communities as relatively passive sites for either appropriating ideas or inserting ready-made solutions, with little reflection on the grassroots as active subjects in innovations and making appropriations of their own. In our view, however, this is a criticism that calls for greater understanding and reflexivity towards grassroots innovation movements rather than circumscribed definitions. It is something we attempt with our case studies in Chapters 3 to 8.

Furthermore, as we argued earlier, even tightly defined notions focusing on grassroots ingenuity have to be careful with the inevitable encounters beyond the communities concerned. When institutions engage with grassroots movements they risk decontextualizing innovation and turning it into an object removed from the originating grassroots processes. Well-intended assistance for scaling up or diffusing instances of grassroots ingenuity can transform it through, for example, the introduction of intellectual property for the purposes of protecting benefits, standardizing for purposes of scaling up and commodification for purposes of attracting investment and marketing. These are institutionalized approaches from mainstream innovation management that imply commercial motivations, identities and values that may be distinct or counter to the motivations mobilizing many grassroots innovation movements. Or such commercial formalizations may be welcomed. But is it still grassroots innovation?

About this book

Our introduction has set out some of the issues and themes motivating this book. The majority of the research was undertaken through a project called Grassroots Innovation: Historical and Comparative Perspectives, which ran from 2012 to 2015. The project was funded by the Economic and Social Research Council's STEPS Centre at the University of Sussex. The STEPS acronym stands for research dedicated to Social, Technological and Environmental Pathways to Sustainability. The Centre's research investigates the social causes and consequences of developments in science and technology as they relate to principles of sustainable development. The research project aimed to contribute to the understanding, debate and appreciation of grassroots innovation movements. The following are the questions we asked for each case study movement, and which we answer in Chapters 3 to 8.

1. Why did this grassroots innovation movement emerge?
2. How did activists mobilize support and activities in grassroots innovation?
3. What dilemmas confronted the movement when constructing alternative pathways, and how did it negotiate those dilemmas?

Given the geographical spread of the team, with members in Buenos Aires, Brighton, Bogotá and Delhi, we were in a position to study grassroots innovation movements in South America, India and Europe. In this way we could extend study beyond the US and Europe (Hess, 2007; Jamison, 2003; Mathie and Gaventa, 2015; Smith, 2005), and combine it with studies in the so-called 'global South' (Gupta et al., 2003; Willoughby, 1990). The movements we chose to study were the following.

The movement for socially useful production (UK, 1976–1986) (Chapter 3)

The movement for socially useful production emerged in the context of economic decline and loss of manufacturing jobs in industrial communities in the UK. It involved an unusual mix of engineers, workers and activists, and arose out of a combination of diverse social movements, including grassroots trade unionism, peace, community activism, radical science and, to a lesser extent, environmentalism and feminism. Activists both provided a critique of the existing institutions for innovation in society and developed a set of practical initiatives that anticipated more directly democratic processes for socially shaping technologies.

The appropriate technology movement (South America, 1970s and 1980s) (Chapter 4)

During the 1970s and 1980s appropriate technology become a worldwide grassroots innovation movement that sought to redefine technology as a tool for development.

Introducing grassroots innovation movements **13**

In South America appropriate technology emerged in a context of social upheaval between the challenge of political repression and the influence of new forms of activism and participation. The movement was able to develop its own local networks, technologies and to reframe appropriate technology ideas in a more suitable way for the needs of the region, as well as pioneering activities that would outlast the movement in areas such as agroecology.

The People's Science Movement (India, 1960s to present) (Chapter 5)

The People's Science Movement (PSM) in India emerged from various popular science movements appearing from the late 1960s onwards. The movement encompasses a range of grassroots networks, organizations and associations, each of which varies in size, history, focus and strategy. The PSM approach emerged from discussions between scientists, technologists and civil society organizations that centred on the potential for upgrading traditional techniques through the application of science. Particular attention was and is paid to the development of the 'social carriers' of innovations for inclusive local development.

Hackerspaces, fablabs and makerspaces (international, 2000s to present) (Chapter 6)

Hackerspaces, fablabs and makerspaces are community-based digital fabrication workshops providing innovative spaces where people come together to learn about and use versatile digital design and manufacturing technologies. Some spaces are run voluntarily, while others receive institutional support (e.g. from universities and libraries), but all share an ethos towards making skills and tools freely available to the wider public, so that they can participate directly in design and making activities. Nowadays, workshops constitute a global network and they can be found in many major cities around the world. Many of them network and share projects and knowledge through social media and meet physically at international events.

The Social Technology Network (Brazil, 2000s to 2012) (Chapter 7)

Originating in Brazil in the early 2000s and suspended in 2012, the Social Technology Network (STN) involved a range of participants, from academics to activists, unions, government representatives, funding agencies and, especially, NGOs and community groups. The STN fostered processes of social inclusion, public participation and income generation by putting community development activities at the centre of developing new, inclusive capabilities in science and technology development. The STN had as its main aim fostering a more democratic process of innovation for development by turning isolated initiatives into broader public policies and application, with attention to income generation and social inclusion for the poorest among the population.

The Honey Bee Network (India, 1990s to present) (Chapter 8)

The Honey Bee Network (HBN) emerged in India in 1989 among a group of scientists, farmers, academics and others interested in documenting and disseminating traditional knowledge and local innovation in local languages. They focused on ensuring that the individual innovators would receive benefits from their local ingenuity. The HBN views grassroots innovation as invention and innovation coming from the grassroots, often among people with little formal training and reliant on local, traditional or indigenous knowledge. The network's main activity is the scouting and documentation of innovations and traditional knowledge based on different actions such as visiting communities, interviews, awards and competitions. A second step is related to the exploration of the commercial potential of products and processes identified during scouting.

There were analytical and practical considerations affecting the selection of these grassroots innovation movements for study. Analytically, in all cases, we wanted to look at movements whose networks were dedicated to promoting grassroots innovation generally, rather than movements doing innovative things as part of mobilizations in particular sectors or on specific topics. So, for example, we chose not to look at movements specific to agroecology, health, housing or recycling. We chose movements whose core aims were to promote and expand the capacity of people at the grassroots to participate directly in innovation, and consistent with the definition given earlier. In fact, the grassroots innovation movements we looked at were active in areas such as housing or food, but they were also working in other areas and bridged these various mobilizations.

Another analytical choice was choosing diverse cases, not simply in terms of locations and therefore contexts, but also in terms of the approaches adopted. We chose different cases in order to recognize the particularities involved: how grassroots innovation looks different for these varied movements, and the development challenges they confront. At the same time, however, any issues or patterns recurring amid the diversity could point to some fundamental and enduring features of relevance to grassroots innovation movements more generally (Flyvbjerg, 2006). Consequently, our comparison is not intended to isolate variables and explain why some movements perform 'better' than others according to some external measure of sustainability. Rather, we want to understand and appreciate these movements on their terms first: an 'insider' ontology (see Chapter 2). In all cases, we wanted to trace movement developments over time, including the rise of the movement, its ability to endure over time and its decline and dispersal where relevant.

Adopting an appreciative comparison requires a framework of analysis that is open enough to account for the diversity of movement-centred perspectives important to us, but nevertheless having sufficient structure that we can work consistently with each movement and identify common patterns. We developed our framework iteratively during the earlier phases of the project. It is explained in Chapter 2. Such appreciation is important when responding to the kinds of policy, business or NGO interest in grassroots innovation noted earlier. As we discuss in Chapter 9, issues emerge that institutions and movements need to think about carefully.

Practically, our choice of case study movements was affected by the need to access each movement, whether in terms of archive materials, interviews with participants or our own observations as participants. Such considerations explain why we overlook movements in Africa, North America, Eastern Europe and South East Asia. In addition to the usual fieldwork activities of interviewing people, gathering documentation about initiatives and searching for materials in archives, we were able to organize workshops in Buenos Aires, Delhi and London that brought together movement practitioners. Here we could convene presentations, discussions and reflections on the experiences we were researching. These were fantastically rewarding engagements, especially for those research team members participating from outside the region. In the cases of movements still active, we also participated in their events and learnt much from the discussions. Our engagements continue. We hope that this book will be of use to them, and to other grassroots innovation movements with which we did not have the benefit of working.

2
AN ANALYTICAL FRAMEWORK FOR STUDYING GRASSROOTS INNOVATION MOVEMENTS

In this chapter we do two things. First, we elaborate our grounds for conceptualizing the field of study as consisting of grassroots innovation movements. Second, we develop a framework for analysing grassroots innovation movements in South America, India and Europe from historical and comparative perspectives. Drawing on a combination of ideas from research literatures on social movements, science and technology studies, and theories of innovation, including recent work on grassroots innovation, we develop a framework for understanding these particular movements' historical antecedents, motivations and strategies for innovation and development, as well as their engagements or disconnects with 'conventional' innovation approaches and mainstream development pathways, as set out in Chapter 1.

Our aim is to provide a framework for studying each case study consistently but flexibly – so that patterns may be identified, but space allowed for the specifics of each history. In our approach to analysing the cases, we alternately move between an 'outsider' and 'insider' (Smith and Stirling, 2007) ontology; in other words, recognizing our positions as analysts of the movements, we describe the movement's broader contexts as we understand them and in relation to the literature. On the other hand, we also carefully describe as faithfully as possible how the movements themselves see and describe their contexts, thus also employing an 'insider's' ontology. Ultimately, in attempting this method, we seek a way of exploring some of the diversity and context sensitivity of grassroots innovation. This also enables us to identify and explore any fundamental similarities or deep-seated features in movements, albeit playing out differently in the varied times and places we study, which will help us to develop understanding of why grassroots innovation movements' activities and influences take the forms they do (Flyvbjerg, 2006). We stress that this approach is not a comparative evaluation for best practices against some common, externally applied metric. Rather, we hope that an appreciation of different movement experiences can be mutually informative and provide fresh ideas, insights and perspectives for thinking about more familiar initiatives closer to home. As such, our aims are to open up the field of grassroots innovation movements for wider appreciation and debate, rather than to close in around particular models and pathways.

As we pointed out in Chapter 1, our interest is as much in the networks between groups that practise or promote grassroots innovation as it is in the grassroots innovations per se. Moreover, we are interested in the ideas and identities that connect and motivate these groups and in the wider social consequences that their activities have. These are all themes prominent in the research literature on social movements, and so it seems reasonable for us to begin the development of our analytical framework there.

Grassroots innovation and social movements

While the grassroots innovation networks that we study in this book do not all self-identify as social movements, they nevertheless involve collective action in civil society and at times link to broader social movements. Social movements are often characterized as a historic form of collective action that is broadly composed of three elements: (a) a collective claim that challenges incumbent elites in society or institutions and opens a controversy about resources, rights or values; (b) forms of organization located primarily within civil society and with a set of strategies or repertoires of actions different from mainstream institutions; and (c) a sustained form of collective action over time that creates bonds of solidarity and identity (Tarrow, 2004; Tilly, 2008). An additional element underlying the formation of social movements that is particularly relevant for this book is knowledge production. As Eyerman and Jamison (1991) highlight, social movements are knowledge producers that can draw ideas from different sources (from science, history and the arts) and translate them into political action. In this process, social movements act as laboratories of experimentation for new ideas, forms of organization and knowledge. In this way, social movements can be regarded as reflexive social actors in two forms. First, social movements are social actors that learn by doing, particularly through reflection and debate concerning experience with movement practices, strategies and forms of organization (and modified accordingly). Second, social movements produce knowledge that 'might be inconvenient to and resisted from those above' and bring it to the public (Cox and Flesher Fominaya, 2009, p. 1), while movements' critique (of existing inequalities) enhances the reflexivity of society (Buechler, 2000). Movements thus also produce alternative ways of thinking about development and social change.

Much social movement literature examines questions around what motivates groups to mobilize, how they pull together, who is involved and what shapes the development of strategies. Earlier literature focused mainly on structural socio-economic factors, with particular attention to struggles for material resources and access to political power. In the 1980s, a wave of literature on 'new' social movements (such as feminism, environmentalism, peace and lesbian, gay, bisexual and transgender rights, in contrast to the older movements based around labour or freedom from colonialism) highlighted additional motivations for collective action. Subsequent literature has highlighted the key roles of social movement organizations in shaping identities and the importance of local, national and transnational networks to help mobilize resources and open up political spaces (Thompson and Tapscott, 2010).

Relatively few studies have linked social movement literatures to studies of science, technology and innovation. Frickel and Gross (2005) have analysed the relationship between social movements and intellectual movements. In the same vein, Scott Frickel and Kelly Moore (Frickel, 2004; Frickel et al., 2010; Moore, 2006) have studied the role of social movements and collective action frames in the construction of alternative science, but also the undone science on issues neglected by conventional scientific institutions (Hess, 2007). Escobar (2004) and other decolonial scholars have highlighted different kinds of knowledge production by social movements. Regarding technology and innovation, others (for example, Hess, 2007; Jamison, 2001; Smith, 2005) have examined the role of social movements in developing alternative forms of technological change. Leach et al. (2010) have brought attention to the politics of knowledge involved in social movements.

Drawing upon the social movements literature, it is possible to suggest three features of grassroots innovation movements, and which further analysis must explore.

1   Grassroots innovation movements are primarily based in civil society forms of organization.

Grassroots innovation movements are informal phenomena that are mainly based in bottom-up initiatives that include different network architectures and a broad diversity of social actors, including non-governmental organisations (NGOs), social movements and cooperatives. Some are focused on social justice and sustainability, though others are not. Grassroots innovation movements are the result of collective action that requires constant collaboration, mobilization and self-recognition among a broad diversity of social actors. Collaboration and coordination between heterogeneous actors requires organizational strategies for mobilization of resources and spatial coordination, but also symbolic arrangements that differ from formal institutions. These forms of organization also require some flexibility and negotiation with mainstream institutions such as governments, development organizations, business and science and technology institutions. As a result, grassroots innovation movements create different spaces of experimentation and follow different strategies and forms of engagement with institutional actors, from extra-institutional forms of mobilization to collaboration to co-option.

2   Grassroots innovation movements use alternative strategies of knowledge production.

A central element of grassroots innovation movements is their focus on knowledge and technology production as a means to explore alternative scenarios of social change. An important component in this endeavour is the open character of knowledge production that the grassroots innovation movements usually try to foster. Grassroots innovation movements experiment with different forms of public participation in the knowledge production process. However, this is not simply participatory innovation towards the same aims as conventional innovation institutions, such as we see in some forms of citizen science. Rather, grassroots innovation movements identify and demand innovation in areas, on topics and directed towards issues neglected by conventional innovation institutions, and even towards a different social rationality and set of criteria. Strategies might include experiments with co-design, participatory research or popular education. These schemes are usually aimed at including a broader diversity of actors in the process of problem framing, knowledge creation and material solutions, which brings different forms of expertise and experience into play. In practice, this means that grassroots innovation movements create spaces where learning how to use and how to create technologies and alternative forms of knowledge is central. Furthermore, grassroots innovation movements prefer non-proprietary forms of innovation and common goods that differ from proprietary forms of intellectual property that dominate mainstream science and technology. As a result, grassroots innovation movements tinker with technology and knowledge and other resources in ways that are often very different from the formal institutions of science and technology. Unattached to the rules of disciplinary bodies, scientific evaluation and for-profit requirements, grassroots innovators are free to explore new directions of technological change.

3   Grassroots innovation movements are political actors.

The ability to experiment with new technologies and forms of organization is an important tool in the critique of incumbent forms of technological development. Grassroots innovation movements can be regarded as initiators or advocates of alternative pathways of socio-technical development. However, these roles are not exclusive, and hybrid arrangements can arise in pursuit of these aims that require engagements with science and technology institutions and development agencies. Pragmatic engagements can involve technical assistance, funding or other kinds of institutional support, but also include symbolic legitimacy, policy design and supportive regulatory structures (Ely et al., 2013). All these activities are ultimately aimed at opening up a discussion about the direction of development and the roles of scientific research and technological change. In this way, grassroots innovation movements raise questions about technological needs in societies, the appropriate directions of technological change and who is enabled to design, own and access a technology, and on what terms. Such questions involve a politics of knowledge that challenges the distribution of resources and power in knowledge production and technology development.

Taken together, these three features – mobilization through civil society, alternative forms of knowledge production and a political pursuit of different rationalities and criteria – instil grassroots innovation with characteristics closer to those of social movements than of conventional innovation institutions. However, there are important differences between grassroots innovation movements and other, broader social movements regarding the forms of knowledge they produce and their means of mobilization. Conventional social movements (old or new) are generally based on claims about class, rights or identity, while grassroots innovation movements challenge specific directions and forms of knowledge production, technological change and development. This focal difference implies an important analytical distinction. Grassroots innovation movements are not reduced to contentious politics (Hess, 2007). While the repertoires of action that grassroots innovation movements might use include, only occasionally, public protest involving rallies and boycotts (Tilly, 2008), such displays of force and unity do not constitute the main means of expression and political mobilization. Instead, in similar fashion to scientific or intellectual movements (Frickel and Gross, 2005) grassroots innovation movements are centrally focused on strategies of knowledge creation and alternative pathways of innovation and development. Grassroots innovation movement repertoires and forms of mobilization are based more on the production of knowledge and technological solutions. As Hess notes, grassroots innovation movements are 'analytically distinctive because the principal means of social change is the development of new or alternative forms of material culture, a means of change that is often associated with calls for significant institutional and policy changes as well' (Hess, 2005, p. 517).

So, in analysing grassroots innovation movements we need to bring in concepts about learning, knowledge creation and technological innovation from innovation studies and science and technology studies, in combination with ideas about mobilization of resources and political strategies from social movement literatures. Such combinations are key to understanding how grassroots innovation movements develop alternative visions and practices of development. Informed by such a combination, over subsequent sections we develop our analytical framework. It will focus on the contexts in which each grassroots innovation movement arises, the framings they bring to questions of innovation and development, the spaces and strategies they create and pursue for turning their ideas and aims into material practice, and the development pathways that emerge from this activity (and that variously grow, disperse or disappear). The remainder of this chapter, and each case study chapter, is thus organized along the lines of an analysis of context, framings, spaces and strategies, and pathways. We draw on research in innovation studies, science and technology studies and social movements in order to elaborate each concept and bring into view some issues for consideration in advance of each case study.

Broader contexts

The importance of broader historical and political-economic *contexts* is a common theme both in evolutionary economic approaches to the study of innovation and in social movement theory. Broader, dynamic contexts shape the opportunities for social movements to arise, flourish and diminish, as well as forming environments that select and shape technological developments and guide their trajectories over time. Contexts can condition grassroots innovation movements in three ways. First, predominant directions in innovation and development deemed problematic by activists can serve as motivation for the creation of alternative visions and directions. Second, dynamic contextual conditions can provide windows of opportunity for the development of grassroots alternatives. And third, dynamic contexts can present constraints to the development of grassroots alternatives.

Contexts may structure opportunities for grassroots innovation movement actions over time by enabling or blocking access to resources, changing dominant development discourses and opening up political opportunities. Mobilization processes often 'emerge from and are strongly shaped by political histories and cultures' (Leach and Scoones, 2007, p. 27). In social movements research, political opportunities might arise when institutions become newly sensitive to an issue that mobilizes grassroots innovators or undergo reforms that are rooted in broader national and international processes such as democratization, which may make state institutions more 'permeable' to action and influence by civil society groups (Thompson and Tapscott, 2010, p. 9). Historical context is also vital for understanding the relation between internal social movement dynamics and wider structures of political power and capital accumulation (Amin, 1993). More recently, neoliberalization – in its multiple and heterogeneous forms – has been a cause for social mobilization, including in the realm of science and technology (Moore et al., 2011).

There has also been increasing attention in the social movement literature to distinct characteristics of social movements in the global South (Escobar and Alvarez, 1992; Thompson and Tapscott, 2010). Despite apparent resource limitations, deemed a prerequisite for mobilization in some Northern social movement literature, there have been extensive movements across resource-constrained communities in Latin America and Asia, suggesting different forms of collective action and approaches to theories of social movements in such contexts (Escobar and Alvarez, 1992). In particular, Escobar and Alvarez argue that economic, political *and* cultural factors are crucial in Latin American social movements. So, in studying the generative contexts for grassroots innovation movements, as well as the opportunities that contexts provide, the lesson from the social movements literature is that this should be historically informed.

In research into technology and innovation, contexts are especially important when thinking about transitions to new 'regimes' of innovation, production and consumption. In the evolutionary economic approach of the multilevel perspective (Geels, 2002; Geels and Schot, 2007; Rip and Kemp, 1998), 'socio-technical landscapes' – including wider society concerns, political-economic crises and changing cultural or ideological discourses – are an exogenous source of change, which can provide windows of opportunity for destabilizing existing socio-technical regimes and opening up possibilities for innovation alternatives (Geels, 2010; Geels and Schot, 2007). Research in this field illustrates how 'sustainability' as a discourse can be interpreted as a landscape-level change that is destabilizing the contexts of operation of existing regimes and underpinning and effectively distributing services in energy, mobility, food, housing, water and so forth in a variety of geographical settings (Garud and Gehman, 2012; Grin et al., 2010; Smith et al., 2005; Voss et al., 2009). New social demands and structural contradictions cast hitherto robust regimes of provision and accumulation into doubt, opening up opportunities for social movements and other agents, including entrepreneurial business leaders and research institutions, to press for alternative social and technological configurations for meeting societal needs.

International or transnational networks can also help to open up windows of opportunity in national and local contexts. Movement actors can leverage influence from internationally based allies for local-level activity. This can be especially important when national contexts are otherwise unfavourable, the so-called boomerang effect (Keck and Sikkink, 1998). The appropriate technology (AT) movement, for instance, arose in the 1960s and 1970s in Europe and South Asia, gaining attention within the professional development community. AT activities were subsequently supported by development agencies at an international level. For instance, sections of the Organisation for Economic Co-operation and Development (OECD) and the International Labour Organization, as well as the World Bank, United Nations Development Programme (UNDP) and United Nations Environment Programme (UNEP), conducted activities around 'appropriate technology' into the 1980s. This mainstream interest helped to foster and open up opportunities for engagement among science and technology institutions and NGOs in other parts of the world, such as South America. However, national political-economic and ideological contexts regionally played an important role in the forms that the AT movement took in South America (see Chapter 4).

Within the current global economic crisis, renewed political focus on issues of inequality and social inclusion has drawn institutional attention at an international level once more to grassroots solutions and varied notions of inclusive innovation. Interest has been claimed within the OECD, the World Bank and the United Nations (Gradl and Knobloch, 2010; OECD, 2015; World Bank, 2012), among others. Such recognition brings with it both opportunities and challenges for grassroots innovation movements.

Thus, adopting our outsider's ontology, we can describe how broader contexts – whether political, economic, social or cultural – shape opportunities for grassroots innovation movements. However, turning to an insider's ontology, we need to examine how grassroots innovation movements themselves problematize the broader development contexts described above, and how they themselves frame opportunities and alternative possibilities.

Framings

In the social movement literature, the concept of framing is key to understanding how, beyond shared grievances, social movements are held together by a collective production of ideas and meaning that creates bonds of solidarity between actors and informs their coordinated action. The concept of framing was taken from its origins in psychology and adapted by social movements research in order to understand the importance of interpretative orientations, values and interests in mobilization processes. According to Snow et al. (1986), framing involves a process of meaning production that enables movements to identify and organize their experience in forms that help them to connect to more powerful narratives. In this way, 'collective action frames are action-oriented sets of belief and meanings that inspire and legitimate the activities and campaigns of a social movement organization' (Benford and Snow, 2000, p. 614). Tarrow (2004) adds that framing processes are enacted by both social groups and states, and can serve to build boundaries of a constituency, develop a collective identity and define 'others'. Frames can be important in influencing how a situation and context is understood either descriptively or analytically, and what types of actions might be employed to address a problem.

The socially constructed character of frames means that their meanings and ideas can evolve and develop as part of a learning process that social movements undergo in relation to different periods of activity and mobilization. As such, the concept of framing allows understanding of how social movements not only act to claim and blame incumbent powers, but also develop a complex process of knowledge production. This aspect of framing is obviously important to understanding how grassroots innovation movements develop alternative forms of technological change.

Work in the sociology of technology and more political approaches in innovation studies emphasize the various 'framings' that social groups bring to innovation activities (Hess, 2005; Leach et al., 2005; Leach and Scoones, 2007; Smith, 2005). Bijker (1995) and others have studied how relevant social actors can draw from one or more technological frames in order to produce innovations. Technological frames consist of the shared problems, strategies, requirements, theories, knowledge, design criteria, exemplary artefacts, testing procedures and user practices that emerge through social interaction in groups. They help us to understand what social actors deem to be reasonable in choosing and developing a technology. Precisely for this reason, technological frames emphasize technical and cognitive aspects of innovation and tend to underplay explicitly political aspects involved in grassroots innovation struggles. Thus, by using technological frames there is some risk that we will regard technology as *the* central concern and output of grassroots innovation movements; whereas the way framings are invoked as a concept in social movement research points to a broader set of social, economic and political concerns within a frame. Including the social movement notion of framing helps us to combine the cognitive aspects of technological framings with symbolic, organizational and power aspects present in social movement framing activity.

In the case of grassroots innovation movements, following Jamison (2001), we argue that an important aspect of their framing involves critique of mainstream science, technology and innovation. In analysing our cases, we employ the concept of framings empirically to uncover what specifically motivated the movement's origins, how movements problematize mainstream models for innovation and development, what alternative visions and aims they develop and promote and how these change over time – through negotiation, or due to changing opportunities and resources, for example.

A broad focus on *framings* helps us to appreciate the discursive and interpretative orientations of different grassroots innovation movements towards their contexts, which informs and shapes their engagements with technology development, innovation *and* values and ideas about social change. Where grassroots innovation comprises heterogeneity of actors and institutions, so the framings in play are likely to be plural also. And where a variety of framings underpin the movement, so we may anticipate tensions and debate about priorities and relations between them. This suggests a need for attention to the existence, operation and influence of different framings within grassroots innovation movements and to how different framings:

- prioritize different motivating factors;
- suggest different roles for grassroots groups;
- guide activity towards different opportunities and possibilities;
- emphasize different kinds of knowledge production and parts of the innovation processes or expected outcomes;
- identify and promote different exemplary artefacts and technologies; and
- point to contrasting strategies for engaging grassroots innovation groups with the state, business and wider civil society.

Plural framings may be an indication of contending normativities. Each frame can inform narratives about the movement and link to storylines about desired futures and goals, such as sustainability, social inclusion and participation (Leach et al., 2010). In this way, framing must be regarded as a key aspect of grassroots innovation movements and the process of building alternative development pathways (Leach et al., 2010).

We are interested in analysing how these different framings and interpretations of innovation, social inclusion and participation are negotiated and contested, and what modes of engagement grassroots innovation movements use in order to forge alternative pathways of innovation (Hess, 2007; Smith, 2007). However, even when frames inform alternative visions, action repertoires and pathways of innovation, they do not necessarily constitute a blueprint for mobilization and sociotechnical experimentation. The plural frames held by social movements can be a source of contestation and debate, as well as flexibility and pragmatism in coalition building. Which frames become pre-eminent in strategies for grassroots innovation can depend upon their adequacy in negotiating spaces for doing and advancing grassroots innovation materially.

Spaces and strategies

Thinking about spaces and strategies helps us to identify, describe and understand the varied arenas where it is possible to do grassroots innovation, as well as the repertoires of action employed by grassroots innovation movements to create or claim such spaces. These spaces need to be relatively sympathetic to grassroots innovation movement framings, as compared to conventional scientific, technological and innovation institutions. They are spaces where the norms and expectations for innovation are different (Kemp et al., 1998; Seyfang and Smith, 2007). These are spaces, for example, where social goals valued by the movement prevail over, say, the market pressure to rush into competitive commercialization and economic growth. In these spaces it is possible to develop the grassroots innovation by mobilizing resources for experimentation and enrolling receptive audiences, alliances and users for improving performance. Ultimately, however, if grassroots innovation is to open up alternative pathways for development, activity has to expand beyond these spaces, push back against the broader, problematic social context and influence the wider world.

Analytically, we want to understand the strategies by which grassroots innovation movements open up spaces for their activities, and how the characteristics of those spaces influence innovation processes and outcomes, including any development pathways that unfold. We use the terms *spaces and strategies* to bring together these different locations and activities that grassroots innovation movements leverage as they try to achieve their goals. Conceptually, we draw upon ideas of participation and repertoires of action (Tilly, 2008) and resource mobilization (McCarthy and Zald, 1977) from social movement literatures, and spaces of experimentation and niches from development studies and innovation studies (Cornwall and Coelho, 2007; Kemp et al., 1998). Ideas about resource mobilization in the social movements literature focus on strategy, agency and organizations for creating or claiming alternative spaces of engagement, which are seen as key to social movement mobilization. From this literature, we draw three key points in relation to the strategies available to grassroots innovation movements for opening up spaces; these are intermediaries and networks, mobilization structures and repertoires of action.

An ability to create *intermediaries and networks* is crucial to opening up spaces. Networks contribute through communicating, coordinating, representing and sharing grassroots innovation. Networks serve as both communicative structures and political actors, enabling flows of ideas, resources, claims and activities, including across transnational locations (Bebbington and Kothari, 2006; Keck and Sikkink, 1998). Intermediaries are key to sharing lessons arising from different grassroots innovation initiatives. Intermediaries network between specific grassroots initiatives and carry experiences, insight and lessons in order that it becomes easier to do the innovation in other settings (Hargreaves et al., 2013). The sharing of lessons and knowledge might be oriented instrumentally towards improving an innovation or oriented to identifying ways to speak to the agendas of policymakers and investors; or lessons might generate critical knowledge about limitations imposed on the innovation by broader social structures and which need to be addressed politically (Smith et al., 2015). Networks and intermediaries are able to operate above specific innovation situations and engage the wider context in opening up spaces for further activity.

Repertoires of action are the forms of organization and activism that movements develop and use to gain access to the spaces and challenge opponents. Grassroots innovation movements adopt specific strategies under certain conditions of opportunity in mobilizing access to resources. Knowledge, skills and capabilities for mobilizing in different ways are required. In social movements, this conventionally involves activities such as rallies and boycotts, linkages with other groups and organizations and cultivating a sense of shared identity, values and solidarity. In the case of grassroots innovation, the repertoires extend to activities such as prototyping, publicizing designs, arguing for inclusion, fund-raising campaigns and protesting against exclusions from science and technology agendas and institutions.

In *mobilization of resources* a group or network may mobilize many different types of resources and institutions in order to pursue its goals. In doing so, grassroots innovation movements must consider the costs and benefits, risks and rewards of different strategies, which are shaped by the conditions attached by resource holders to the deployment of those resources. Types of resources can include both material (such as financial, material goods and services) and non-material resources (for example, leadership, trust, skills, shared culture, historical tradition and ideology) (Oberschall, 1973). Shared identity, values and solidarity can also be mobilized to persuade other forms of commitment, particularly material resources (Jenkins, 1983). Other resources include outsider support or linkages with other groups and organizations, including investors and businesses, and even government strategies, all of which can selectively and conditionally furnish resources with a view to appropriating, co-opting or limiting social movements' aims, activities and accomplishments (McCarthy and Zald, 1977). Hess (2005) points out that science and technology can be one of the resources a movement may be interested in accessing but to which access is structured by the norms of scientific and technological institutions. The point is that structures of political, economic and social power, as well as geography, may render some resources more elusive than others for grassroots innovation groups.

Spaces may be physical, such as workshops, fields, buildings, factories, villages or neighbourhoods where groups can work on their innovations. Spaces may be social, in the sense that there are social groups, social networks and social activities able to provide support, lend resources and platforms for furthering grassroots innovation or become lead users of the grassroots innovation. Examples here might include social movements, such as peasants' movements, environmentalists, workers' groups and community activists. Spaces could be institutional, in the sense that an institution provides support and opportunity for grassroots innovation. Universities, for example, might open their doors and lend their research and education capacity to community initiatives and grassroots innovators, as has been the case with science shops. Political parties, trade unions or business associations might commit to grassroots innovations and bring attention, publicity, investment and advocacy. Consumers in niche markets might emerge who further help a grassroots innovation. So, spaces can range from cognitive spaces receptive to alternative ideas and methods (such as the development of new scientific ideas in the margins of academia) to physical, political and institutional spaces where it is possible to develop and experiment with tools and forms of organization.

There is an important difference between spaces and strategies here and our earlier explanation of *contexts* described above. The difference turns on the agency of social actors. Contexts imply structural conditions that can restrict (or favour) the availability and locations of resources and opportunities for grassroots innovation activities; whereas the idea of spaces and strategies tries to understand how grassroots innovation movements can also be proactive in opening up new arenas or actively seizing and shaping platforms for alternative innovation activity.

Helpful here is research into niche spaces for alternative forms of innovation. Niches are spaces where the rules are different, or the conventional norms of innovation are suspended, perhaps partially. This allows social actors and institutions to build – sometimes only temporarily – protective spaces to tinker and experiment with innovative ideas and practices. Niches are the locus where it is possible to mobilize resources to nurture and test new technologies and new forms of organization. In this way, niches can be considered a source for path-breaking innovations (Smith and Raven, 2012). Grassroots innovation movements may be conceived as constructing temporary protective niche spaces where people can experiment with new technologies, knowledge practices and forms of organization (Seyfang and Smith, 2007). The act of constructing niche spaces encompasses both discursive practices and framing activities as well as material practices, including technological developments, funding strategies, infrastructure and network development. Importantly, processes and platforms for learning are vital to the development of these innovative spaces.

Niche spaces can be created by taking advantage of relatively 'passive' arenas, not generated or opened up by the grassroots innovators themselves but found to hand and actively exploited for their favourable possibilities. Conversely, niche spaces may be opened up much more deliberately and actively, in order to generate dedicated opportunities and situations, by pushing for support from other actors and institutions. In either case, it is important to understand that spaces of experimentation often involve negotiation and struggle with incumbent powers and entrenched practices that might otherwise close down such spaces.

Thus we ask how spaces – physical, social, discursive and institutional – are opened up by and for grassroots innovation movements in order that their alternative approaches can be put into practice; how framings and wider discourses are mobilized in each case, alongside other resources, in order to open and further these spaces; and how experiences in these spaces, and the success or otherwise of influencing the wider context, prompt reflection, reframing and some renegotiation of strategies.

Pathways

A final aspect to our understanding of grassroots innovation movements is to explain how they contribute to alternative developments over time. We do this by using the concept of pathways. The STEPS Centre (Leach et al., 2010), where the research project leading to this book was based, makes the case for a plural approach to sustainable developments by arguing that plural development pathways are possible. In any given situation there is never one self-evidently best way to develop. STEPS research recommends that greater attention be paid to opening up and constructing 'alternative' pathways, either existing or imagined for the future. The Centre makes this case on the scientific grounds of recognizing diversity and difference and on normative grounds for environmentally sustainable and socially just developments.

So, how can the framing of contexts and innovation, and the active opening of spaces for doing grassroots innovation over time, contribute to alternative development pathways? How do grassroots innovation movements develop activities and respond to changes over time, and with what consequences for the pathways they build? Particularly interesting here is how encounters between grassroots innovation movements and mainstream institutions for science, technology and innovation can lead to the construction of alternative pathways of development (Fressoli et al., 2014; Hess, 2007; Smith, 2007): pathways with greater attention to issues of social inclusion, diversity and difference, and social justice.

The STEPS pathways approach emphasizes the multiple narratives that arise in sustainable development debates, shaped by a range of discursive framings (including scientific knowledge), and which in any given context can generate a plurality of possible development pathways. Different framings are more inclusive of some issues, criteria and knowledges than others, and framings can differ in their recognition and responses to the uncertainties inevitable in all social choices about the purposes and directions of development. Not all framings and associated narratives are equally influential, however; some may be linked to dominant pathways or directions, while other narratives may be side-lined or hidden, associated with more marginalized pathways (Leach et al., 2010). The STEPS approach calls for identifying the actors involved in different pathways, how each actor or group of actors frames their reality and their goals for change, and thus which features are prioritized and what strategies they choose to leverage development and change (Leach et al., 2010). This can extend to framings of the past and present, and visions for the future, all of which can have a function in the building of pathways, doing work to help construct them (Garud et al., 2010). Furthermore, pathways are not necessarily linear in time or space. There can be an element of 'back and forth-ing', truncation and renewal, in the durational journey along pathways (Garud and Gehman, 2012).

We draw on the STEPS pathways approach when considering the consequences of grassroots innovation movements. It involves us returning to an outsider ontology and attending to the intersections of power, politics and institutions that influence which pathways dominate (i.e. pathways that exhibit lock-in towards particular directions of development and lock out others), which pathways are marginalized or excluded and, hence, the associated successes and failures of contributions to alternative developments from our case study grassroots innovation movements. To do this, we examine the relations (e.g. supportive, antagonistic, indifferent) that exist between grassroots innovation movements and mainstream innovation agendas and institutions: how do alternative movements, often situated on the margins in relation to prevailing political and economic structures, try to influence or respond to such asymmetric relations? What are the controversies, politics and power relations that challenge (or perhaps support as well as undermine) alternative pathways; what enduring influences or traces do these pathways leave? What are the lessons for grassroots innovation in future pathways?

However, we also seek to push the pathways framework beyond its emphasis on framing and narrative to include more explicit attention to the material aspects of pathways and the importance of interaction between the discursive and the material features in pathways. A significant body of work in science and technology studies more broadly calls for attention to the relations between the material and the discursive and the co-constitution of the social and the technical (Jasanoff, 2004; Latour, 1993). Whatever the values in play – be they the requirements of intended users, the ideas of grassroots innovators or the democratic ideals of activists – all have to confront the materiality of the technologies that feature in the solutions. Technologies themselves become agents in pathways: their material properties affect whether and how they are accessible to grassroots innovators, and thus how models, for example, of participatory design, can be applied to those technologies (Asaro, 2000). The materiality of the objects and concrete practices developed by grassroots innovation movements must therefore be considered a key component in the construction of alternative pathways.

An emphasis on the more material aspects of pathways is evident in the sustainability transitions literature (Schot and Geels, 2008; Smith et al., 2010). Some of this work emphasizes an iterative modulation between vision and practice, discursive and material components (Loorbach, 2007; Voss et al., 2009). This mix of adaptation or reorienting of goals through experience in material experimentation involves multiple actors, including intermediaries and outsiders, in 'steering' or shaping pathways (Kemp et al., 2007). For example, Kemp et al. (2007) recognize the sometimes conflicted encounters between actors at multiple levels and over multiple timescales that shape development pathways. Scholars developing the transitions framework point to various roles for intermediary actors – from government departments, local, regional and national-level NGOs, different kinds of research and development institutions, and the private sector, whether as firms, associations or investors – in steering, coordinating action and aggregating lessons arising in niches and for wider application (Geels and Deuten, 2006). Empirical work suggests that the realities of niches are complex and varied, and identifies the considerable work of intermediaries in helping to grow, consolidate and diffuse grassroots innovations (Hargreaves et al., 2013). Intermediary actors implement various methods to try to coordinate support and generate lessons for alternative pathways from very diverse, context-specific local projects, but drawing lessons across these varied circumstances and among a plurality of social actors with diverse interests is challenging (Hargreaves et al., 2013). Moreover, an emphasis on scaling up, growth and mainstreaming in niche management can eclipse some of the more critical and oppositional motivations of the grassroots innovation movements. Easily co-opted elements of a grassroots innovation might be supported, especially those that align with dominant development pathways, to the detriment of grassroots elements criticizing and seeking alternatives to those dominant pathways (Smith et al., 2015).

Thus, for grassroots innovation movements, we need to trace the framings of pathways and the narratives for their development *as well as* the material objects and spaces they develop when trying to create alternative pathways. In other words, we want to attend to the actual material doing of projects and how these connect over time. We do this with the use of specific illustrative examples for each movement; projects that feed back and become resources (or cautionary lessons) for subsequent movement mobilization and help to shape or maintain movement identities. The strategies involved in working across projects or linking between broader aims and specific activities on the ground are part of what constitute innovation pathways over time. Grassroots innovation movements learn and develop their knowledge bases, skills and capabilities through the actual development of grassroots enterprises, case studies, pilots, experiments and technological objects, as well as through the lessons gained (and dilemmas raised) from taking advantage of public programmes or resources, addressing pressures to formalize or scale up, or seeing some practices co-opted or diffusing widely but in forms diverging from the original intent. All these experiences are also part of building pathways. Pathways may not go in the directions desired by some activists, or they may fail to incorporate some cherished values. How grassroots innovation movements perceive, reflect and respond to these pathway experiences becomes a focus of concern and the way that such reflections inform continued attempts to build alternative pathways.

Conclusions

In this chapter we have developed a framework for analysing grassroots innovation movements by introducing and discussing a number of interrelated concepts that are useful for thinking about the aspirations, activities and consequences of grassroots innovation movements. These concepts were as follows.

- *Context* covers the historical circumstances in which the grassroots movement arose, the issues and situations that were generative for the movement and the opportunities available to the movement within those contexts.
- *Framings* focuses on the shared meanings, interpretations and narratives for doing innovation differently that hold the movement together and orientate its activities.
- *Spaces and strategies* are the collection of sites and arenas – physical, institutional, organizational and cognitive – where grassroots innovation movements actively open up material activity and do innovation and get support for promoting further grassroots innovation.

- *Pathways* considers the development of the grassroots innovation movement over time, both in discursive terms (the fate and influence of its ideas and aims) and in material terms (the creation of new artefacts and new development trajectories).

In the next six chapters, we analyse our case studies of grassroots innovation movements in detail, including their encounters with mainstream institutions of science, technology and innovation. In each case, we carefully set out the context for the movement. We analyse how different framings and interpretations of innovation, social inclusion and participation are negotiated and contested, and what spaces are opened up through different strategies in order to realize their activities and forge alternative pathways (Hess, 2007; Smith, 2007).

Each of our case study chapters is structured so that it considers the above concepts in turn. Although this risks implying a linear process – framings inform spaces which enable pathways – the realities are movements whose contexts, framings, spaces and strategies are much more interactive, and whose dynamics carry implications for the kinds of grassroots innovation that get done, and the pathways involved.

3
SOCIALLY USEFUL PRODUCTION

In January 1976 workers at Lucas Aerospace in the UK published an Alternative Corporate Plan for the future of the company. This was an innovative response to management announcements that thousands of jobs were to be cut in the face of industrial restructuring, international competition and technological change in design and manufacturing. Instead of redundancy, the workers argued their right to socially useful production, and in so doing spawned a grassroots movement.

Industrial restructuring and relocation by the owners of capital threatened many manufacturing livelihoods and communities in industrialized countries in the 1970s. Workers in the UK were fighting closures and redundancies at factory level through strikes, occupation and work-ins (Coates, 1981). The Lucas Plan was unusual in that, through careful analysis of their skills, machinery, work organization and economic potential, the workers proposed innovative alternatives to closures in manufacturing.

Around half of Lucas Aerospace's output supplied military contracts. Since this business area depended upon public funds, as did many of the firm's civilian products, workers argued that state support would be better put to developing more socially useful products. Arms conversion arguments attracted interest from the peace movement and social activists more widely. Additional proposals in the plan, such as for human-centred technologies that enhanced skills rather than displaced labour, caught the attention of some on the Left, and broader arguments for socially shaping technology for community benefit resonated with the emerging radical science movement.

The *Financial Times* described the Lucas Plan as 'one of the most radical alternative plans ever drawn up by workers for their company' (*Financial Times*, 23 January 1976, cited in Wainwright and Elliott, 1982). Or, as the Minister for Industry, Tony Benn, put it in an Open University film at the time, 'one of the most remarkable exercises that has ever occurred in British industrial history'. The plan was nominated for the Nobel Peace Prize in 1979.[1]

Despite this attention, the workers themselves, and especially their leaders in the Shop Stewards Combine Committee, suspected (correctly) that the plan in isolation would convince neither management nor government (Lucas Aerospace Combine Shop Stewards Committee, 1979). In the meantime, and as a lever to exert pressure, the workers embarked upon a broader political campaign for the right of all people to socially useful production. As one of the leaders put it afterwards, the Lucas workers wanted to 'inflame the imaginations of others' and 'demonstrate in a very practical and direct way the creative power of "ordinary people"' (Cooley, 1987, p. 139).

Links were forged with workers adopting similar initiatives elsewhere in the UK, and also in Germany, Scandinavia, Australia and the USA. The plan also found willing support among newer social movements in radical science, community activism and the environment. Arguments in the Lucas Plan 'went far beyond the confines of the company, industry, trade unions and even the country concerned' (Pelly, 1985, p. 107). The plan became symbolic of a wider critique of mainstream policy towards technology and economic development (Bodington et al., 1986). Over the next few years, initiatives for socially useful production emerged from the bottom up, in shop floors, in polytechnics and in local communities (Blackburn et al., 1982; Collective Design/Project, 1985). It is in this sense that socially useful production was a grassroots innovation movement. However, it was also a movement that, with hindsight, was swimming against the political and economic tide. The alliances struck, the spaces created and the initiatives generated were ultimately swept aside by the rise of Thatcherism and the installation of neoliberal ideology.

Analysis begins in the next section by explaining the economic, political and social background from which the movement emerged. The following section analyses the movement's framings of technology and development. Analysis then moves to movement spaces and strategies for socially useful production. Specific initiatives provide further illustration, before the penultimate section discusses critical features in pathways towards socially useful production. The chapter concludes by reflecting on some lessons for grassroots pathways.

The industrial background to the Lucas Plan

The 1970s were a turbulent and transformative period in the UK socially, economically and politically (Beckett, 2010; Sandbrook, 2012). Heightened international competition, technological change and the restructuring of capital were placing UK manufacturing under increased pressure. Changes in investment practices and ownership brought manufacturing under additional pressures. Industrial policy reliant upon state-directed development through nationalizations, and upon loans and subsidies to industrial champions, was in difficulty. Plant closures were growing. Unemployment passed one million in 1972 and kept rising.

Investment decisions by capital were central to restructuring, but so too was state power through tax breaks, grants and subsidies to enterprises 'rationalizing' their operations and investing in new technology. Indeed, Lucas Aerospace emerged from a series of mergers in the industry in the 1960s that were supported by government grants. The relocation and consolidation of factories onto larger sites, the introduction of new working practices through technological change, and outright closure of facilities, were reshaping the industrial landscape. Workplace resistance manifested in shop stewards organizing occupations and work-ins aimed at overturning restrictions on pay and work, and plant closures (Coates, 1981; Darlington and Lyddon, 2001; Ferris, 1972). Workers were also concerned about the consequences of new technology for employment, work rates and skills, particularly with computer-controlled and automation technologies. New forms of worker awareness and initiative were required in order to negotiate new technologies (Thompson and Bannon, 1985).

Politically, the post-war consensus over Keynesian economic policy was fragmenting between a rising new Right and a disoriented Left. The Right was increasingly laissez-faire towards economic restructuring: management should be liberated to make profitable choices, and 'lame duck' firms should be allowed to fail; unburdened enterprise, especially in services, would generate new jobs. On the Left, alternatives were sought in renewed interest in popular economic plans, industrial cooperatives and workers' control (Tuckman, 2011).

Out of this industrial background emerged the Lucas Plan. In an attempt to coordinate and strengthen responses, shop stewards transcended historic divisions of role, craft and profession and were 'combining' workers from across trade unions and industrial sites. Early victories over pay and redundancies enabled the Lucas Aerospace Shop Stewards Combine Committee to demonstrate the advantages of coordinated solidarity. The Combine Committee began discussing socially useful production among the workforce as an alternative to redundancy. It was hoped that government intervention (forthcoming in past industrial rationalizations) would bring management to negotiations along these lines.

Input to the Alternative Plan was solicited initially through a letter to leading authorities, institutions, universities, trade unions and other organizations that the Combine thought would be sympathetic to developing alternative products. Only three responses were received. Dave Elliott, from the Open University, proposed renewable energy and energy-efficiency product alternatives that the workers might develop. Meredith Thring, from Queen Mary College, proposed that Lucas should redeploy its capabilities into telechiric products (devices for working remotely). Richard Fletcher, from North East London Polytechnic, proposed a hybrid road–rail vehicle. Each proposal was incorporated into the plan, but the Combine was disappointed in the low response rate (Wainwright and Elliott, 1982). When it turned to its own workers, with a wide-ranging questionnaire distributed via shop stewards, the response was much stronger. The questionnaire prompted discussion about the equipment, skills and organization available at Lucas plants. It led to ideas way beyond the development of alternative products and into considerations of the planning and organization of production, issues related to labour processes and training, and economic management.

It took a year to put the plan together. The plan ran to six volumes of approximately 200 pages each. Designs and descriptions for over 150 products were accompanied by market analyses and economic considerations. Proposals were made for employee training that enhanced and broadened skills, and suggestions were put forward for restructuring work organization into less-hierarchical teams, breaking divisions between practical shop-floor knowledge and professional engineering knowledge. The plan challenged fundamental assumptions about how innovation and business should be run. Senior management rejected it. Meetings with the Combine were delayed, cancelled and evaded. National trade union leaders were similarly unhelpful when it came to practical, material assistance. There was opposition to the idea of grassroots initiatives upsetting the conventions of union demarcations, hierarchy, procedure and activity – even though grassroots trade unionists were interested and actively organizing. Similarly, despite government continuing to provide public money to Lucas in the forms of deferred taxation, grants and public financing for new factory infrastructure, the Lucas Plan was consistently overlooked.

A tripartite meeting was finally initiated by the government in February 1979, but made little headway (Wainwright and Elliott, 1982). Senior industrial managers, the presidents of trade unions and civil servants were not open to the idea that workers and grassroots agendas should shape the criteria and directions to which technical know-how and manufacturing should be put.

However, the plan attracted a great deal of attention and discussion beyond the company. The *New Statesman* claimed (1 July 1977) that 'The philosophical and technical implications of the plan are now being discussed on an average of twenty-five times a week in international media' (cited in Forrester, 2012, p. 12). After several years of campaigning, a debate on the plan was held in the House of Commons. As Bob Cryer MP[2] put it in opening the Commons debate:

> It took the shop stewards three years to meet the management to discuss the corporate plan, because they were challenging the hierarchical nature of our society, which is that the bosses shall make the decisions and the workers shall accept them, and woe betide workers who question those decisions and perhaps even produce better ones. That sort of attitude challenges the whole nature and structure of our society.
> *(Bob Cryer MP,* House of Commons Debates, Hansard, *vol. 962, cols 899–932, 12 February 1979)*

More than the practical, socially desirable products it contained, the plan symbolized a radical reordering of industrial processes and purposes in society. For elites on all sides, that vision seemed simply incredible, or, more seriously, was discomforting, unwelcome and even threatening.

For others, the plan resonated with their aspirations for social change. The demands of new social movements for peace, the environment, community activism and women were becoming increasingly prominent in social and political life. The Lucas Plan came to the attention of these different social movements in various ways. The peace movement's demands for disarmament generated debate about converting the arms industry to civilian production. Environmentalists sought alternative technologies for an ecological society, especially in response to the energy crisis. Radical scientists wanted socially responsible technological development. Feminists were interested in less-patriarchal technologies. Community activists in manufacturing towns were linking neighbourhood deprivation to economic decline. A broader coalition of groups began discussing and promoting ideas for socially useful production.

Institutional support came through the leadership of a handful of radical Left local authorities, including the Greater London Council (GLC), who provided resources and facilities for putting ideas into practice. They hoped that socially useful production combined with popular alternative economic strategies could present a platform for challenging a rising right-wing agenda nationally.

The resulting movement flourished only briefly. The election of the Conservative Thatcher government in 1979 and the emergence of an eventually hegemonic neoliberalism over the 1980s took politics and socio-economic development in a very different direction. The economic and manufacturing fate of the country was to be left to the market and not to popular planning. The industrial recession of the early 1980s saw trade union bases decline sharply, and legislative measures restricted trade union practices and emboldened management. Local authority autonomy over economic development was restricted severely through new legislation, and metropolitan authorities such as the GLC were shut down completely. The struggles that helped to forge the movement ultimately overwhelmed it. But not before it had demonstrated the importance and possibility for democratic technological development.

Framings for socially useful production

Reflecting upon workers' plans at a conference on Alternatives to Unemployment in 1978, Mike George, from the Centre for Alternative Industrial and Technological Systems (CAITS), summarized the framing of socially useful production:

> These workers maintain that manufacturing industries need to be revitalized through the conversion of the productive apparatus to achieve a number of aims:
>
> - to fulfil social needs, products or services which are not exclusive to the rich or any other elite, which maintain or promote health, welfare etc;
> - to use technologies which are interactive with human skills, which enhance those skills, which can be controlled by the worker;
> - to design for need, to stress maintenance, re-use, re-conditioning – against high-volume, obsolescent products;

- to work on products which can be 'sold' in a socialized market, e.g. design and production of medical equipment with direct contact with medical staff and patients.

(George, 1978, p. 176; see also Cooley, 1987, pp. 154–155)

Activists from social movements fed ideas into this framing, and their elaboration through practice evolved over time. As such, activities in socially useful production were informed through a variety of intersecting framings:

- arms conversion, alternative technologies and community activism;
- human-centred technology and the labour process;
- industrial democracy and participatory design;
- alternative economic strategy and social audit.

In this section, each framing is elaborated in turn.

Arms conversion, alternative technologies and community activism

The Lucas Plan had obvious attractions for the peace movement. The Plan not only made salient the movement's moral critique of violence, but also addressed the thornier issue of unemployment arising from government cuts in military spending. The swords-to-ploughshares conversion argued by defence workers themselves was fantastic (Pelly, 1985). Peace activists promoted the development of alternative plans at other defence firms too, including Vickers and British Aircraft Corporation.

The Lucas Plan also resonated with activists in radical science, centring on the British Society for Social Responsibility in Science, who were questioning the vested interests that were setting scientific priorities in society (Asquith, 1979; Levidow, 1983; Reilly, 1976). Whether informed by Marxist analysis of the structures of science and technology or by the cultures of science in society (Asdal et al., 2007), the radical science movement shared with the Lucas workers an interest in developing an alternative framework for science and technology. The movement for socially useful production was consequently not framed solely as a campaign for jobs and products but, rather, about the culture, structure and direction of technological change in society. Such attention provided philosophical and analytical resources concerning the importance of plural knowledge, including tacit and practical expertise, public decisions about the funding of product research and development and participation in the processes that shape technological agendas (Cooley, 1987).

Ideas for alternative technologies were also salient among environmentalists. However, environmentalist interest in smaller-scale technologies appropriate for a decentralized, ecological society was ambivalent towards trade unionists interested in jobs arising from the industrial production of eco-friendly technologies

(Smith, 2005). Even when technological artefacts were essentially the same, such as wind turbines, heat pumps and solar panels, tensions arose in the way these technologies were related to different kinds of production, use and ways of living; and that further complicated interaction across differences of class and ideology between environmentalists and workers (Brachi, 1974; Elliott, 1975). Nevertheless, as a social issue, the environment, and especially energy, became included within the ambit of the socially useful.

In similar respects, women's perspectives and gender issues were raised as important absences in the initial framing of socially useful production and which arose in the male-dominated sector of manufacturing. Feminists pointed to gendered perspectives within industry and urged socially useful production to look beyond manufacturing settings, arguing the importance of consumption activities, as well as production in other sectors. Furthermore, they contributed ideas that went beyond 'products' to consider the undervalued social production already going on in homes and through care work (Huws, 1985; Liff, 1985). These important perspectives broadened the movement's framing and presented a view on production that drew on its relations with different forms of consumption (Blackburn et al., 1982).

A final broadening beyond the impetus of the Lucas Plan arose through connections with community development. Activists were increasingly seeing community problems in structural terms of class and economic relations (Community Development Project, 1977). A strategy of integrating community and industrial struggles and forming alliances between local trades councils and community groups 'was a central part of the strategy of the new radical community work' (Loney, 1983, p. 150; see also O'Malley, 1977). Socially useful production needed to direct industrial, technological and economic resources to needs identified and defined by local communities. At the Coventry Workshop, for example, shop stewards' committees and grassroots community groups joined to 'explore the links, in concept and practice, between industry and the community, the economy and the state, production and consumption, home and work' (Coventry Workshop, 1978, pp. 6–7; see also Field, 1985).

Human-centred technology and the labour process

The movement found its first expression in manufacturing workplaces. Here, technological changes, particularly computer-integrated manufacturing, were impacting on work skills, quality and jobs (Brödner, 1990). Influential studies argued that automated technologies introduced by capital, such as computer-aided design systems, production controls and numerically controlled machine tools, were reshaping the labour process to the disadvantage of workers (Braverman, 1974; Cooley, 1987; Noble, 1979). There were fears about dehumanized workplaces and workerless factories (George, 1978).

Technological change was conventionally seen as an evolutionary process relatively autonomous from society (Winner, 1977). Policy efforts for working people ought therefore to promote the best accommodation around inevitable developments towards automation (Freeman and Soete, 1994; Kaplinsky, 1984). Workers' leaders saw their task predominantly in first resisting changes and then negotiating a share of the productivity gains in terms of redundancy payments for those laid off by machines, retraining packages for work in the services sector and better pay and conditions for those remaining to tend the machines (Thompson and Bannon, 1985; Wainwright and Elliott, 1982).

However, the movement saw nothing automatic to automation. A plurality of technological pathways were plausible, including more flexible and skill-enhancing uses of computer-assisted machine tools (Piore and Sabel, 1984; Rauner et al., 1988). Workers and radical researchers argued that computer-controlled machinery should allow programming on the shop floor, machines should enhance rather than substitute operator skill and initiative and production should be organized by teams of workers who schedule the work required (Rosenbrock, 1989). Significantly, workers themselves should be involved in the design of new socio-technical systems (Ehn, 1988).

Not all automation was necessarily advantageous to management and capital. Automation required oversight, debugging and adaptation; systems designed without thought for user skills resulted in serious failures, as well as resistance; and production programming in centralized offices could be inflexible and lead to slow and costly retooling that was unresponsive to customer demands (Brödner, 1990; Cherns, 1976; Senker, 1986). The practical know-how underpinning any complex task provided a potential lever for increasing creative input from workers.

As such, the socially useful framing expanded to argue democratic control, and direct participation was required over the design and social use of technology (Cooley, 1987; Ehn, 1988; Murray, 1985a). The movement articulated opportunities for workers and communities to become involved in new forms of production (Mole and Elliott, 1987; Thompson, 1989).

Industrial democracy and participatory design

In the mid-1970s a union's right to negotiate wages and working conditions was a standard feature in industrial relations (Coates, 1981). Rights to negotiate product design, including decisions on technology investment and the organization of production, were not part of mainstream union, corporate or government policy. Yet this was key in socially useful production. Design, development, investment and marketing decisions were a matter for participation, debate and negotiation. Workers and communities had to be involved. Brian Lowe, at the Unit for the Development of Alternative Products in the West Midlands, explained:

> The central feature of socially useful production is the development of ideas and organisation forms that encourage involvement, generate self confidence and release new-found or rediscovered skills during the examination of how productive resources should be used to meet social needs. Initiatives promoting socially useful production must, in turn, be extremely

responsible and very supportive throughout the complete process if working people are to successfully take on the tasks and challenges of responding with alternative plans.

(Lowe, 1985, p. 69)

In the workplace, this meant involving workers from 'all levels of staff from the high-level designers and engineers through to the skilled craft workers on the shop floor' (Cooley, 1981, p. 54). A departure from conventional notions of industrial democracy was the argument for extending participation outside the workplace into local communities and social movements. Wider participation in the development of alternative design criteria, organization of production and R&D for social use was envisaged as arising through local branches of trades councils needed to build alliances with community groups, organizations of the unemployed, pensioners and consumers and socialist, feminist and anti-racist bodies (Blackburn et al., 1982). The desire to produce in a socially useful way, and to place skills and production technologies at the service of communities rather than capital, became a key framing.

Alternative economic strategy and social audit

Arguments to invest in socially useful products in terms of use values rather than exchange values were well and good; but how to secure these investments in practice? On this matter, framings focused on the direct and indirect social costs of unemployment, and argued that it was more cost-effective to put people to socially useful work than to pay them benefits on the dole. The government was spending billions in direct grants, subsidies and deferred taxes in order to help large firms restructure and shed jobs, and then further billions in unemployment payments and social benefits to those laid off. Moreover, it was society, and not the producer, that bore the externalities of harmful and dangerous technologies, such as weapons, and the escalating defence costs associated with their development. Why not redistribute public funds to designing, making and marketing socially useful products? A variety of bodies used these 'social audit' arguments to justify public investment in socially useful production (Barratt Brown, 1978; Eastall, 1989; Murray, 1985b).

Sympathetic left-wing local authorities adopted this alternative economic strategy for jobs and created enterprise boards for investing funds into product prototyping, the development of cooperatives and rescuing failing enterprises (Greater London Enterprise Board, 1984b). While socially useful production became framed within these alternative economic strategies, the strategies themselves were not specifically promoting socially useful production (Bodington et al., 1986; Palmer, 1986; Rowthorn, 1981). These strategies introduced questions of economic calculation into socially useful production (Rustin, 1986). How was one to prioritize development efforts between the wide varieties of socially useful proposals that were emerging through alternative plans and community activism? And, crucially, how could initiatives leverage the very large investments needed to move from prototyping and demonstration and into full-scale production? While alternative economic plans were operating 'in and against the market' (Murray, 1985b), they were, nevertheless, public programmes under pressure to demonstrate value for money.

Some attempts were made to formulate socially useful production economically (Bodington et al., 1986; Rustin, 1986). However, activists were reluctant to go too far because they feared that calculation would distort founding ideas about grassroots participation and turn the ideals for democratic decision into codified, technocratic procedures little better than existing industrial production. Under this view, what constituted social use was left to open and accessible considerations through locally specific deliberation in ways that allowed more tacit understandings to come into much more socialized processes of innovation. However, the lack of an alternative institutional framework for economic investment in products consistent with socially useful criteria left activities susceptible to selective dismissal and capture under more conventional economic criteria (Palmer, 1986).

Spaces and strategies for socially useful production

Spaces for socially useful production were created within grassroots trade unionism, research institutes and radical local authorities. Each provided distinct strategic opportunities. However, they were also spaces that were being squeezed by the wider political and economic changes underway in the UK.

Grassroots trade unionism

Working conditions at Lucas Aerospace were conducive to the development of an alternative plan. A large proportion of workers were highly skilled, accustomed to working with (unionized) design and technology professionals and where research and product development were important components in complex batch production that retained craft elements. Work on new products involved mixed teams where the tacit knowledge of operatives, fitters and so forth was apparent to the more propositional and codified theories of attentive engineering design professionals. Developing alternative designs and proposals was something that workers were confident could be organized effectively. Less-organized workers in smaller firms, or workers on mass production lines, less familiar with product development, had further to travel.

Workers at Lucas were proactive in supporting workers in the trade union movement and sharing their ideas and experience. The Combine Committee helped to create CAITS for these purposes (see below) and helped workers' plans at Vickers, British Aircraft Corporation, Dunlop, Parsons and Chrysler (North East Trade Union Studies Information Unit, 1980; Speke Joint Shops Stewards Committee, 1979). Support worked through the grassroots trade union activity, including local trades councils, and created space by organizing teach-ins among the workers, distributing information and analysis, publicizing activity through the labour movement press and seeking help from motions of support, funds and policy proposals at trade union meetings (North East Trade Union Studies Information Unit, 1980).

The movement for socially useful production was also noticed internationally (Rasmussen, 2007). Metalworkers in West Germany used UK experience to inform Alternative Product Working Groups in a number of firms, including Blohm & Voss, AEG, VFW, MBB, Krupp and MAK. They proposed combined heat and power systems, transport systems, and, at Voith in Bremen, designed tyre-recycling equipment. Innovation and Technology Centres were set up in Bremen and Osnabrück in collaboration between trade unions, universities and local authorities.

Research and education institutes

The Lucas Combine Committee created CAITS in October 1977 with funding from the Joseph Rowntree Foundation and support from North East London Polytechnic (NELP). The initial idea was to use NELP facilities and worker input to develop prototypes proposed in the Alternative Plan and furnish economic and industrial analysis. It was believed that this would strengthen the bargaining position of workers. CAITS facilities were extended to workers at other companies and in other industries. CAITS was joined by other research units that could provide union members with access to independent analysis about firms, sectors and technological trends.

Conferences and projects coordinated research, educational and campaign activity in socially useful production (e.g. Open University, Coventry Polytechnic, NELP). Movement activists at a variety of polytechnics linked their facilities to local communities, including through student projects. Ideas and initiatives for socially useful production also featured in educational programmes at the time. Open University materials, for example, explained the Lucas Plan to thousands of design students.[3]

Activists attended European conferences and, in turn, hosted overseas union researchers at UK events (CAITS, 1978). In Bremen, for example, a symposium on Work and Technology brought together academics from the humanities and engineering with trade unionists, managers and politicians (Rasmussen, 2007). Notable among these links were those with Scandinavia. Worker research projects in Denmark, Sweden and Norway were exploring how computer-based technologies could be designed and introduced into the workplace in ways that both extended democratic control over the labour process and enhanced the skills of the workers involved. Pelle Ehn, a key figure in this 'Collective Resource Approach', wrote how:

> As a political commitment our tradition shares many of the values and ideas of the alternative production movement; we have especially been influenced by the strategy of quality of work and product developed by workers and engineers at Lucas Aerospace in Britain.
>
> *(Ehn, 1988, p. 25)*

Left local authorities

A few local authorities supportive of socially useful production provided space for putting movement ideas into practice. Activity at the GLC was particularly intensive. With unemployment heading towards one in eight workers, and manufacturing in steep decline in the city, Londoners had voted an avowedly socialist Labour council into power in 1982. Its manifesto noted:

> Groups of workers such as the Lucas Aerospace Shop Stewards' Committee have, with the support of the Labour Party, begun to develop ideas on alternative production – using technologies which interact with human skills; making goods which are conducive to human health and welfare; working in ways which conserve, rather than waste, resources.
>
> ... We believe that these initiatives – which constitute a fundamental rejection of the values inherent in capitalist production – must be supported by a Labour GLC. We shall therefore be prepared to assist groups of workers seeking to develop alternative forms of production, with finance, with premises, or in other ways.
>
> *(Labour Manifesto, Greater London elections, 1981, quoted in Mole and Elliott, 1987, p. 81)*

Once in office, council leaders created the Greater London Enterprise Board (GLEB) to implement this policy, with an annual budget of £32 million (Eastall, 1989). Recipients of GLEB support were encouraged to promote worker involvement and seek cooperative business models (Greater London Enterprise Board, 1984a; Murray, 1985b).

Mike Cooley, sacked by Lucas Aerospace in 1981, was appointed Technology Director at GLEB, where he was able to use the resources, including political commitment, to enable others in the movement to network and make the case for aspects of socially useful production. It was through his creation of five Technology Networks, with a GLEB budget of £4 million, that facilities were provided for socially useful production (see below). Thames Technet was based in the south-east of the city, and the London Innovation Network (LIN) in the north-east. The other networks were the London Energy and Employment Network (LEEN), the London New Technology Network (LNTN) and Transnet (focusing on transport issues). The aim of these Technology Network workshops was to bring together the 'untapped skill, creativity and sheer enthusiasm' in local communities with the 'reservoir of scientific and innovation knowledge' in the polytechnics (Greater London Enterprise Board, 1984c, pp. 9–10). Similar initiatives were created elsewhere. In the West Midlands, the council opened the Unit for the Development of Alternative Products (UDAP); further north, Sheffield Council and Sheffield Polytechnic created the Centre for Product Development and Technological Resources (SCEPTRE) (Lowe, 1985); and a Centre for Alternative Products was proposed by Cleveland County Council and Teesside Polytechnic.

44 Socially useful production

Illustrative examples

Movement strategy took a variety of forms. Three were particularly emblematic: promoting particular artefacts or objects; the provision of facilities; and the practice of methodologies consistent with movement ideals. Examples of each strategy illustrate the different challenges in the development of pathways for socially useful production.

Objects: the road–rail bus

Included in the Lucas Plan was the proposal from Richard Fletcher at NELP to develop a bus that could run on both road and rail. These affordable vehicles increased the flexibility with which public transport could use infrastructure in both developed and developing-country situations (Lucas Aerospace Combine Shop Stewards Committee, 1978). As with other proposals in the Lucas Plan, the bus went to prototype on 'borrowed' company time and equipment. When Lucas created CAITS the road–rail bus was developed further.

While the viability of a road–rail bus was open to question, an advantage with this prototype was that it could be used in a Lucas Plan roadshow. The press was invited to join the bus as it toured industrial sites, shopping centres and local communities around the country. Other exemplary prototypes and designs were carried aboard the bus. The bus and displays engaged people in discussions, and visitors were invited to propose their own ideas for socially useful products. Prototypes on display included electric bicycles, small wind turbines, loading machinery, storable play equipment, catering services, medical equipment, robotic vision systems, products for people with disabilities and other designs. The idea was for these 'technological agitprops' to prompt discussion and debate about the wider framings surrounding socially useful production.

The road–rail bus was not developed further in the UK.[4] Nor were many of the other prototypes. Reflecting on experiences in the West Midlands, Brian Lowe wrote,

> [investment and marketing] require particular skills which were not available from within UDAP nor from within the other existing support groups. Consultants hired at great expense did not appear able to do a satisfactory job because they did not seem to appreciate the social criteria which were being applied.
>
> *(Lowe, 1985, p. 68)*

It proved difficult to align investor interest in returns on capital with the social goals that activists were realizing in their prototypes; and few people had the skills and capabilities to negotiate across these two worlds (Palmer, 1986; Rustin, 1986).

Nevertheless, the designs were considered an indicator of the untapped ingenuity residing within the grassroots, as well as being emblematic for issues of concern to people. Prototyping objects openly, through practical activities at places of work or in community life, engaged people in social issues differently, as compared to discussions at public meetings (Cooley, 2007). A GLEB leaflet about Technology Networks explained, 'Already there is no shortage of proposals for products and services . . . to excite interest, widen horizons, and ensure a continuing flow of practical and job-creating *challenges to economic fatalism*' (Greater London Enterprise Board, 1984a, emphasis added). This quote is quite typical in blending practical, object-oriented activity with political aspirations to rise to social challenges (Linn, 1987).

Facilities: Technology Networks

Technology Networks facilities considered the prototyping of alternative technologies to be a significant activity. Each workshop developed differently, but the broad aims were similar. They provided physical spaces, access to shared machine tools and assistance from technical staff in the service of local communities, enterprises and cooperatives. Attempts were made to recruit staff who 'appreciate the tacit knowledge of local residents and workers' (Greater London Enterprise Board, 1984c, p. 12). Workshops were governed by representatives of local communities, trade unions, tenants' groups and academia (Cooley, 1985). In an attempt to break down barriers between workshop staff and local communities, the London networks were sited away from 'alienating' educational campuses. The facilities provided walk-in venues intended for anyone wishing to get involved. Training was provided to boost access, inclusion and involvement. LNTN undertook training initiatives, for example, exploring how communities could network information and communications technologies (ICTs) to generate and share information, to engage with expert systems and enable groups to communicate and coordinate more effectively. A women's cooperative was established to address gender bias in microelectronics. Technology Networks hosted visits and machine-tool training for visitors. Mary Moore, from the London Innovation Network, described Technology Networks as:

> making sure that what you do is going to be of real use to the intended users which means somehow getting them to take part in the design process . . . You'd actually get them in the workshop and enable them to learn more about how such things are made and designed and repaired and modified.
> *(Quoted in Mackintosh and Wainwright, 1987, p. 214)*

Dissemination and sharing of knowledge and prototypes was encouraged through a 'product-bank'.

> Each centre contributes a product-bank of innovations patented by the networks for use by working people and for socially useful purposes. Machine-banks, consisting of second-hand machinery refurbished as part of a training programme, will be available for use by client enterprises.
>
> *(Greater London Enterprise Board, 1984c, p. 12)*

The plan was for profit-making enterprises to pay royalties on non-exclusively licensed products, which would contribute to network running costs and cross-subsidize the socially useful mission. Other sources of revenue were identified through the provision of useful products and services to the public sector and returns from the spin-off development of cooperative enterprises under the wider activities of GLEB. A user-friendly electronic heating controller, designed to improve efficiency, was fitted at County Hall to improve energy performance. However, proposals to manufacturers for its wider commercialization were resisted: the design reduced the need for lucrative maintenance and servicing contracts. In practice, marketing challenges like these sometimes proved intractable. Other activities, including IT manufacture and toys for schools, did go into successful local manufacture. Others, such as an electric bicycle, found developers and investors in other countries, including Germany and Italy, but without benefit for jobs in London. Even where a commercial market looked promising for prototypes, the investment required to move into manufacturing was simply beyond the means of GLEB, and financial institutions either were not interested in providing the industrial capital or refused to locate production in London.

The difficulty of developing products so directly was recognized, and the product-bank idea was adapted by an offshoot from the networks. A Technology Exchange was created that matched technology designs to firms seeking new products. This technology-transfer service was opened up successfully to commercial technology offers internationally. This commercial offshoot was deemed a success for the more business-oriented overseers of the Technology Networks at GLEB (Rustin, 1986). In contrast to the more radical aspirations of activists, the business emphasis rested in using workshop facilities to develop businesses. Brass Tacks, for example, repaired and reconditioned broken furniture and consumer goods for distribution to disadvantaged households. The Technology Networks worked with it to manufacture replacement components on a bespoke basis.

Here was an aspect to the movement that brought in business leaders and linked to their interest in small-scale enterprise (Davis and Bollard, 1986; McRobie, 1981). Business leaders took ideas and activities beyond the ideological confines of 'socially useful' and inserted them more widely into the spirit of enterprise that Thatcherism was trying to cultivate. Similar links were forged through training programmes and where practices generated by ideals for democratizing technology could be realigned with providing people with skills to enter new technology job markets (Palmer, 1986).

Not everyone in Technology Networks was agreed upon this direction. One of the first networks, starting in 1983, was LEEN. As various community, tenant and energy organizations became involved in the network, so the focus of the workshop opened up. As Dave Elliott explained:

> It was found that the rationale for the establishment of the networks, the promotion of alternative products and the provision of access to workshop and technical facilities leading to socially-useful employment was not the main problem regarding energy related issues discovered by LEEN. In the field of energy, at least at the local level, the main factor is not the lack of socially-useful technologies; rather the technology exists, but what is required is the political, institutional and financial commitment to the redistribution of resources that would allow the implementation of these technologies.
> *(Mole and Elliott, 1987, p. 87)*

Susie Parsons from LEEN explained how,

> Partly in light of these problems, many people involved in the technology networks quickly came to the conclusion that they had other useful roles besides product development. One of these was the use of existing technology to provide services to people, and helping people to understand and use existing technology more effectively.
> *(Mackintosh and Wainwright, 1987, pp. 208–209)*

Working with others under a 'Right to Warmth' campaign, LEEN provided energy audit and advice services for people, which involved developing convenient energy monitoring and modelling devices and assembling packages of energy-conserving technologies for installation in homes. The campaign drew attention to particular needs in apartment blocks and organized community energy initiatives aimed at job creation through the implementation of energy improvements (Greater London Enterprise Board, 1984c).

Activists involved in other technology networks recognized the political nature of forging links between technological development, community activism and local economic regeneration. Attempts were made to identify and then mobilize behind socially useful initiatives by linking to parallel developments in popular planning. The GLC Popular Planning Unit was attempting through community engagement to prioritize bottom-up socio-economic development priorities. Community workshops elsewhere were on a similar journey (Lowe, 1985).

Tensions emerged between those looking to the development of revenue through commercialization of products, a view associated with GLEB boards overseeing the networks, and the popular planners seeking to mobilize the networks for socialist transformation. Reflecting from their position in popular planning at the GLC, Maureen Mackintosh and Hilary Wainwright wrote:

> GLEB, for its part, put an increasing emphasis on commercial skills and product development, worried that money might be wasted, and the networks not survive, if products were not produced and marketed fast enough. They saw the products themselves as providing a sort of 'technological agitprop' capable of stimulating a further input by example. They argued that such practical demonstrations of the potential for socially useful job creation had to take priority over open-ended outreach work . . . Network staff, members, and users, however, take a more complex view than this. They acknowledge the importance of commercial skills, and having a plan of development of the networks. But they see on the whole a too early concentration on new products as counterproductive. What GLEB calls 'outreach', they see as the essence of networking, and the factor which can in the end generate real innovations. While recognising the tensions, they [network staff] see them as creative: the only way to democratise inputs to technological development.
> (Mackintosh and Wainwright, 1987, pp. 212–213)

It became increasingly apparent that the more radical aims required a transformation in the culture and institutions of innovation. 'Constructing an open door to planning and decision-making procedures is not enough' (Linn, 1987, p. 116). The networks and resources for design, prototyping and product development needed to also be culturally and socially accessible to Londoners. Socially speaking, that meant working around or transcending the daily demands on people's energy and time by providing them with the opportunities to participate (to patterns set by participants, in the evenings, weekends, etc.). Culturally, it meant the gradual process of building egalitarian relationships that crossed lines of expertise, class, race and gender. Workshop practices, language, attitudes and expectations needed careful and open reflection in order to overcome unintended exclusions. GLEB-appointed boards overseeing the networks were accused of having 'employed high numbers of technically experienced trade union men whose language, bureaucratic ways of working and emphasis on the product rather then the community process act to exclude even technically qualified women' (Linn, 1987, p. 121). The practicalities of bringing diverse communities together with engineers, machinists and designers proved considerable. As Mary Moore put it, 'You will not find this group coming together naturally after a CND demonstration or a football match, for a quick drink or an exchange of ideas' (quoted in Mackintosh and Wainwright, 1987, p. 214). Democratizing decisions required the resolution of conflicts between different groups, whether workers, neighbours, consumers, investors, professions, communities, and across divisions of class, gender and race (Blackburn et al., 1982).

Such challenges extended beyond the workshops. Pam Linn, at ThamesNet, described vividly the intimidating power relations in play when an unemployed grassroots innovator met the executives of a large manufacturer suspected of pirating his design for safety lighting (Linn, 1987). The networks alone could not resolve these deep-seated societal issues. Some networks did attend to the cultures of innovation within their workshops by developing more inclusive practices (Clark, 1983).

But the opportunity to do so proved short lived. Hostile to radical local authorities, the Conservative central government abolished the GLC and similar authorities (e.g. West Midlands) in 1986. It also curtailed local government powers and budgets over economic planning more generally. In the universities and polytechnics too, reductions in funding and a harsher environment eroded already fragile academic alliances. Community workshops struggled on with reduced funds, but those that did had increasingly to adapt to a commercial, self-financing logic, such as providing training and consultancy that aligned their services to the needs of private enterprise (Eastall, 1989).

Methodologies: human-centred technology

Mention was made earlier of movement links with projects in Scandinavia that were seeking methodologies for human-centred technologies (Asaro, 2000; Howard, 1985). Through these initiatives, researchers and workers began to consider more participatory ways of designing and negotiating the introduction of new technologies. Together they developed the use of mock-ups, scenarios and prototyping, and joint study of workplaces and the labour process and its socio-economic basis (Ehn, 1988; Kraft and Bansler, 1994). The aim was to empower workers through participatory methodologies in technological change.

In the UK, similar discussions finally came to fruition in 1986 with a European Commission European Strategic Programme on Research in Information Technology (ESPRIT) project to develop human-centred computer-integrated manufacturing (Rosenbrock, 1989). The idea was to develop programmable machine tools and devices that followed and enhanced operator skill and control. Reflecting emerging industrial interest in flexible specialization (Piore and Sabel, 1984), project collaborators at the University of Manchester Institute of Science and Technology (UMIST), the Innovation and Technology Centre at Bremen and the Danish Technical University involved industrial partners who would host the pilot systems. However, while usability, work teams and skills enhancement were part of the project, any framing for the purposes of industrial democracy and socially useful production receded and was displaced by a more commercially minded logic.

Rasmussen recalls how research and practice generally over time became dominated by investigating 'how humans interact with computers, rather than looking the other way around, how the technology can be shaped to support enrichment of human skills and socially useful products' (Rasmussen, 2007, p. 475). He noted how initiatives in the 1980s and 1990s 'focused on the microlevel only. The societal perspective of the Lucas Workers' Plan or the attempts made by Greater London Council in the 1970s and 1980s get lost' (Rasmussen, 2007, p. 491). As such, the full significance of human-centred technological methodologies was reduced (Rosenbrock, 1989). Practical elements that were easier to absorb into industry informed subsequent developments in a more pragmatic user-centred design.

Aspects of the methodologies pioneered through movement initiatives have become standard features in user-centred design approaches and, hence, the marketability of technologies (Asaro, 2000). While the democratic intent developed much less fully, the spur provided by such intentions nevertheless generated ideas and practices taken up in industries that were restructuring for flexible specialization, working groups and seeking more effective human–computer interaction (Asaro, 2000; Piore and Sabel, 1984). Flexible machine-tool technologies afforded some operational autonomy to workers within shop-floor work teams, even if team conditions and targets were set by central management and, ultimately, capital rather than social need (Brödner, 2007). To some, this was a diminished, technical application of democratically motivated aspirations for human-centred methodologies (Buchanan, 2001).

Pathways for socially useful production

Four features were prominent in the development pathways pursued by the movement for socially useful production. These were, first, addressing the structural changes enabling and constraining pathways; second, how the characteristics of the spaces where initiatives materialized influenced the possibilities for moving beyond those spaces; third, the practical reasoning afforded by grassroots alternatives; and finally, the legacy of the movement, given its loss of momentum and dispersal.

Restructuring for socially useful production

Debates about socially useful production recognized repeatedly that its viability required deeper-seated political and economic changes; yet recognizing these changes was beyond the agency of the specific initiatives. The triple challenges of transforming the institutions of innovation for community participation, redirecting substantial investment into production for social use and articulating economic demand to social use value ultimately eluded the movement (Lowe, 1985; Mackintosh and Wainwright, 1987; Mole and Elliott, 1987).

The hegemonic rise of neoliberalism, and the specific antipathies of the Thatcher government, industrial management and capital towards the movement, proved insurmountable. The restructuring of industry, and changes in society and economy, continued in a different direction to that sought by the movement. These political and economic challenges were in debate in the 1970s. Indeed, resistance to emerging market orthodoxies nourished the spaces available for social alternatives and provided impetus to specific initiatives. Ultimately, however, the new orthodoxies undermined possibilities for consolidating and expanding movement initiatives. Activists tired, or moved on, or their pathways succumbed to these structural forces; spaces closed down, and activities dissipated into other spaces and forms (see below). Initiatives that outlasted the movement did so because they also worked under the new structural orthodoxies, and their diffusion could be presented technically as socially innovative fixes, rendered palatable by stripping them of overt political intent.

Moving beyond alternative spaces

As the movement moved into the spaces of community workshops and alternative economic strategy, so activities became imbued with framings that included popular planning, community involvement, gender and environmental issues. The prototypes were envisaged by activists as moving into production under less-alienating industrial forms, organized through democratic planning, underpinned by state spending in socialized markets and using human-centred technologies in socially and ecologically progressive societies. Organizations and institutions sympathetic to these aims were able to orchestrate spaces for bringing grassroots needs and ingenuity into equitable contact with advanced design and manufacturing tools.

However, some spaces (transmitting structural changes noted above) introduced pressures for more business-oriented approaches. Social prototypes became objects for commercialization. Technological citizenship became skills provision. Forced to operate beyond its (shrinking) alternative spaces, socially useful production dissipated into a world of technological commercialization, user-centred design, training programmes and flexible specialization. In terms of the movement's radical framings, these moves were limited and limiting.

Activists had taken seriously the idea of pursuing a different kind of innovation and using concrete experience to explore, rethink and transform social relations and institutions. The movement was building among the grassroots the power to do innovative things. But becoming mainstream would require power over economic agendas. Debates concerning the purposes of prototypes in workshops were typical of the considerations in moving beyond alternative spaces. Was the goal to use grassroots innovation to stretch and transform the institutions of innovation, or to refine specific grassroots innovations to fit and conform to prevailing market institutions? In the end, it became increasingly difficult to sustain the more transformative strategy. The more tactical and pragmatic negotiation of specific initiatives for entrepreneurship, training and local economic development became the course of action available.

As such, pathways beyond pioneering spaces need to be understood in a porous and pluralistic way, so that the complex relationships with other processes can be appreciated. Part of the complexity apparent in this case is that pathways must not be considered solely in instrumental terms. The instrumental view sees spaces and pathways in terms of generating a reservoir of ideas, designs, methodologies, objects and so forth that offer up appropriable instruments for fixing social problems. However, movement activities also involved people in the practical reasoning of broader social issues through material activities, and thereby in developing critical thinking towards political and economic relations in their social worlds.

Practical reasoning and socially useful knowledge

Even where initiatives appeared not to leave substantial consequences, activists' practical confrontation with social and economic issues generated a rich plurality of knowledge. Whether highlighting and addressing the exclusions and inequities in existing grassroots innovation (e.g. hitherto unspoken privileges in workshops) or pointing to injustices in society, a figuring-out of issues through material projects proved both informative and expressive for participants. Movement initiatives and spaces permitted finer-grained and more richly textured forms of knowledge production as compared to, say, more rarefied analysis and argument in manifestos, reports and policy documents. Material projects involving hands as well as minds brought in more varied participants, allowed wider forms and channels of expression and addressed different audiences as compared to, say, speeches and texts evoking an abstract revolutionary agent, entrepreneurial state or overseeing governance framework.

Arguably, some prototypes proved to be diversions (e.g. the road–rail bus). But they nevertheless allowed the gathering and accommodation of new and unusual allies, including engineers and community activists, and so should not be dismissed without consideration for the social processes they helped to catalyse. The Right to Warmth campaign at LEEN illustrated this vividly. Monitoring methodologies developed at LEEN validated in technical form acceptable to public authorities something that householders already knew: their homes were damp, cold and inadequately heated at great cost. Conversely, it required the knowledge and skills of tenants' associations, community organizers and the households themselves to mobilize a campaign to win the public funds for refurbishing their homes with the technical remedies developed at LEEN. All were mobilized through the process, but it is worth pointing out that the grassroots innovators would not have implemented their techniques and devices without the power of the tenants' campaigns.

In that respect, pathways in this case involved a practical figuring-out of the complexities of motivating framings. Deliberations ranged far beyond the focal activities to which people were attending in the development of objects. Prototypes were devices for engaging wider socio-technical systems and broader alliances, and presented a broader perspective on technologies in societies. Participants learnt and demonstrated by doing how technologies were not neutral tools but, rather, devices shaped by social structures. While the movement eloquently articulated and popularized arguments for democratic design and human-centred technology, its prototype devices were both material input and manifestation of such arguments. Socially useful pathways drew out the tacit knowledge of people that was conventionally overlooked by innovation institutions. The movement wanted to uncover the ideas, skills and resourcefulness of workers and communities, and to try to empower them in ways that demanded constructive responses by more powerful institutions, without becoming engulfed by the logics and codes of those institutions.

The social shaping of technology

Given the discussion above, the overall legacy of the movement has to be seen in its pointing clearly and committedly to the fact that there is nothing natural or inevitable about technological trajectories; social choices shape our technological worlds. The movement pointed to this social shaping and, in a very practical and grounded way, explored how people might develop greater agency over alternative shaping processes for more socially useful purposes. In so doing, activists anticipated ideas and analysis that were to consolidate into science and technology studies over the coming years; indeed, for some contributors to those studies, the movement for socially useful production was a formative inspiration.

Although it is now largely forgotten, returning to the movement for socially useful production nevertheless proves instructive. Recalling the radical origins of ideas about participation in technology development begs questions about just how sufficient are polite policy recommendations today for, say, inclusive innovation, as compared to calls for shaping technology democratically. The experience of socially useful production is one of the practices being selectively appropriated by more powerful political and economic structures. The more challenging features of the pathways pursued were locked out by these structures, while other features were co-opted and reconfigured.

But the other instructive aspect to the history provided here is the very practical attempts to involve people materially in technology development. Whereas methodologies such as constructive technology assessment seek predominantly discursive approaches and arenas to shaping technology, the movement for socially useful production created (physical) spaces for practical and direct engagement in the development of technology. Despite their limitations, Technology Networks did enable people to engage in technology directly in extra-discursive ways, and thereby to reflect on the wider social, economic and political processes that made some workshops' aspirations more elusive than others.

The current flourishing of hackerspaces, fablabs and makerspaces (Chapter 6) suggests that this urge is insistent, and that pathways for shaping technology directly from below and beyond formal institutions can re-emerge. The possibilities opened up by the more rapid, extensive and versatile networking possibilities of the new digital fabrication technologies operating across social media platforms recast these earlier ideas into interesting new forms. That said, the emphasis on tacit knowledge, skill and learning by doing through face-to-face collaboration involving material objects, which caught the attention and imagination of the earlier generation of activists as a way of resisting automation, raises questions about the possibilities of codification and transmission of experience and know-how through digital social media today. It suggests that the new movements cannot and must not under-estimate the offline, local community-based activism component in any democratization of a technology commons (Smith, 2014b).

Conclusions

The movement for socially useful production consisted of an unusual mix of people acting in a remarkable set of circumstances. Movement framings picked up ideas from grassroots trade unionists revitalizing industrial democracy for the purposes of human-centred high-technology, and in so doing met ideas arising from newer social movements, the Left and radical scientists. What the movement shared was opposition to the contemporary direction of technology and a search for alternatives. In this respect, activists were pursuing pathways ahead of necessary structural changes identified in their own critique of capitalist innovation. This prefiguring of restructured social relations through technological prototyping presented activist pathways with two related challenges.

The first challenge involved holding together practical, project-based initiatives while lacking the full means to achieve their emancipatory goals, because those goals required structural changes. Nevertheless, the movement sought out and developed spaces committed to similar political and economic changes, which enabled initiatives in socially useful production that illustrated what these changes could underpin practically.

The particularities of the spaces available for practical projects had an influence on the kind of grassroots innovation that was materially possible. Reliance upon a mixture of material resources in the spaces to hand, the skills available and allied social goals, or whatever features opened up a degree of socially useful possibility, introduced specific relationships that could be built upon and which became internal to the initiative. Examples included dependence on local government grants for workshops, on trade union resources for educational campaigns or on the prototyping infrastructure of sympathetic polytechnics. Each also entailed conditions for commitment.

Some initiatives proved viable beyond these spaces and commitments, under prevailing structures, and spawned small businesses, product banks, methodologies and products. Herein lay the second challenge. Some of the relationships and commitments with the alternative spaces had to be shed in order for the initiative to diffuse beyond the pioneering setting. It is a challenge that we see across subsequent case studies. Should activists modify the output of the initiative so that it could flourish in the wider social world, such as its commercialization into a commodity? Or should they try to expand the supportive conditions found in protective spaces into the wider social world, such as through networking and mobilizing for a socially useful restructuring of industry or, more modestly, the popularization and spread of community-based workshops for grassroots innovation? Which brought activists back to the first challenge concerning pursuing pathways ahead of structural change.

These twin challenges constituted the central dilemma facing the movement. It was a highly productive dilemma. Even if swimming against the broader political and economic currents of the time, the ideas and practices bursting from the movement were formative for subsequent, more enduring arguments and approaches in the social shaping of technology. We see that legacy today in attempts to instil more open and deliberative approaches to innovation policy, but also in renewed grassroots interest in community workshops and shared technology projects (Chapter 6).

Timing and contingency always feature in the social shaping of technologies, but the ready provision of plural possibilities is a never-ending requirement. Even if alternative pathways are vague and less powerfully articulated than conventional institutions for innovation, they nevertheless cultivate ideas and practices that can resonate through time and can have real material consequences when the moment is right. In the case of socially useful production, we find rich repertoires of activities worth reconsidering today for their instructive potential. This movement pioneered ideas and activities for a more constructive and democratic relationship with technology development in society. It pushed against received views about technologies evolving apparently autonomously from society. The practices cultivated by activists anticipated those in constructive technology assessment, participatory design, community workshops, critical making and other arrangements for opening the direction of technology development to wider scrutiny and influence. Insisting upon democratic technology developments, and attempting to advance this practically, was probably the most socially useful product of the movement.

Notes

1 Mike Cooley, prominent in the Lucas Plan and wider movement, was awarded the Right Livelihood Award (also known as the alternative Nobel Prize) in 1981, 'for designing and promoting the theory and practice of human-centred, socially useful production'. The prize money was donated back to the Lucas Combine.
2 His Keighley constituency neighboured the threatened Lucas plant in Bradford.
3 More popularly oriented materials included TV programmes, such as *Look No Hands*, in which Mike Cooley argued for human-centred technology. All this served to raise the profile of the movement.
4 Although the CAITS prototype was never commercialized, there was some interest in developing it in Germany. Attempts to develop this type of public transport recur periodically. A version of the technology is used in rail-maintenance vehicles. *Wired* reported trials of a bus by Hino Motors and Japan Rail Hokkaido in 2008 (Lew, 2008).

4
THE APPROPRIATE TECHNOLOGY MOVEMENT IN SOUTH AMERICA

Born in the 1960s, appropriate technology (AT) began as a reaction against wholly blueprint developments involving large-scale Western technologies, whose industrial contexts were ill-suited to the poor (Carr, 1985). The basic idea of AT was to try to help people develop out of the situations they were in by providing technologies appropriate to those situations, conservative in their use of materials and resources, but which afforded some improvement in the users' economic and social circumstances. What started with just a few centres of experimentation in AT during the 1960s grew during the 1970s until it became a global grassroots innovation movement in the 1980s, with an estimated thousand institutions worldwide (Whitecombe and Carr, 1982).

In South America[1] the rise of an AT movement coincided with a period of dramatic social changes, including cases of political repression and social mobilization. The idea of development and the role of the state began to be questioned as endogenous industrialization and social services infrastructure were slowed or even halted in some countries. Furthermore, most South American countries were affected by a 'debt crisis' that provoked economic restructuring and gave way to what was regarded as the 'lost decade' of the region.

Nevertheless, the AT vision of self-reliant economic activity through technological autonomy resonated well with practitioners, non-governmental organizations (NGOs) and some scientists in the region. But it also attracted suspicion, as it smacked of 'second-class' development for some elites (including scientific communities) (Dickson, 1974) and a technologically deterministic theory of development (see Willoughby, 1990) that suggested that if the right kind of tools could be developed, then more egalitarian economic and social development would automatically flourish.

Perhaps these prejudices were some of the reasons why the history of AT in South America has remained largely untold. Apart from some personal communications and brief mentions there has been almost no reflection on the extent, results and legacy of the AT movement in the region. Many AT centres have now closed, and archives and libraries have been lost in some cases, which reinforces both the impression of failure and the difficulties of researching more nuanced genealogies and hopeful consequences of AT activity.

In 2016, at a time when the debate on sustainable development and technological development is raging on, we need more than ever to understand the visions, frames and strategies of AT. We also need to comprehend what kind of barriers and dilemmas AT practitioners faced as they attempted to challenge the mainstream idea of industrial, large-scale development. The history of AT ideas, forms of mobilization and technologies is interesting in and of itself, but it also might bring important lessons to current grassroots innovation movements.

In this chapter we look at the AT movement in South America, exploring the context in which it arose and waned, who were involved, how they conceptualized AT, what strategies they used, types of projects that were experimented and the obstacles or dilemmas they faced. In doing so, we attempt to trace some of the lasting influences or pathways that were constructed.

We draw on interviews in Argentina, Brazil, Chile and Colombia and a review of primary and secondary sources of information, including archived documents. The text is organized as follows: the next section will focus on the historical background of the AT movement in South America, followed by exploration of the framings of AT and how these ideas were translated and reshaped in the region. We then describe the spaces and strategies where AT ideas and practices were developed, and follow that by describing briefly some of the exemplary technologies of the movement. The penultimate section analyses the pathways that AT practitioners attempted to forge in South America, highlighting some of the difficulties they faced. Finally, we conclude with some remarks on the legacy of AT in the region and its implications for other grassroots innovation movements.

Historical background

As in many parts of the world, South America during the 1960s, 1970s and early 1980s experienced a dramatic period characterized by revolutionary ideas, the emergence of new social actors, novel political demands and intense contradictions within strategies for development. The influence of Latin American dependency theory and interest in economic sovereignty, peasant movements, changing political consciousness within universities and the 1973 oil crisis made for a context that was receptive to ideas about AT. In the 1970s, the exhaustion of import substitution and increasing political struggle led to political confrontation and violence in many countries (Collier, 1978; Levy, 1981). Alternative visions of the purpose and practice of science and technology among some intellectuals, peasants and students, while often suppressed, were also notable at this time and were key to the spaces and contexts for AT in the region.[2] It is in this complex scenario that practitioners in South America sought to develop AT as a tool for empowerment and development.

Dependency theory and technological autonomy

Since the 1950s, economic independence, industrialization and technological autonomy have been a key part of the debate about development in Latin America. Some scholars in the region questioned the international economic model that placed Latin America in a peripheral position, dependent on Northern markets and technologies; a situation that was maintained through international political-economic and social structures.[3] These scholars proposed industrialization through substitution of imports as an escape from chronic underdevelopment. In this context, researchers and practitioners of the so-called Latin American school of thought on science, technology and development emphasized technological autonomy and local and endogenous technological development as a way to foster an integrated development process that was attentive to broader sectoral and national policies (Vidal and Mari, 2002). Members of this school of thought were particularly interested in linking science and technology (S&T) with the basic needs of socially and economically marginalized groups. They criticized existing research and development (R&D) systems for being severely disconnected from social realities in Latin America at the time and for failing to draw on domestic capabilities, while also calling attention to environmental concerns (Herrera, 1973). Amílcar Herrera and Oscar Varsavsky, in particular, called for a science that was committed to addressing pervasive social inequalities. Herrera was an early supporter of AT ideas and became an important influence for some AT practitioners.

Politics, economic development and activism

The political upheaval of the 1960s, 1970s and early 1980s would affect almost every aspect of economic, political and social life in many South American countries. Even countries that did not have dictatorships, such as Colombia, were nonetheless experiencing massive political unrest.

In general political terms, the aim of the various authoritarian regimes was to dismantle the structural base of organized mobilization of the 1960s and 1970s – which included a national popular alliance based on the working class, students, peasant movements and other actors – through 'repression, marginalisation and increasing informality of the economy' (Garretón, 2002, p. 11).

In economic terms, neoconservative policies sought to end the period of endogenous development through autonomous industrialization and state regulation (Schamis, 2009). Dictatorships also introduced pro-market policies that cut or reduced social welfare programmes, suspended workers' rights and opened up the economy to imports. As a result, import substitution diminished and imports grew, resulting in increasing unemployment and loss of the industrial workforce (Hirschmann, 1986). Finally, Latin American countries accumulated massive foreign debts at the end of the 1970s, which hampered economic growth and political stability during most of the 1980s. (On the crisis of foreign debt and its consequences see Cavarozzi, 1991.)

Rural economies and the poorest portion of the population were particularly hard hit by the opening of the economy and retreat of the existing welfare state. In countries such as Argentina and Chile, state-funded programmes of technical assistance and technology transfer for the rural population were generally cut and dismantled (Gárgano, 2013; Gomez and Echenique, 1988).

For Argentina, Brazil and Chile, the 1980s made clear the dramatic (and more or less structural) consequences of the dictatorships in terms of demobilization and increasing economic crisis (Cavarozzi, 1991) but also highlighted the need to seek new forms of organization and social work. As the period of more violent repression came to an end, civil society organizations and social movements took the opportunity to regroup – although they did so by turning 'more towards cultural and social problems than economy and politics' (Garretón, 2002, p. 11; our translation). It is in this context that practitioners and former activists started to experiment with AT ideas, technologies and forms of organization.

AT in the world and in South America

The umbrella term of 'AT' involved, broadly speaking, a set of common characteristics that attempted to shape technologies for development: low in capital cost; reliant on local materials; job-creating, employing local skills and labour; small enough in scale to be affordable for small groups; understood, controlled and maintained by local people wherever possible, without requiring a high level of Western-style education; involving some forms of collective use and collaboration; avoiding patents and property rights; and so on (Darrow and Pam, 1978). In essence, proponents of AT sought a more situated, environmentally concerned and socially just set of design and operational principles for diverse technology choices by involving local communities (Kaplinksy, 1990; Willoughby, 1990).

An important inspiration for practitioners in the AT movement was the economist Fritz Schumacher, who founded the Intermediate Technology Development Group (ITDG) with colleagues in 1966 in England[4] (Willoughby, 1990) and wrote the influential book *Small is Beautiful* (Schumacher, 1973). Schumacher's views, along with related arguments by Ivan Illich (1973), the Dag Hamaarskjöld Foundation (Dag Hamaarskjöld Foundation, 1975) and others, resonated with the frustrations many development workers in the field had with post-World War II industrialization blueprints through North–South technology transfer (Rist, 2011).

Between the 1970s and early 1980s, as the notion of AT gained recognition, international institutions such as the Inter-American Development Bank, the World Bank and the UNEP established AT departments. Over this period, the plethora of programmes, projects and interests supporting The World of Appropriate Technology (the title of an OECD report in 1982) were substantial (Jéquier, 1982). In this context, as South American countries also experienced increasing expectations about democracy and development, some individuals and groups were able to attract support from international aid organizations, and many AT centres were created in the region.[5] Regional AT proponents adapted global ideas to the local context and combined these with home-grown visions for technology, empowerment and mobilization. Interestingly, this was also a time when ideas about AT were reaching their peak globally and started to be challenged by the rise of market-based development and neoliberalism (Pursell, 1993; Rist, 2011).

The history of AT in South America is rich and diverse, involving various institutional assemblages, areas of interest, technological domains and political goals. Almost every South American country had some AT activity during this period (Table 4.1). Apart from a few exceptions (most notably in Brazil), AT centres in the region were autonomous institutions, with an NGO-like status that depended on external funding to carry out their activities. These centres included engineers, economists, sociologists and social workers; in some cases they also included the work of volunteers and students and had a few links with academic institutions. Importantly, some of the regional social actors and AT centres were connected to the global AT movement, linking regional developments and international opportunities.

In the following sections we analyse this experience by focusing on the framings, strategies, knowledge and technologies involved and the dilemmas that AT cases experienced in Argentina, Chile, Brazil, Uruguay and Colombia.

Framings for appropriate technology

As AT practitioners started to develop capabilities and technologies in the region, they soon discovered that the AT ideas from Europe and South Asia did not exactly fit the complex realities of South America at the time. So, one of the first tasks for AT centres was to translate and reframe AT ideas in terms relevant to local problems, actors and situations.

Development intervention

In the early 1980s, most Latin American countries were suffering a general retreat of state social policies. In this context of increasing inequality across the region, AT centres aimed to provide solutions to urgent problems that the population was facing in terms of food security, energy, healthcare and social housing by developing simple, accessible technologies. In some countries, such as Argentina, Chile and Uruguay, this strategy also fitted well with the need to find new forms of engagement amid the demobilization of earlier social activism and the gradual emergence of new civil society organizations.

Development interventions involving AT in the region were widely varied, including: alternative energy generation in rural areas; productive urban communities; livelihood generation; nutrition and food-harvesting and -processing technologies; and water and sanitation. These efforts were in response to a sense of failure in attempts at technology-transfer projects, which ignored local knowledge, needs and constraints, including local politics. Thus, such AT efforts focused on acknowledging and honouring the skills and knowledge of poor and excluded

TABLE 4.1 AT organizations/centres in South America

Name of centre or organization	Location	Year founded	Exemplar technologies
Soluciones Prácticas (associated with Practical Action UK)	Peru, but active across Andean region	1985	Housing, agriculture, sustainable livelihoods, water and sanitation, food-processing technologies
Environmental Development Action in the Third World (ENDA) ENDA – Colombia	Colombia, but other national ENDA organizations exist in the region as well	1983	Urban recycling, food security, environmental protection
Centro de Estudios sobre Tecnología Apropiada para América Latina (CETAL)	Valparaíso, Chile	1982	Solar collector, compost toilet
Centro de capacitación y experimentación en Tecnología Apropiada (Tekhne)	Santiago, Chile	1983	Rural and water management
Centro de Estudios sobre Tecnologías Apropiadas de Argentina (CETAAR)	Marcos Paz, Argentina	1985	Agroecology, medicinal plants, solar collectors
Centro Científico Tecnológico Barrancas (CECITEB)	Jujuy, Argentina	1982	Agroecology, indigenous knowledge
Centro Uruguayo de Tecnología Apropiada (CEUTA)	Montevideo, Uruguay	1985	Agroecology, solar collectors, witch cook stove
Instituto de Transferencia de Tecnologías Apropiadas para Sectores Marginales (ITACAB)	Based in Lima, Peru, but with links across South America	1986	

(continued)

TABLE 4.1 (continued)

Name of centre or organization	Location	Year founded	Exemplar technologies
Servicios Múltiples de Tecnologías Apropiadas (SEMTA)	La Paz, Bolivia	1980	Agroecology, water recollection
Red Colombiana de Tecnología Apropiada	Bogotá, Colombia	~1987	Urban AT, self-construction, technological alternatives to public services
Universidad de Los Andes, Facultad de Ingeniería	Bogotá, Colombia	~1974	Cassava processing, health technologies, water filtration, ceramic stove
Centro para la Gestión Tecnológica Popular	Lara, Venezuela	1988	Smokeless stoves, organic compost, hydroponic crops
Centro Experimental Gaviotas	Bogotá, Colombia Vichada, Colombia	1971	Solar water heater, micro-hydro, small wind turbines, biodiesel generation, agroforestry
Participatory Research in Agriculture Project at Centro Internacional para la Agricultura Tropical (CIAT)	Based in Palmira, Colombia. Oriented to tropical countries worldwide	1967	Cassava processing and preservation technology
Fundación Ecuatoriana de Tecnología Apropiada (FEDETA)	Ecuador	1984	Solar energy, rural management
Centro de Tecnología Apropiada (CTA), Catholic University	Asunción, Paraguay	1981	Building techniques, agroecology

Source: Authors' own.

Note: This list does not aim to be comprehensive, but highlights an array of institutions we identified as engaged with AT in South America.

people who were understood to be 'constantly experimenting and innovating in a struggle to survive' (Gamser et al., 1990, p. 3).

Changing social and political consciousness

In the face of political violence, economic retreat by the state and the economic crisis that followed, some AT practitioners transformed their former political activism into material practices in order to avoid confrontational action. This meant moving from the work of political formation to less visible popular resistance and a focus on basic needs, also as a political strategy of survival.[6] As the Centro de Educación Tecnológica (CET) in Chile described: 'there is a need to approach the basic needs of popular sectors, and not only through organization and social conscience' (CET, 1985, p. 5).

AT ideas provided a concrete set of tools to intervene and continue former social activism in shanty towns and poorer, working-class neighbourhoods, although through more concrete means.[7] There was a sense that, by promoting local capabilities and the ability to solve their own problems, civil society organizations would be able to establish certain autonomy from the state, which itself did not provide the solutions required. AT groups envisaged a concrete, material technological practice that allowed community development as a way to recreate solidarity bonds, restore lost self-confidence and promote local leadership.

In this sense, many practitioners strove to experiment with social participation, enabling communities to define their problems and experiment with their own solutions. This differed significantly from traditional models of technology transfer. The influence of scholars such as Paulo Freire and Orlando Fals Borda[8] helped to shape new approaches to participation (Kaimowitz, 1993). Thus AT programmes often included sociologists and social workers as part of their team. Some also devised methodologies that pointed to co-design of technologies, also leading to self-organization and construction by users of technologies. In the case of Tekhne, an AT centre in Chile, its method of intervention involved allowing local communities to express their own needs, including some participants in the development of technologies and taking decisions together with the community regarding the adoption of proposed solutions and the necessary steps for implementation; the implementation and process of starting up the technology is done together with the community, along with shared tasks of supervision and technical support (Leppe and Velasco, 1985).

However, the new approaches did not come easily and were sometimes adopted as a result of earlier failure with technically focused AT methodologies. In other words, the design of workable, participatory AT methodologies implied a long process of learning by doing. As a former member of Centro de Estudios sobre Tecnología Apropiada para América Latina (CETAL) describes:

> More than theory, we started to make technologies, real artefacts and then we realized that working with people in the field was indeed more related to social

engagement, that you had to include social work. Technological transfer was not possible without social engagement. Then we realized that it was more important to have an organized community than technology; that technology in itself was useless, and therefore that appropriate technology was not correct as a definition. That is why we started to call it Socially Appropriate Technologies.

(Interview with Pedro Serrano, 2014)

Thus, in some contexts in South America, learning how to do AT became intrinsically related to social participation in the processes of technology development. Furthermore, as practitioners assigned other meanings to AT, such as political resistance to dictatorship, autonomy or solidarity, so the idea of participation took on deeper and stronger significance.

Funding institutions did not always understand this approach to AT. Large international organizations sometimes pushed for a more industrially focused vision of AT, even questioning the 'alternative movement' as limiting opportunities and the interest of national governments because they were associated with the 'off-beat', 'counter-culture' movement (Reddy, 1979). In South America, international funding institutions also pressured grant recipients to scale up experiences, a process that some regional AT organizations thought would undermine public participation schemes (Interview with Pedro Serrano, 2014).

Participatory AT approaches also underwent their own conceptual development, as some practitioners started to talk about AT as 'socially appropriable' technologies (Serrano, 1985), implying that appropriateness was a social process that had to be constructed during the initiative, rather than an a priori definition based on technical requirements.

Of course, AT centres in the region also drew from the traditional use of directories of technologies and static solutions to complex social problems. However, the effort to devise distinctive, participatory approaches that used technology as a tool for autonomy and empowerment stands out as characterizing various nodes of the AT movement in South America.

Traditional knowledge and indigenous communities

Regional redefinitions of AT did not stop at its conceptualization. The terms for identifying problems, choosing materials and sources of knowledge were also adapted. In South America, and especially in the Andean region, this process of adaptation sometimes meant an emphasis on the needs and traditions of indigenous communities such as the Mapuches in Chile or the Quechuas in Peru.

From its early years, definitions of appropriate technologies in Latin America include references to the importance of local knowledge and available solutions. For example, in a paper originally written in 1979, Manuel Baquedano describes the cultural features of AT: 'Whenever possible, they should try to re-value local culture, by using all the knowledge accumulated by the community throughout its existence' (Baquedano, 1985; our translation).

Therefore, as part of AT tasks and aims, there was an element of retrieving and revaluing popular knowledge and indigenous knowledge, which appealed to a social memory of technology. By bringing indigenous knowledge into AT workshops, groups of engineers and practitioners attempted to systematize local knowledge, seeking to validate it with a certain scientific base. Much of the work of retrieval involved the collection and study of botanical and agricultural knowledge from indigenous communities. This aligned with another framing close to AT in South America: agroecology and sustainable development.

One of the more radical approaches was that of Grupo Talpuy in Peru, which started as a typical AT group offering off-the-shelf technology, but rapidly realized the need to adapt its technologies and communication strategies to the indigenous population through its bilingual (Spanish and Quechua) magazine *Minka*. *Minka* magazine ran between the early 1980s and the late 1990s; its content was selected and developed in collaboration with local communities. For instance, a potato pest affecting local farms was described in Quechua and also by its scientific name (Paucar Santana and Zambrano, 1991). According to the editors of *Minka*,

> Indigenous knowledge can provide the basis for an Andean technology system that allows communities to produce more, at lower cost, without damage to the environment and without external dependency. Modern scientific knowledge has a role to play in this process. The key is to use it to explain and develop Andean farmers' own technology. We work to uncover the scientific basis of Andean knowledge, while at the same time popularizing other types of scientific knowledge.
> *(Paucar Santana and Zambrano, 1991, p. 58)*

For *Minka* editors, modernizing indigenous knowledge was important for building an 'authentic indigenous science' (as the subtitle of the magazine affirmed). For many AT centres the process of retrieving local knowledge was associated with 'scientific validation' in more formal settings such as universities and R&D institutions.

Environmental crisis and alternative development

Concern about the environment and the negative effects of technological development were at the heart of the original vision of AT worldwide and also influenced AT groups in the region. Latin American scientists such as the eco-economist Ignacy Sachs in Brazil and the agroecologist Miguel Altieri from Uruguay were important influences in the design of strategies for, respectively, low-cost and no-waste technologies, and organic agriculture (Kaimowitz, 1993).

The diagnosis of the situation included both macro and micro aspects of a crisis in the rural sector. At the macro level, concerns about the social and environmental effects of the Green Revolution and large-scale, industrialized agriculture pointed to the need to develop more sustainable, alternative methods suitable for small farms. Practitioners worried about a development strategy based on the increased use of synthetic inputs (e.g. agrochemicals) that were expensive and were not necessarily produced locally or even nationally – thus increasing foreign dependency. Furthermore, the concentration of land ownership accompanying modernization worsened access to land for small farmers and increased pressure on the environment (Altieri and Yurjevich, 1991). On the micro level, there were concerns about the marginalization of the rural population in national development agendas, the increased process of acculturation that resulted from industrialization of the rural space and the loss of traditional practices. It was argued that these processes undermined the social identity of rural communities and had an impact on its resilience and autonomy.

Agroecological knowledge, complemented with the task of retrieving indigenous technologies and farming practices, provided AT centres with a programme to foster autonomy and economic self-reliance. Having important synergies with organic farming, agroecology was a farm-level systems approach to tackling poverty and producing food with the tools available to the community, focusing on the complex interactions between ecological and socio-economic components of the system, and thus promoting sustainable development (Altieri et al., 1987).

Agroecological ideas and methods were regarded at the beginning as a complement to other AT technologies. However, as AT centres became increasingly involved in rural development, agroecology gained further importance and eventually became one of the legacies of the movement in the region.

One of the challenges for AT practitioners in South America was to translate global ideas about alternative development in a complex reality involving diverse political scenarios. In doing so, they inevitably drew from the local ideas and debates mentioned above, including popular education, participatory action research, emerging agroecological ideas and the relevance of indigenous knowledge. While more focused on concrete action than ideology, the process of framing was flexible and reflected in part the learning process in the field. It nevertheless resulted in a regional reconceptualization of AT.

Spaces and strategies for AT in South America

AT practitioners in South America were able to create centres and regional networks with financial support from international institutions. They did so by focusing mainly on rural areas and to a lesser extent on urban settings. Regional spaces for AT included international and regional networks of AT centres, universities and links with R&D institutions and the rural development arena. Work in these spaces was key to experimentation with technologies and approaches. Furthermore, through their networks, AT centres in the region were able to share learnings and designs, creating a movement of ideas and people who advocated for AT.

Regional and international networks

At the beginning of the 1980s, appropriate technology was still at its peak in the international arena and a number of international aid agencies were promoting

AT around the world. In South America these institutions were key supporters, funding events, debates and some field activities including by international NGOs and bilateral aid organizations (for example, the International Development Bank, Oxfam, CAFOD and USAID).

International networks of practitioners (for example, ITDG, the German Appropriate Technology Exchange and Volunteers in Technical Assistance) were also important in spreading AT ideas and technical knowledge in the region, especially in the initial stages, including through membership of international bodies, or through publications such as ITDG's quarterly journal *Appropriate Technology*, started in 1974.[9] Additionally, some international agencies were also concerned about the political situation in various countries in the region, making funding available for grassroots activities and poverty relief (as well as human rights).

Contacts and learning from international networks were also important in setting up leading AT centres in the region, as was the case in Chile. These centres would later become regional hubs that pioneered the process of reframing AT ideas and disseminating them around the region. AT institutions such as CETAL and Tekhne in Chile were originally built by former political refugees who had found asylum in Europe and subsequently returned to their home countries (Leppe and Velasco, 1985). In the case of CETAL, the founders' first encounter with AT ideas was at the University of Louvain in Belgium. As these former political activists returned to Chile, they drew from AT ideas to create their own centres. Lacking any state funding support, Chilean AT centres relied on international cooperation from Germany, the Netherlands and France, through institutions such as Diakonia or Hivos. Paradoxically, the retreat of the state and social services – which was especially acute in poor rural areas – created a sort of niche where Chilean AT institutions were able to work almost untroubled (Hirschmann, 1986).

As AT centres grew in Chile, they tried to expand their activities to other spaces and other countries through training courses and regional networks. One of these networks was created by CETAL and was based at a summer school organized from 1983 to 1988 and directed by Pedro Serrano. Every year around thirty students from Argentina, Uruguay and Bolivia went to Valparaíso to receive training in AT technologies and organic farming and to debate ideas underpinning their work. The school was an important hub for the diffusion of AT ideas in South America (Interview with Pedro Serrano, 2014). Former students of the school later created their own centres in their countries, as was the case for Centro de Estudios sobre Tecnologías Apropiadas de Argentina (CETAAR) in Argentina and Centro Uruguayo de Tecnología Apropiada (CEUTA) in Uruguay. Another Chilean centre was Centro de Educación Tecnológica (CET), which specialized in organic farming and agroecological techniques. From the early 1980s, CET started to offer training in organic farming in Chile and then in other countries in Latin America. Later, at the beginning of the 1990s, it formed a Latin American agroecology network, the Latin America Consortium of Agroecology and Development (CLADE).

In Colombia, AT projects at the AT centre and eco-community Centro Experimental las Gaviotas (founded in 1971 by a Colombian development practitioner, Paolo Lugari) were supported by Colombian–Dutch collaboration, ITDG, the United Nations Development Programme (UNDP) and UNESCO, in particular (CIFI, 1985; Loboguerrero, 2008). Like other regional AT organizations, Gaviotas contributed articles to the ITDG journal *Appropriate Technology* and helped with Spanish translations of other ITDG publications (UNEP, 1979). Gaviotas involved researchers from the University of Los Andes and the National University to develop a wide range of technologies – from solar-powered water heaters to wind-driven rural water pumps and low-cost hydroponic urban agriculture (Bradley, n.d.; Zapp, 1991) as well as a large-scale reforestation project in the area surrounding the eco-village, Centro Experimental las Gaviotas, in Colombia's eastern plains (Weisman, 1998). Gaviotas founder, Paolo Lugari, drew high-profile visitors to the community, including Nobel prize-winning author Gabriel Garcia Marquez, and it also achieved recognition from the UN as a model of sustainable development.

Formal, organized networks overlapped with more informal networks based on the work and travel of a few Latin American intellectuals who supported AT and carried their ideas transnationally. These included Amílcar Herrera, Miguel Altieri, Ignacy Sachs and Bonsiepe Gui. Ideas and concepts from these scholars circulated widely within AT circles and helped to diffuse AT ideas to a wider public.

Scientific knowledge and the academy

A setting different from the AT centres and their practitioner networks, but sometimes linked, was that of academia. Scientists often thought of AT as 'second-class development', based in low-tech knowledge, and thus far from the more exciting frontiers of scientific knowledge production (Willoughby, 1990). As a result of such disparaging views, most AT centres were established in independent institutions and NGOs. However, in some cases in Brazil, Chile and Colombia AT practitioners gained support from scientists or became included in academic spaces such as universities or scientific funding institutions.

In Brazil AT activities began in the late 1970s under the influence of the ecological economist Ignacy Sachs and were promoted by a group of designers from the Fundação Centro Tecnológico in Minas Gerais (CETEC). In 1978 CETEC tried to implement a series of appropriate technologies in the city of Juramento (Brandão, 2001). By the early 1980s, this initial experiment had been adopted by the National Council for Technological and Scientific Development (CNPq), where an Appropriate Technologies Transfer Programme (PTTA) for rural areas was created. Working with cooperatives, farmers and communities, the ultimate goal of the PTTA was to promote 'technological autonomy' and economic self-reliance among the rural population. The PTTA ran a series of activities until the end of the 1980s, including an AT bank, a survey of AT in local communities and R&D activities for AT (Brandão, 2001). In the 1990s the programme was closed and then reprised and reformulated as the Programme for Support of Appropriate Technologies, but its aim was reduced to the production of information and diffusion of AT.

In Chile, links with scientific institutions were sporadic and ephemeral during the 1980s. The CET started collaborating with agroecologists in the early 1980s. This collaboration led to the creation of the Organization for Research in Alternative Agriculture (CIAL), which led to research on organic agriculture and produced several academic theses. Only during the 1990s, as the CET started to lose international funding, did the organization turn increasingly to academia in order to create a series of teaching courses that helped to establish new spaces for training and funding (Personal communication with A. Yurjevich, 2014).

In Colombia, attention to scientists' contributions to social needs was evident among some university departments, such as at the University of Los Andes in Bogotá. Different research groups at the university's Faculty of Engineering showed interest in AT and 'intermediate' or appropriate technologies, as evidenced by the creation of a Group on Rural Development, projects involving the Group on Technological Development and the development of a seminar on S&T policy. Project-based courses encouraged students to develop final projects on AT in collaboration with NGOs and government bodies, and particularly linked to the AT centre and eco-community mentioned above, Centro Experimental las Gaviotas.[10]

In this way, formal scientific institutions provided significant support in some instances, as in the cases of Colombia and Brazil. However, this support was not widespread and was limited to particular institutions where practitioners and sympathizers pushed academic institutions to provide some kind of technical support or funding.

Rural development

Many AT centres in South America focused mainly on rural areas, and to a lesser extent on urban settings. Indeed, the rural or semi-rural space became a niche for AT partly in response to the generalized abandonment of rural development by government and S&T institutions. Furthermore, governments pushed market-led policies that weakened existing aid programmes for the poor (see, for instance, Gárgano, 2013). Finally, the rural population often lacked access to basic services such as energy, potable water and healthcare, some of which could be ameliorated by AT.

The general lack of policy attention to rural areas meant that AT practitioners could address rural problems without clashing with government. For example, in Chile:

> In some way, the NGOs that worked with AT were solving a problem for the state. Notwithstanding the fact that they (the militaries) could have disapproved if people got too organized, they did not make any waves. Because these NGOS were working in a space where the military was absent. They did not work with the farmers, fishermen or indigenous communities, and these NGOs started to work with these populations.
>
> *(Interview with Pedro Serrano, 2014)*

For the CNPq in Brazil, it was probably easier to justify funding of applied science and R&D in mature technologies for the rural sector, rather than a scientific or technology development agenda involving rural communities (Brandão, 2001). In Colombia, the Faculty of Engineering at the University of Los Andes justified a focus on rural areas by identifying specific needs for technologies for crop processing and in housing, health and nutrition (CIFI, 1985).

This does not mean that AT centres did not attempt or carry out projects in urban areas, such as Tekhne in Chile (Tekhne, 1990). ENDA-Colombia and Gaviotas in Colombia also had urban projects – the latter including the largest installation of solar water heaters in Latin America (Weisman, 2008).

Nonetheless, the rural development arena, as a relatively neglected area under political repression and technological modernization, provided open ground for AT experimentation for several technologies, including solar and wind energy, water collection, agroecological techniques, housing and sanitation.

Illustrative examples

AT centres in South America experimented with different technologies that were intended to be simple, easy to build and operate, and low cost. These technologies were chosen or designed to address local needs and also with regard for their potential to generate appropriation and solidarity. Experimentation with technologies varied according to regional needs, as well as local capabilities and interest. Nonetheless, many technologies were developed in response to perceived environmental problems and the needs of the poorest population. These included energy (in particular solar energy), sanitation and agroecology. Almost every AT centre in the region developed technologies in these areas.

From solar to social housing technologies

Solar technologies. The design and implementation of solar technologies is related to the cost of fuel and the lack of access to energy for housing and production in rural areas. The use of some solar technologies provided a source of energy that could be complemented by other sources such as biomass. Some of the solar technologies developed in the region included solar heaters, solar dryers for fruit and solar cookers. These were generally based on a simple design that tried to make use of available material and avoid costly inputs. For instance, a solar heater designed by CETAL is described as a provisional, low-cost artefact that could last up to two years and could be made using discarded water bottles, wood and glass (Interview with Pedro Serrano, 1985). In Colombia, the Gaviotas Centre was a pioneer in solar technologies, installing solar water heaters in big urban developments and hospitals. Variations on these designs are widespread in South America and have been adapted to other uses such as water purification (see, for instance, Fressoli et al., 2013). Another heating technology that was fairly common in the region was the so-called witch cooker (in Spanish: *cocina bruja*). The witch cooker insulates a cooking vessel that has already been heated to temperature, extending cooking by conserving the heat, even after the heat source is removed.

Sanitation. Sanitation was (and in some cases remains) a particularly persistent problem, due to the lack of infrastructure in shanty towns and rural regions. In response, AT centres such as CETAL developed a composting toilet design based on a 200-litre recycling tank that allowed for anaerobic fermentation. The tank provided a controlled environment that after three months could be harvested for safe, dry compost ready to use in the organic garden of the house. With variations in design, the composting toilet was also promoted in Argentina and Uruguay, and later in Brazil.

Other technologies developed in South America included social housing models, low-cost building materials, bamboo water pipes, water pumps, recycling techniques and biodigestors. An AT survey produced at the end of the 1990s shows more than forty different ATs (including the aforementioned) in use in Brazil, Colombia, Venezuela and Bolivia (Tratado de Cooperación Amazonica, n.d.).

Beyond the diversity of technologies, it is important to note the repetition of the same designs in several countries in the region. One of the reasons for this repetition is that most of these technologies were taught and shared in regional workshops such as CETAL's AT summer school, or through manuals and courses offered through the regional network of the Convenio Andrés Bello. Multiple technologies also sometimes formed part of the same strategy of intervention. For instance the witch cooker was combined with other technologies, such as the composting toilet and organic farming, into a rural AT 'package'. By offering a set of technologies instead of a single solution, AT centres also aimed at addressing the complexity of social needs, especially in rural settings and emergency scenarios (for example, earthquakes in Chile) (see, for instance, Serrano, 1985). In any case, definitions of what technology was to be used for, and how to use it, were aimed to be developed in a dialogue with social actors on the ground, be they impoverished communities, isolated rural populations, indigenous communities or other NGOs working in the field. To do so, AT centres built a set of approaches that attempted to foster community participation. These approaches varied, depending on whether they were dealing with vernacular technologies (indigenous knowledge), AT designs from other parts of the world (for instance, imported solar or wind technologies) or new, locally developed technologies (Serrano, 1985; Tekhne, 1990). In some cases, they included at least one member of the user community in the process of the design or adaptation of the technology (Leppe and Velasco, 1985). Once the technology was designed and built it was still subject to a process of cultural and technological evaluation by the community that was to use it. Eventually, the technology might be modified or discarded by the community. The aim of many South American AT centres was to ensure the engagement of the community in the process and encourage its self-organization (and solidarity) in order to produce the appropriation of the technologies. As Serrano argues: 'Any process of technology transfer that did not take into account in depth the human factor of social actors is bound to fail, especially if it involves issues of development and the lifestyle of the community' (Serrano, 1985, p. 66).

However, building participation was a laborious process that took a lot of time. Where there was the need to design a new technology, this process could take years. This timescale presented a lot of challenges to AT centres in terms of resources, time allocated for projects and funding. External funders did not always understand this process and pressed for outcomes to be produced quickly, disregarding the time and subtleties involved in working with communities. Furthermore, as AT centres depended on external funding, the continuity of projects was precarious.

Beyond the process of participation, there was also the challenge of how to design technologies that could be improved and upgraded over time, and eventually could compete with market-based solutions. With a focus on low-cost and simple solutions, this was not an easy task. And that is perhaps why some of the technologies survived the passage of time and others did not. As Nicolas Espinosa put it:

> AT ideas were thought of as solutions and technologies for the problems of the 1980s. But, as access to certain goods was massive, technology started to lack its appropriateness and innovative characteristics. It did not make any sense to build a solar collector when you could buy it ready made.
> *(Interview with Nicolas Espinoza, Santiago de Chile, 5 June 2014)*

Despite this fact, some original AT designs survived, and some of these technologies are still in use today.

Agroecological methods

Agroecology became a centrepiece for many AT strategies in the region and most institutions developed training courses or applications. The 'hands-on' and relatively accessible experience of farming allowed centres to introduce agroecology along with other technological developments. In some contexts, such as Colombia, agroecology was not the centrepiece.

Agroecological methods drew from previous experience (and in some cases from the social memory) of the population. Training was focused on small farms and involved techniques such as composting and crop rotation and the introduction of local varieties of cultivars. AT centres usually provided a basic training, which could later be upgraded to widen the scope of technologies and concerns about agroecology, including in food production, animal husbandry, tree cultivation, basic water-pump technology or fruit drying.

These developments were usually accompanied by the production of manuals and dissemination materials such as the series *Aprender a hacer* (Learning to Do) from CET, *Cuadernos Populares* (Popular Textbooks) at CETAL or the *Minka* magazine of Grupo Talpuy in Peru.

More than any other technology in the region, the development of agroecological methods placed the AT vision in between its scientific, rational background and the need to connect with local and indigenous knowledge. AT groups tried to bridge this space in two steps. First, there was a systematic effort to retrieve indigenous agroecological knowledge, including about ancient crops, seeds and medicinal plants. AT centres tested plants in search of their chemical properties, as in the case of CETAL and herbal plants, or selected some cases for academic research, as in the case of CET. At the same time, retrieving indigenous knowledge was seen as a tool to empower local communities by highlighting the cultural value of their practical knowledge. Agroecological techniques combined with indigenous knowledge and scientific attempts at 'validation' eventually led to the creation of new learning and advocacy networks that overlapped and complemented AT.

Pathway construction

AT ideas in South America were pursued amid economic crisis, the 'lost decade' of development in the region and the need to devise new forms of political mobilization and engagement. In this context, AT advocates were moved by the urgency of local needs but worked towards a long-term vision of creating alternative pathways of development based on political autonomy and sustainability.

Global decline and transformation of AT ideas

During the 1980s the favourable context for the AT movement began to change internationally. As neoliberal policies pioneered in Chile began to unfold elsewhere in the region, in the USA, UK and other countries, ideas of 'structural adjustment' hit development agencies (Rist, 2011). But the full force of their effects in Latin America was especially felt in the 1990s. By the mid-1980s, funding agencies and international donors also started to abandon the idea of appropriate technologies, and official development attention worldwide 'lost momentum' (Pursell, 1993, p. 629). In the USA, the Reagan administration dismantled AT institutions and icons, including the solar panels that the previous president, Carter, had installed on the roof of the White House (Pursell, 1993). The lack of interest in AT internationally inevitably affected AT efforts in South America, where international aid was an important support. However, this did not immediately stop the AT movement, as centres in the region remained and some even grew during the 1980s. For example, in Colombia, the World Bank withdrew finance offered to the Colombian government to help establish a new rural eco-village on the model of Gaviotas, further east (Weisman, 1998). But even as international support dwindled, some national support persisted. Inspired by the Gaviotas model, Colombian President Betancur had solar panels installed on the presidential palace in the early 1980s, Bogotá's energy company had solar water heaters installed in its main offices and in 1983 an airmail stamp was issued showcasing Gaviotas (Weisman, 1998).

AT practitioners in other countries in the region took advantage of a new context of political opportunity, freed from dictatorship and moving towards democracy in Chile, Brazil, Argentina and Uruguay. In this context, AT centres benefited from shifts in international cooperation that sought to support the democratization process in the region. In some cases, such as Tekhne in Chile, CETAAR in Argentina, CEUTA in Uruguay or Instituto de Transferencia de Tecnologías Apropiadas para Sectores Marginales and Soluciones Prácticas in Peru, international funding of projects lasted until the 1990s and 2000s, with some remaining today.

The 1990s was perhaps the moment when existing connections and projects started to dwindle. South American countries increasingly adopted neoliberal approaches to S&T, emphasizing the establishment of productive links between research and industry, rather than local socio-economic problems (Thomas et al., 2000). This approach was opposite to the goals of participation and inclusion proposed by AT practitioners. Those centres that survived did so by reducing the space and scope of their activities, offering courses or consultancy and trying to insert their activities into universities. For example, while the population of the Gaviotas eco-community dwindled somewhat (Romero, 2009), at least partly due to the Colombian conflict and fiscal crises in the 1990s (Weisman, 2008), its international recognition persisted. In 2002, a US-based non-profit, Friends of Gaviotas, was established to support the community and facilitate exchanges. Yet awareness of its presence in Bogotá today persists primarily through its work as a technical provider of renewable technologies, as well as other commercial ventures.

From AT to agroecology

AT centres in South America started in most cases by developing a broad range of technologies, including solar cooking, social-housing techniques, sanitation technologies and agroecological methods. However, as some of these technologies – such as solar heaters and solar cookers – became widely available through market means during the 1990s, AT attracted less and less attention. The fact that anyone could access the technologies promoted by AT centres could also be interpreted as a sign of their success. However, it is perhaps better to think of it as a partial success, since these ready-made technologies lacked any participatory process.

Agroecology was also arguably different from other AT technologies, since it was already connected with local knowledge and traditional practices and linked with the needs and interests of peasants and small farmers. Proponents also sought to enrich this knowledge with scientific ideas and methods. Moreover, agroecology as an approach was clearly opposed to the practices and methods of agribusiness (Wezel et al., 2009). These elements created a niche where agroecological techniques were developed both in the field and in academia (although it generally remained marginal in universities and R&D institutions). As the AT movement dwindled in the region, the newly formed agroecological networks such as CLADE, the Agroecological Movement of Latin America and the Caribbean and the Latin American Network for Action on Pesticides and their Alternatives picked up the baton of grassroots innovation, linking with other peasant movements such as Via Campesina. These networks shared connections and were sometimes formed by the same practitioners from AT centres. In this way, agroecology helped to continue some of the ideas, technologies and frames of AT.

The movement towards agroecology thus shows the continuity and adaptation of some of AT's practitioners as they navigated difficult changes in the political, cultural and cognitive scenarios of the 1980s and 1990s.

Technology for autonomous citizenship

AT activism in South America was somehow a pragmatic answer to the shortcomings and risks that traditional political activism posed at the end of 1970s in many countries. At the same time, a new context of economic crisis and impoverished populations required immediate solutions to basic needs. After the political repression of dictatorship, economists, engineers, architects, agronomists and former activists decided to revise ideas about mobilization and political formation. In countries such as Chile, dominated by an authoritarian regime, the classic demands for political autonomy and social integration through an increased share of state resources and popular control over political economy were meaningless and dangerous (Garretón, 2002). In cases such as Argentina and Uruguay, AT centres became part of a new wave of mobilization around NGOs and concrete social development activities that marked the return of democracy.

AT ideas provided some tools to confront paternalistic, large-scale social programmes and envisioned development on a 'human scale'. Suited for small-scale and do-it-yourself application, AT technologies became a fertile ground for participatory experiments and designs that attempted to include beneficiaries in several stages of technological development. Certainly, not every effort fell into these development patterns or was able to develop inclusive approaches. As the experiences of Grupo Talpuy, CETAL and others show, in some cases AT groups also struggled with a strong technical rationality and lack of understanding of the cultural context, although eventually they challenged these limitations and learnt from experience to focus on participation instead of technology prowess.

The importance attributed to participation and empowerment is central to understanding the effort of some AT institutions in South America. As AT practitioners realized the difficulties and structural modification posed by the new political scenario of economic crisis, they turned to building immediate solutions to poverty and exclusion. They did this by developing artefacts, techniques and material practices in order to replace former strategies of political action. Translating old political ideas about mobilization into the technical clothes of AT was also part of a new strategy that sought to promote autonomy from the state. In this way, hidden beneath the social work and technological solution lay an attempt to recreate forms of political conscience and participatory activism, and the use of technology as a means to empower citizens. Ideas about participatory research and technological autonomy were also taken on by subsequent grassroots movements or networks, most notably the Social Technology Network in Brazil at the beginning of the twenty-first century.

However, as the AT movement was disbanded and practitioners were isolated, knowledge and experience about participation became diluted and forgotten. Without a shared space in which to learn and advance participation, empowerment and 'socially appropriate' technologies, new AT enthusiasts struggled with the very same problems of technical rationality and paternalism that had affected the first wave of AT activism in the early 1980s. (For a recent example of the struggle of AT enthusiasts with technical rationality, see Fressoli et al., 2013.) Lacking a social movement to foster experimentation and new approaches, the idea of AT became just a phantom of its former self.

Furthermore, as AT and participatory development ideas became inserted in some academic or research institutions and NGOs, their aim of empowerment was sometimes 'captured' to demonstrate adoption of technologies that were already developed and 'off the shelf'. For example, participatory research and innovation methods were sometimes leveraged as a way to convince farmers to use existing technologies, thereby diluting the notion of co-research (Ashby, 2009).

In this context, it is not surprising that the memory of AT has become that of a paternalistic approach that dismissed local knowledge and participation. This image of AT was fostered by early studies of AT which criticized the underlying inference of 'technological determinism' that permeates AT's ideas of development and well-meant but problematic attempts to experiment with the development of poor countries (Rybczynski, 1980). More recent critiques also carried a similar image of the AT movement in the region and their goals in terms of empowerment and development (Thomas, 2012). What these critiques seem to be missing is not the lack of technological determinism but the constant tensions between technical rationality and participatory approaches. AT practitioners usually reconciled these tensions and made notable efforts to experiment with approaches that enabled social participation and some instances of co-design. In this sense, following Willoughby (1990, p. 250), we think that attempts to posit AT as technological determinism are misleading, since they 'artificially separate technological factors from political factors' and the broader framings under which AT centres were operating. By doing so, they fail to understand the importance of AT as a social movement that sought to experiment with empowerment and technological *and* political autonomy.

Moreover, in contexts where AT work was combined with political formation and ideological debates, it was transformed into a politics of technological resistance to the structural changes that had been imposed by neoconservative policies in the region. At this point, technology became a tool for AT centres in what was in reality a fight against exclusion and inequalities. At the same time, AT advocates were building ideas, knowledge and technologies that ultimately pointed to alternative pathways of development. The capacity of AT centres to spearhead alternative visions and practices of development in the region is perhaps the less understood aspect of the movement.

Conclusions

With some exceptions, the AT movement arrived in South America in the 1970s in the midst of turbulent times characterized by political repression, economic adjustment and the foreign debt crisis. Internationally, by the 1980s AT was already passing its peak of interest and the decline of the movement was close, due to the wave of neoliberalism (Kaplinksy, 1990). And yet, in South America AT practitioners found fertile ground to develop technologies and new approaches for the particular realities of the region. Even swimming against the current, the AT movement in South America was a vibrant social experiment that thrived in some rural settings and was replicated in different countries. Two elements of this history are particularly interesting contributions to ideas about the construction of alternative pathways of development and might bear lessons for other grassroots innovation movements.

First, in many contexts, AT practitioners experimented with participatory methods and created their own approach to technological design. They did so by drawing from regional intellectual influences such as Paulo Freire and Orlando Fals Borda and a history of social and political mobilization. They also took on the difficult task of combining local and indigenous knowledge with scientific principles. Thus, the AT movement in South America devised a participatory approach where technology became an instrument to foster social empowerment, create solidarity bonds and strengthen local identities. Interestingly, the participatory approach was almost forgotten after the movement started to lose momentum, and the image that remained of the movement regarding technology design was that left behind in handbooks that gave the impression of, and criticisms that focused attention on, AT as technological fix.

Undoubtedly, some of this fixation with technology was present – and with the social movement absent, this has probably been aggravated today. And yet, when the Social Technology Network retook some of the ideas, frames and technologies of AT in Brazil, an inclination towards technology fixes was not a real concern.

A very different critique highlights the difficulties of scaling up experiences and sustaining activities over time. This point was raised, for example, during discussions about the Social Technology Network in Brazil (see Chapter 7).

The dilemma of how to produce structural changes while depending on project-based funding was a major problem for AT centres. However, it would be misleading to think of AT outcomes as a failure to scale up, in light of the new scenario of public policies for social inclusion of the early 2000s – something that was notoriously absent or challenged in the 1980s. In fact, we should note that strategies of mobilization by the AT movement in South America relied on a very different set of resources, namely NGOs, regional networks and international aid funding. This meant that the framing of mobilization was often based precisely in gaining autonomy from the state. Therefore, apart from attempts in Brazil and, earlier, in Colombia, the idea of developing public policies to allow the continuity of AT initiatives was largely out of the question.

Instead of trying to address the problematic issue of impacts and outcomes, it is indeed more interesting to note how, at the time, the AT movement in South America showed a remarkable capacity to learn and modify its frame and pathways. Overall, the analysis of framing, spaces and pathways of AT in South America shows that grassroots innovation activities were not a fixed endeavour that relied somehow on established theories or pure technical rationality. Instead, we have tried to show how AT practitioners, due to dynamic political-economic contexts, shifted their political and mobilization strategies from social conscience and mass mobilization of the past so as to develop new, more pragmatic strategies for advancing ideals, with an acute awareness of opportunities and limitations under the political economy of the time.

As a result, the AT movement in the region (and worldwide) was able to give impetus to ideas about technology whose subsequently quiet, often hidden influence over the years is visible in sustainable innovations today. Moreover, processes for public participation and the inclusion of local knowledge, made so apparent by AT principles, have become common practice in development projects (Chambers, 1997; Pieterse, 1998) and subsequently subjected to their own associated critiques (Cooke and Kothari, 2001; Hickey and Mohan, 2004).

So, while AT as a category slipped away from the development agenda, the movement practitioners, fieldworkers and development professionals dispersed into multiple new development debates, agendas and currents of funding. And yet some of them remained engaged in different activities that planted the seed for current grassroots innovation efforts. In this way, well beyond technologies, both participatory methods and the new networks and ideas that sprang from the AT movement are perhaps its most important legacy in South America.

Notes

1 South America is a complex and diverse region with important differences between its countries (Cardoso and Faletto, 2003). To avoid a homogeneous view of the region we have tried to highlight some particularities of each country's historical context in relation to AT experiences.
2 Most of Latin America experienced military dictatorships during the 1960s and 1970s, including Brazil (1964), Uruguay (1973), Chile (1973) and Argentina (1976). There were few exceptions, for example: Colombia, Costa Rica, Mexico and Venezuela.
3 The structural dependency theorists (e.g. Raúl Prebisch, Carlos Furtado, Osvaldo Sunkel and Pedro Paz) described a situation of 'centre–periphery' relations (i.e. North–South) that led to structural dependence.
4 ITDG formally changed its name to Practical Action (http://practicalaction.org/) in 2008.
5 Periods of relative political openness allowed social and political activists to come back from exile in foreign countries (e.g. Chile, Argentina). As they returned, they brought back new ideas and experience with technology and politics, which combined with regional ideas that had been repressed during the period of dictatorships. In countries such as Colombia that did not have the same experience of the dictatorships, opportunities for AT took place through links and exchanges with international researchers and institutional networks.

6 In the context of dictatorship, mass mobilization and protest against elites were met by severe repression. Therefore AT practices created a convenient cover to do social work while introducing new forms of empowerment. But, even with the return of democracy in Argentina and Uruguay, AT ideas drew from new strategies of mobilization, in particular related to the rise of NGO practices. In this sense, AT can also be seen as part of a larger grassroots and cooperative development movement (Hirschmann, 1984).
7 Authoritarian regimes sometimes tolerated these grassroots movements and organizations (as in Chile and Brazil). As Hirschmann explains, some smaller initiatives were 'considered as "diversionary" by the Left, so they were welcomed by the new authoritarian regimes as social formations likely to absorb energies that might otherwise take more dangerous forms' (Hirschmann, 1984, p. 99). The same idea of intervention was also present in other spaces and had some connections with the social doctrine of the Catholic Church.
8 Paulo Freire was a highly influential Brazilian scholar and early proponent of critical pedagogy, which sought to avoid the universalism of modernity in education and instead called for collective actors (such as students, peasants, indigenous people) to participate actively in the co-creation of knowledge through intercultural dialogue and to appropriate to themselves mainstream culture as a medium to become free subjects. Orlando Fals Borda was an influential Colombian sociologist and founder of participatory action research, which called for the political and social responsibility of the researcher, including the participation of both the researcher and the researched in producing new transformative knowledge. Both Freire and Fals Borda contributed significantly to thinking from the perspective of the oppressed or periphery (see Fals Borda, 1979; Freire, 1973).
9 In 1986, Manuel Baquedano from CETAL became a member of the international committee on Socially Appropriate Technology International Information Services.
10 A report by the Faculty of Engineering at the University of Los Andes describes eighty-nine thesis projects on AT conducted between 1972 and 1982 (CIFI, 1985).

5
PEOPLE'S SCIENCE MOVEMENTS

The contributions of People's Science Movements (PSMs) in India for the creation of 'alternative' technologies and forms of organization are best known through the work of Kerala Sasthra Sahithya Parishad (KSSP), a state-wide active PSM group (to be introduced later), but are much broader. Academic writings focus on the state-wide introduction of decentralized people's planning, diffusion of fuel-efficient smokeless cook stoves and hot cases for food storage, mass installation of biogas, promotion of micro-hydro systems and electronic chokes, and the establishment of Kudumbashree (women's self-help groups) and labour collectives in the southern Indian state of Kerala (Chathukulam and John, 2002; Chattopadhyay and Franke, 2006; Franke and Chasin, 1997; Parayil, 1992; Prasad, 2001; Zachariah and Sooryamoorthy, 1994).

Significant additional contributions exist on the part of PSMs that do not have a state-wide reach in many other states. PSMs are active in the districts of Mandi in Himachal Pradesh; Dehradun in Uttarakhand; Patalkot, Sheopur and Kanker in Madhya Pradesh; Puducherry, Kanyakumari and Ramanathapuram in Tamil Nadu; Guntur in Andhra Pradesh; Koraput in Odisha;[1] Agartala in Tripura; 24 Parganas in West Bengal; and Mumbai, Thane and Pune in Maharashtra (Abrol, 2014b; Giri, 2005; Pattnaik and Sahoo, 2006). Grassroots innovation activities under the PSMs are thus diverse. The variety of challenges that PSMs have tried addressing and their contributions to the landscape of pro-poor grassroots innovation in India in the sphere of livelihood development are listed in Table 5.1.

Without trying to cover the PSM activities exhaustively, the chapter studies the contribution of PSMs, with the aim of understanding the dynamics of development of alternative technologies and forms of organization that have contributed to innovation emerging in collaboration with the rural poor, who presently constitute the majority of the grassroots in India. We show how the PSMs' framings and strategies define the ideological and material spaces in various parts of the country

TABLE 5.1 Challenges addressed by People's Science Movements

Challenges addressed	PSM contributions	Illustrative examples of real-world experiments
Rural industrialization	Improving traditional techniques by blending modern with traditional technological knowledge	Leather processing, fruits and vegetables processing, non-edible oilseeds processing, fibre processing in Himachal Pradesh, Uttarakhand, Madhya Pradesh and Odisha
Rural energy	System building for the local manufacture of renewable energy devices	Cook stoves, biogas, micro-hydro systems and electronic chokes in Kerala
Low-cost construction	Development and diffusion of value-added technologies for construction of environmentally friendly buildings which use mainly locally available construction materials	Energy-efficient buildings and energy conservation in West Bengal and Kerala
Development of teaching aids for science and mathematics education	Development of low-cost teaching aids and dissemination of innovative methodologies of learning by doing multi-play, magic mirror, ball and mirror solar projector, sundial, geosynchron, nano solar system, etc.	Diffusion of Jodo 3D polyhedral kit, the Mathemat, the Experimath kit, Navrang puzzle, daytime astronomy kit, in the schools of Mumbai, Delhi, Bihar, Punjab and Tripura
Functional literacy and continuing education as a mass activity	Learning, teaching methods	Total literacy campaigns, Jan sikshan (vocational and literacy training outside formal educational sector) and library movement in more than twenty states
Science communication in India's numerous mother tongues	Low-cost educational resources, educational campaigns and joy of learning methodology	Comprehensive programme of daytime astronomy containing dozens of 'wow' experiments that children perform using self-constructed equipment
Experiments in alternative technologies and organizational forms for the rural non-farm and farm sectors	Cooperation in production and agroecological approaches and socially just water management systems	Kudumbashree (women's self-help groups in Kerala), Malar groups in Tamil Nadu, agroecology, bio-farming, water management bio-inputs in West Bengal, Tripura, Odisha, Maharashtra and Andhra Pradesh
Nutrition	Group entrepreneurship	
Nutrition, mid-day meals and sanitation	Mobilization of people for local area planning and implementation of essential public services in the fields of nutrition and sanitation	Low-cost latrines in Puducherry and Tamil Nadu, solid waste management in Kerala, design of systems for providing mid-day meals in Delhi, nutrition in Jharkhand, Bihar and Odisha
Innovations in the organization of healthcare systems	Strengthening of public sector in the field of health services, women's health	Replication of field experiments in Chattisgarh, Odisha and Jharkhand
Local self-governance and local area planning	Decentralized planning systems	Systems for decentralized planning of rural infrastructure, health services and agriculture in Kerala

and contribute to ecological, social and technological justice for the Indian poor. We discuss the challenge of pathway construction with the aim of reflecting on the potential of PSM experiments in achieving self-reliance within the sphere of local economies in order to advance the wider process of structural change in India.

Origins and background

Constituted as the mainstream approach of the Congress party, the 'Nehruvian' path of development of the economy – focusing on heavy industries in general and machine tools in particular and food self-sufficiency – was in crisis by the beginning of the 1980s. With parliamentary democracy in place for the purpose of political governance of development, the state priorities were beginning to shift to the introduction of new and emerging technologies available in the form of personal computers and automation, biotechnology and non-conventional energy resources, and to the development of appropriate and alternative technologies in the case of rural industries to promote the pathway of 'production by the masses' to accelerate the pace of employment generation and poverty reduction.

The government was trying to mobilize the publicly funded science and technology (S&T) sector to link itself, on the one hand, with the local industry in sectors such as pharmaceuticals, automobiles and information and communications technologies and, on the other hand, with non-governmental organizations (NGOs) for the development of S&T for economically and socially weaker sections. The policy of external liberalization of trade and investment was still on hold. Grassroots innovation movements were beginning to find takers within the S&T departments. Decentralized governance of the development process was gathering strength. The polity was getting ready to adopt the idea of implementation of political democracy at the village and district level. India adopted the 73rd and 74th amendments to the Indian constitution in 1992.

During the Sixth Five Year Plan period under the Scheme of Science and Technology for Weaker Sections (established in 1983–84), the Department of Science and Technology (DST) provided a window of opportunity to PSMs for the development of alternative technologies and forms of organization. The technology policy statement of 1983 identified the need to push S&T institutions to take up the challenge of technology development for 'production by the masses'. At that time, due to the prevailing rigid framework of division of labour within the government, the Council of Scientific and Industrial Research (CSIR) was mainly interested in contributing to the technological upgrading of rural non-farm occupations. Agriculture also offered far less scope for the diffusion of non-conventional technologies. The DST's funding mechanisms were less tied. At the level of ideological and material conditions, favourable space for the exploration of alternatives to the PSM was available in the sphere of rural non-farm occupations.

When the PSMs began their experiments in grassroots innovation, a constant refrain was that it was inappropriate to sell to the poor those marginalized solutions that the rich and powerful themselves would not be willing to adopt. In India, the focus of practitioners of the appropriate technology (AT) movement was still limited to the implementation of intermediate technologies that were being created either through the downsizing of modern technologies (as in the case of CSIR) or through the upsizing of traditional technology (as in the case of the Khadhi and the Village Industries Commission in India) (Abrol, 2004). Experience of 'walking on two legs', using alternative technologies along with heavy industries (based on the implementation of backyard furnaces, fertilizer units and many other such artefacts in China), also existed as the other reference point.

Amid all these concerns, with the pioneering help from Upendra Trivedi, P. N. Chowdhury, Dinesh Abrol, D. Raghunandan, Joginder Walia, M. P. Parmeshwaran, T. Sundraraman, Ajay Khare, S. R. Azad, Satish, Dinesh Pratap, T. P. Raghunath, Gautam Roy and many more, the PSMs were beginning to get involved through the efforts of some of the key members of the All India Peoples Science Network (AIPSN).[2] Kerala Sasthra Sahithya Parishad in Kerala and Delhi Science Forum in Delhi, Society for Technology and Development in Himachal Pradesh, Centre for Ecology and Rural Development in Puducherry, Madhya Pradesh Vigyan Sabha, Eklavya in Madhya Pradesh, Society for Promoting Participatory Ecosystem Management (SOPPECOM) in Maharashtra, Jan Vigyan Vedika in Andhra Pradesh, Lok Vigyan Sangthana in Maharashtra, Paschim Bengal Vigyan Manch and Forum of Scientists, Engineers and Technologists in West Bengal and Centre for Social Research in Tripura were beginning their individual journeys of linking their own researchers to the S&T institutions, with a focus on the problems of technological upgrading of the peasant-artisan economies as a system in itself. In order to illustrate and discuss the wider lessons from this work, we first introduce two pioneering examples of PSMs: the Delhi Science Forum (DSF) and the KSSP.

Delhi Science Forum

The Delhi Science Forum (DSF) began to formally interact with the Science and Society Division (SSD) of the DST in the development of alternative technologies and forms of organization from 1985 onwards, through specific R&D projects. To date, most of the PSMs retain their distinct place in the programmes of the SSD. Similarly, the schemes started by the S&T leadership for the benefit of the application of science and technology for rural areas during the Sixth Five Year Plan continue to be in place to date within the DST. Even today the PSM interventions continue to be coordinated in the DST, in many cases for India-wide programmes by the Centre for Technology and Development (CTD), an organization set up by the DSF.

The efforts of the DSF were supported by P. N. Haksar (Vice Chairman, Planning Commission), Dr Y. Nayudamma (Director General of the Council of Scientific and Industrial Research [DGCSIR]), A. Rahman (Chief, Planning, CSIR) and Prof. P. N. Chowdhury (Head, Centre for Management and Development, CSIR). The CSIR system was keen to use the space being opened up for the creation of alternative technologies and forms of organization in India. Dr Upendra

Trivedi of DST and Prof. Chowdhury of CSIR helped to forge the collaborative arrangements organized between Central Leather Research Institute scientists and PSM activists. Dr Trivedi, the founder of SSD of the DST was a founder member of the DSF. The first set of DSF projects was stirred by a publication entitled *Gaon Ke Karigar aur* [Village Artisans and] *Science*, containing the proceedings of a workshop jointly sponsored by the DST and the CSIR (CSSTD [CMD] and CSIR, 1981). It was organized by the Centre for Studies in Science, Technology and Development (CSSTD) in 1980. In 1981 the CSIR renamed the CSSTD as the National Institute of Science, Technology and Development Studies, where the author worked until his superannuation.

The very first PSM project that the DSF took up, related to the development of vegetable tanning, involved the upgrading of the East India bag tanning method. It focused on the development of carcass utilization for obtaining value-added products from the meat and bones of the carcasses of fallen animals. This project involved implementing the ideas put forward for the development of heuristics (in the form of process flow charts and system designs) at the CSSTD workshop on Gaon Ke Karigar and Science, in collaboration with the regional S&T field groups established in Mandi, Dehradun and Rohtak with the help of local PSMs. In this way the DSF started to build its real-world experiment for the creation of an alternative technology system for leather tanning. Development of the S&T field groups, technology-generating groups and a system design group in the form of the CTD was undertaken with the help of the DST. Evidence suggests that these heuristics have had a far-reaching influence on the practice of S&T-focused voluntary organizations across the country. Efforts based on the DSF approach have spread to fruit and vegetable processing, pottery, blacksmithery, economic and medicinal plants, rural energy, non-edible oilseeds, agro-processing, agroecology-based activities in farming and so on.

Kerala Sasthra Sahithya Parishad

The KSSP is a leading PSM that has been characterized as the harbinger of 'ecological Marxism' by Gadgil and Guha (1994), due to its role in the protection of the Silent Valley forest reserve, threatened by damming in the 1970s. Founded in 1962, KSSP was already a major PSM organization, having a mass base of thousands of activists in Kerala during the early and mid-1980s. At that time it was conducting experiments in alternative forms of rural energy, particularly on smokeless cook stoves (*chullahs*) (see below). The KSSP's activities around rural S&T linked to other work on the development of Village Science Forums in various parts of Kerala.

In the early days of this rural work, the limitations on spreading 'scientific temper' (an approach to life based on scientific thinking, first coined by Nehru) and outlook were being realized in the KSSP. In the battle for liberation of the masses from impoverishment, scientific understanding was not enough. Technical ability was needed. The idea that science should be taken to the people through increased application of science and technology within the economic activities of society began gaining momentum among the PSMs in the 1980s.

With this objective the KSSP started its S&T activities for the transformation of rural areas, setting up 'rural science forums' all over the state of Kerala. Attempts in the 1970s to initiate alternative development approaches at the micro level, interventions for self-reliant villages and so forth, had all struggled with a severe dearth of personnel, limited technical capabilities and the formidable nature of the real problems in the field. The KSSP was slowly coming to terms with the reality in the field: the enormous gap between science and society. The necessity for efforts in integration, alternative forms of data and even new methodologies was becoming evident.

As a science movement the KSSP realized the importance of in-house research and development quite early. Like the DSF, which had established the CTD in 1986, the KSSP had also started thinking about establishing an R&D facility of its own (IRTC, 1993, p. 2). The genesis of the KSSP's R&D efforts can be traced back to its research programme for developing the wood-burning cook stoves. The cook stoves developed by KSSP, widely known as the Parishad *chullah*, have the highest recorded level of acceptance and functionality among the various *chullah* models propagated in the country, and the lowest drop in fuel efficiency from the laboratory to the field.

The resounding success of the Parishad *chullah* is attributed to the unique methodology of participatory technology diffusion adopted by the KSSP, involving extensive field testing of the prototype and design modifications based on feedback from the field. The encouraging results of the *chullah* development programme inspired the KSSP to undertake a further research programme to develop ashmoh cement, an alternative to ordinary cement. The KSSP also took up the challenge of diffusing biogas generation from kitchen waste, but both these initiatives were a failure in the initial phase. The setback in the programmes of cement and biogas was a key trigger for the KSSP to set up its own central research facility, the Integrated Rural Technology Centre (IRTC). The IRTC, an important in-house R&D organization for the development of alternative technologies and forms of organization, began its work formally in 1987 (IRTC, 2001, p. 1). It was started with core support from the SSD of the DST, Government of India.

PSM activities multiply with and without government help

By the mid-1990s the DST was supporting a great number of PSM groups active in the area of alternative technologies, including the CTD and IRTC described above.[3] An overlapping set of PSMs was being supported by the Ministry of Rural Development.[4] Beyond the DST and Ministry of Rural Development support, Bharat Gyan Vigyan Samiti was collaborating with the Ministry of Human Resource Development during this period in the areas of functional literacy, continuing education and science education, and this effort enabled the PSMs to develop into wider social movements working for people's science and technology during a very short period of one decade. Other educational networks such as Nav Nirmati, the Society for Promoting Participatory Ecosystem Management (SOPPECOM), Jodo Gyan and the Free Software Foundation, all started in the 1990s and are still active.

The collaboration between the policymakers and the PSMs described above continued actively until the late 1990s, after which the National Democratic Alliance government (led by the Bharitya Janata Party) took over and the collaboration of PSMs with the Ministry of Human Resource Development declined. This support was revived to some extent after the formation of the United Progressive Alliance government at the centre, following the 2004 general election. In the context of a rightward shift in the polity and the adoption of the strategy of neoliberal global integration of the economy by the mainstream actors today, the PSMs are again in the midst of confronting the challenge of framing their strategies for the diffusion of alternative technologies and forms of organization. Today the AIPSN plans to deepen its collaboration in this sphere, with the help of the wider democratic movement (Thrissur Declaration, 2014).

Framings of grassroots innovation according to the PSMs

When the PSMs began their efforts in the mid-1980s for the creation of alternative technologies and forms of organization, two terms were actively under discussion in the discourse on science, technology and society, namely, 'appropriate technology' and 'alternative technology'. The earlier framings of Fritz Schumacher (1973) and Masanobu Fukuoka (1978) come to mind, although Gandhi was clearly a pioneer and ideological inspiration in India. For the followers of these inspiring figures, technologies involving the modern factory production operations evolving in the extant markets were totally inappropriate for the development of underdeveloped countries such as India, on account of their higher intensity of capital and use of non-local resources.

Alternative responses included, for example, the efforts of Professor A. K. N. Reddy, the founder of the Centre for Application of Science and Technology for Rural Areas at the Indian Institute of Science, Bangalore. Attention has been drawn by the author elsewhere to the strengths and weaknesses of the initiatives being undertaken in the Khadi and Village Industries Commission, CSIR, Ministry of Rural Development and Appropriate Technology and Development Cell of the Ministry of Industrial Development (Abrol, 2004). Evolving as a social movement from the 1970s onwards, the appropriate technology framing focused on the creation of grassroots innovations in the context of farm and rural non-farm livelihoods. Appropriate technologies (also famously called 'intermediate technologies' by Schumacher, 1973) meant specially designed, context-specific (locational or user) technologies, as opposed to conventional technologies aimed at the usual forms of industrial development.

The term 'alternative technology' also came into use in the environmental context of reducing resource use and waste, with a major thrust towards renewable energy and energy conservation, and promoting social forms in harmony with nature – more specifically moving towards 'environment-friendly development' and 'ecological agriculture'. Although there was a growing realization that (apart from the expected economic gains) positive values of environment-friendliness and poverty reduction would have to be realized through the development of alternative technologies and forms of organization, the debate focused on how, through the mere adoption of these technological options, their social carriers would be able to achieve desirable and alternative social relations within society. It was clear that the appropriate and alternative technology movements urgently needed to reconsider their framings.

The distinctive origins of the PSM framings need to be traced to the experiments initiated by the DSF and the KSSP during the 1980s, with their focus on the co-evolution of 'alternative technologies and organizational forms'.

Delhi Science Forum

The DSF began its efforts with a focus on how to get small producers to strengthen their interlinkages (which were already present in rudimentary form within the bounds of traditional manufacturing). To this day, the DSF continues to concentrate on the challenge of upgrading traditional techniques, and targets all those sectors where the small, informal producers and labour are able to obtain access to improved technologies relatively easily. The framing underlying its approach remains that, under competitive conditions, the self-employed small producers not only have to come together for access to resources, but also have to emerge as a multi-sectoral collective of producers, cooperating in production, because economies of scale are required in order to overcome adverse competition. The DSF solution is that the rural poor should raise the scale and scope of their collective production by cooperating across interrelated sectors of traditional manufacturing. Change in scale and scope is considered a key requirement to allow the participating members of the PSM to lower the barriers that the small producer faces.

The framings of the DSF remain in its efforts and experiments focused on how to avoid mutual competition among small producers. As cooperation on a large scale occurs only infrequently on its own (and even when it does, it seldom sustains on its own), the DSF experiments posit that, in order to upgrade, the poor must first develop local markets that are accessible to them and where they are themselves both producers and consumers. Only then should they diversify to non-local markets. The planned scope of DSF experiments has rested on the premise that the rudiments of local economy exist as a taluk-wide (sub-district), multi-sectoral network system of production, and that these rudimentary systems can be strengthened through upgrading the collective production of small producers and workers. Improvement in productivity, increase in incomes and reduction of drudgery require a radical, qualitative shift from household modes of production to science-based industrial forms of productive organization – that is, involving collective production with the organized division of productive activities. Collective industrial forms require managerial and supervisory skills for which local, educated youth (from artisanal or linked agricultural labourer and peasant families) are a potentially sound and available human resource. Artisans and rural labour have been the pivots of small-scale production. They have the potential to develop as the human resource/skills base for science-based industrial forms of organization.

Since, according to this approach, the initial leadership capability requirements are high, the envisaged shift is a big leap for artisans, peasants and agricultural labour. Under the framings of the DSF, S&T-focused voluntary agencies have to take the initiative to build the local teams of leaders that are to be selected from among the small producers and workers. According to the heuristics described above, the DSF's experiments have consciously focused on the establishment of the following organizational structures at local levels: (a) S&T field groups; (b) S&T system design group; and (c) technology generators. The formation of the S&T field group is seen as a critical organizational requirement because it performs the crucial role of interaction with artisans, landless labour and small farmers at the grassroots. The S&T field group participates in production to ensure continuity in these interactions and to foster the development of innovation capabilities. The S&T field group interacts with technology-generating institutions to support the upgrading of the skills of producers in new, improved technologies. It also helps to upgrade their organizational and management capabilities and requires the involvement of activists with formal S&T training, work experience in production, and master craftsmen, artisans, technicians, skilled workers and others who are able to convene and mobilize.

In all its experiments the DSF consciously targets the existing traditional occupations to become the social carriers in the experiments for grassroots innovation.

Kerala Sasthra Sahithya Parishad

As outlined by K. P. Kannan, one of the founders of KSSP, the framings of the organization explicitly give attention to the environment and indigenous knowledge, within the PSM approach to technology development. In *Towards a People's Science Movement*, K. P. Kannan wrote:

> Technology should incorporate in its use the use of indigenous resources including the abundant supply of human labour power and the knowledge that have been accumulated over a period of time. If the human race as a whole is seriously interested in its survival, it can no longer neglect the issues which affect environment, of the land, of the water and of the air. Danger to the environment as a result of indiscriminate use of technology could arise in a society where decisions are signalled through the horse-eyed working of the market mechanism or where decisions are taken by a few in the name of majority. Therefore, the concept of Appropriate Technology cannot but take into account the need for protecting the environment.
>
> *(Kannan, 1979, pp. 132–133)*

The KSSP framings emphasized that an understanding of the 'alternative' demands a clearer understanding of 'alternative to what' in the case of development. In the report of the workshop organized at Palakkad during 1–4 March 1996 entitled, 'Integrating Alternative Development Efforts in Asia (IADEA)', the KSSP/IRTC team articulated its view on the alternative. It stated,

> it is self-evident that with the demise of centrally planned socialist approaches to development, the dominant form is that of aggressively pursued capitalism at global levels . . . [It] is an intricately integrated enterprise of modes of production, production relations, goods and services, legal, educational and cultural structures, values and lifestyles situated within an appropriate philosophical thought, and has evolved over a period of three centuries. Ideally, seeking an alternative would imply an alternative to this integrated dominant [model of development].
>
> *(Raina, 1997, p. 15)*

Experiments prioritized by the KSSP continue to consciously pursue the challenge of establishing alternatives to a market-based approach to development. Experiments for the advancement of decentralized people's planning, solid waste management through decentralized urban governance, initiatives for self-sufficiency in vegetable production, total literacy, reorientation of science education, palliative healthcare for the elderly on their doorstep, and so on, reflect the influence of the framings developed, with the aim to explore the values of integrated models of human development. The concept of appropriate technology was linked by the KSSP to premises such as a search for a new life, a search for a new philosophy and a value system.

Under these framings, alternative technology development is radically different from the existing forms of technological development based on the assumption of an infinite reservoir of natural resources, of unlimited capacity of environments to absorb effluents and of the capacity of societies to adjust to any technological changes. Instead, the IRTC

> calls for the following: (i) industries based on rural raw materials specially agro-waste and untapped forest resources; (ii) technologies which are energy saving; (iii) preference for labour intensive and capital saving technologies; (iv) reorientation of west oriented technological approach in India to Research and Development (R&D) set up; and (v) a system of management of appropriate technologies which will ensure redistribution of wealth in favour of poorer sections of society.
>
> *(Kannan, 1979, pp. 132–133)*

Grassroots innovation and common elements of PSM framings

What distinguishes the PSM initiatives from the efforts of all the other grassroots innovation networks is its distinctive framing that, as the market economy is adversely integrating the small producer, the small producer is at a disadvantage, particularly when trying to compete individually against large enterprises. Alternative technologies and forms of organization need to aim for the organization of unorganized small producers, without which they will not succeed. Small producers need to be made powerful. The ideas of cooperation and local area planning played a critical role in the development of the PSM heuristics, with their focus on upgrading the capabilities of the poor. While the PSMs started their interventions in the sphere of production by focusing on the organization of the rural poor, which includes poor peasants, landless labour and artisans, their experiments have subsequently included workers in urban areas.[5]

The PSMs realized that grassroots innovation for structural transformation needed the organization of a new type of social carrier to provide entrepreneurial leadership that helps the poor to directly develop their own access to markets, capabilities and resources. The PSMs recognized the critical role of S&T voluntary organizations and have treated them as a crucial element of enterprise and group development. This organizational feature is a common element in the experiments of the S&T-based voluntary organizations supported by the DST. In the DST SSD schemes, the S&T voluntary agencies collaborate as intermediaries with the formal sector S&T institutions to incubate entrepreneurial leadership among the poor.

Spaces and strategies

The PSMs have followed the strategy of seeking returns from the technologies developed by multiplying the number of social carriers of grassroots innovation as rapidly as possible and fostering organized leadership to compete in the market place. Their revenue model involves the use of project grants and the earnings that the PSMs have been able to realize via the sale of products and by charging customers for the provision of knowledge-intensive business services. The CTD, IRTC, STD, CERD, MPVS, Jodogyan, SOPPECOM and many other PSM entities have sustained their set-ups by means of this strategy.

Alternatives to a stronger system of IPRs as an innovation incentive

The PSM strategies have assumed that the S&T community and the grassroots innovators do not seek exclusive intellectual property rights as an incentive, and have occupied this space throughout their history. Open dissemination of the contributions created by the S&T voluntary organizations (in collaboration with the formal sector S&T institutions) is regarded as an important and developing policy space for the benefit of grassroots innovation in India. Recently Dr Samir Bramachari, Director General, CSIR, offered the rural technologies of the CSIR to interested parties as an open resource (Abrol, 2014a).

The PSMs are in favour of keeping the mechanisms of intellectual property out of the field of grassroots innovation. The interventions of the PSMs began by organizing artisans for the upgrading of rural non-farm systems and related occupations. Grassroots innovations do not need intellectual property rights as an incentive. Technology-implementing organizations can sustain themselves in the case of grassroots innovations by developing the competence for know-how generation and providing services required for technology implementation.

Formation of S&T voluntary groups under the SSD schemes

Today the core support programme of DST's SSD involves more than 200 S&T voluntary groups. About twenty-five of these organizations receive DST support as core groups. An assessment of the initiatives underway on behalf of the DST core groups suggests the emergence of an enormous diversity of perspective. This is illustrated by the varied responses of diverse groups to the wide assortment of problems thrown up by local populations. Evidence exists of a wider impact of the PSMs' approach to innovation on the activities of organizations such as Vigyan Ashram in Pune, the Society for Rural Industrialisation in Ranchi and Technology Informatics Design Endeavour in Bangalore, none of which is formally a member of the AIPSN. An even wider impact is visible through the diverse contributions of the voluntary organizations supported by the SSD Core Group Support Scheme of DST. Not all of these S&T-based voluntary organizations (which, as discussed above, focus on upgrading capabilities) are capable of supporting the diffusion of innovation. The SSD trusts the capabilities and outreach of PSMs and continues to use these organizations as reliable partners in the implementation of its developmental programmes, especially in a large number of states where the state governments lack the appropriate capabilities. Most of the SSD programmes are still implemented by the S&T voluntary organizations, an institutional mechanism that is known to have yielded rich dividends in terms of location-specific solutions to problems, generic technologies and, above all, a methodology for technology innovation and dissemination.

S&T voluntary organizations take up challenges not addressed by the mainstream

The PSMs have engaged with S&T policymakers around R&D for sustainable livelihoods in rural areas by undertaking 'S&T not done in the mainstream', to be understood as 'undone S&T' (Hess, 2005). Within the space of 'undone S&T' that is undertaken by the PSMs, their in-house R&D establishments have worked in collaboration with the S&T institutions of the public sector R&D system in India. Grassroots activities of technology implementation, development of models for the creation of alternative technologies and establishment of group enterprises of artisans, workers and peasants are all alive because the PSMs as a social movement are interested in continuing them. Significant lessons exist specifically in respect of the implementation of the strategy of developing social carriers of grassroots innovations.

Given below are brief descriptions of the policy spaces in which various PSMs have engaged in producing technological alternatives and forms of organization, focusing on the cases of Delhi Science Forum/CTD and KSSP/IRTC.

Centre for Technology and Development of Delhi Science Forum

The Centre for Technology and Development has often played the role of a nodal organization for the DST in its several All India Coordinated Programmes, namely leather tanning, carcass recovery, fruit and vegetable processing and non-edible oilseed processing. The CTD has been recognized for the development of expertise in a wide range of squashes, spices, pickles, preserved fruit products, murraba and massage oil. It has been marketing this range of products under the Farmers brand. The DST recommends this brand to user groups when they receive support and technical assistance from the DST via the CTD.

The success of the CTD's work in this area has been derived from the fact that it addresses several major problems faced in the horticulture sector. The technology package has been designed for the maximum involvement of women in all its operations. A processing unit catering for a cluster of about 15–20 villages networks women from small growers and landless households. The unit, conforming to the national Fruit Products Order quality assurance standards and methods, uses suitably scaled and adapted equipment and innovative technologies to make a wide range of processed products from produce available at different seasons. Wherever appropriate, pre-processing is also undertaken at home, village or satellite-unit and nodal taluk levels to add value locally. Packaging and marketing are undertaken centrally, adopting a suitable brand name with appropriate labelling. Products are mostly marketed in local and nearby villages, towns and cities, thus minimizing transportation and other marketing overheads, while tapping into the demand for processed products. Local PSM organizations perform the necessary technical and managerial functions, including motivation and networking of growers, training of women in processing and preservation and so on.

The technology package described above was first demonstrated through an All India Coordinated Programme at the DST under the leadership of CTD during the period 1994–97. This involved setting up such units in eleven locations in different states covering a wide range of raw produce. In subsequent phases of the programme, more units were set up in the north-east, and in western and southern India. Most of these units are running successfully and are self-sustaining. The package has also been taken up for dissemination by other diverse developmental agencies, including the Council for Advancement of People's Action and Rural Technology, District Rural and Development Agency under different state governments and Asia and Pacific Centre for Transfer of Technology. In all, forty-three such units have been set up covering practically all the states of India.

Integrated Rural Technology Centre (IRTC) of KSSP

Thanks to the wider social movement in Kerala, which is strong and supportive of the PSM efforts and their hands-on contribution to grassroots innovation activities in the field, the KSSP has succeeded better with regard to the diffusion of alternative technologies and forms of organization. Its contribution in the difficult areas of renewable energy, solid waste management, horticulture and agriculture, and construction confirms this point very well. In search of alternative technologies that would bridge the gap with solutions that are affordable and sustainable, the KSSP activists have been successful in diffusing the alternatives of biomass-based cooking stoves, micro-hydro, solar lighting and many other energy-saving devices.

The IRTC pioneered the programme of panchayath (village-level) resource mapping with people's participation, undertaken in collaboration with the Centre for Earth Science Studies. The Kalliasseri Development Programme and Kalliasseri Total Energy Planning came as logical follow-ons, leading to the Participatory Panchayath Level Development Planning project sponsored by the Kerala Research Programme of CDS Trivandrum. This effort was followed up in the preparation of master plans for watershed-based development for various panchayaths in Kerala. All these efforts became the basis of the people's planning programme of the state government formed under the left-wing administration in Kerala, where the state government implemented the devolution of 40 per cent of the state budget for the management of development processes at the level of the district, block and village panchayaths.

In the states of Kerala and Tripura, where left-wing and democratic groups have given much attention to the promotion of alternative technologies and forms of organization, momentum is growing in the area of agriculture. Larger successes are due to the introduction and acceptance of technologies that are explicitly beneficial to women, such as paddy transplanters, winnowers, weeders, threshers and seeders, and which have reduced labour drudgery. In the area of agriculture, new forms of organization developed in collaboration with the local PSMs include women's collectives, labour cooperatives and associations of water users that ensure rights to dalits (previously known within the caste system as 'untouchables') and other marginal communities. Alternatives in agriculture, led by peasant organizations and PSMs, have matured only over the last decade.

Technology implementation model developed by the PSMs

Today the PSM continues to occupy the space of social movements undertaking S&T not done by the mainstream. The PSM strategy has consciously used the building of in-house capacity for research, development and design, while creating local S&T field groups and system design groups. These carry out intermediation for technology implementation at the level of the grassroots and diffuse alternative technologies and forms of organization, with the sole aim of upgrading the access of socially and economically weaker sections of society to new S&T capabilities, markets and resources. The PSM heuristic continues to focus on development of

S&T voluntary organizations, helping the social carriers of multi-sectoral interventions to emerge and contribute to the establishment of group enterprises in different parts of the country. PSM-linked R&D institutions have worked in collaboration with mainstream S&T institutions towards this end.

The PSM initiatives now extend to the implementation of agroecological approaches for rural development in India. For example, the PSMs are implementing the All India Coordinated Programme of the DST on Biological Integration of Farming Activities and Resource Management (BIOFARM), a distinct approach in the sphere of implementation of agroecological approaches, with the aim to create a viable and appropriate model in India for agrarian transition to sustainable agriculture (DST, 2012). The University of Kolkata is starting a six-month course in agroecology with the help of the Society of Agro-ecology, India, in which the PSM leadership is actively involved.

The PSM technology-implementation model is supportive of the formation of more equitable social relations. For example, gender relations are better in the enterprises that are being set up for fruit and vegetable processing, due to forms of organization that promote equity and dignity. The model of worker-owned group entrepreneurship can be seen in operation in Mandi, Dehradun, Puducherry, Patalkot and elsewhere. In India, within the resource-constrained conditions of the agro-industrial environments where even today modern forms of management are quite scarce in large-scale operations, the PSM model of technology implementation represents a real advance in frugal engineering and inclusive innovation. Although most of the alternative technologies and associated forms of organization that the PSMs have been able to develop practically have until now been only at the district level, the PSM models are now slowly beginning to get wider attention from practitioners of social development (Thrissur Declaration, 2014).

National and international agencies support the efforts of PSM

The United Nations Development Programme is also now supporting the fruit-processing model that the PSM-linked S&T voluntary agencies have developed. The Central Leather Research Institute promotes the leather-technology package developed by the PSMs to those parties interested in commercializing the technology. The Council for Advancement of People's Action and Rural Technology promotes the packages and supported technology resource centres based on PSM technologies for STD and CTD. Technologies for fruit and vegetable processing developed by the PSMs have been duly supported by the Small Industries Development Bank of India and other such financial institutions. Green natural products are on the way to gaining acceptance in the competitive, non-elite markets. In the fruit-processing sector, the PSMs have been able to launch green, healthy products very rapidly at competitive prices. In almost all these cases, both the technology system and the business system are transforming the relations of rural labour, peasants and artisans in production.

Pathways

The achievements and limitations of the PSM framings can be better understood from the scale and scope of the activities of core groups that are funded by the SSD of the DST. The development of organizational capabilities for successful technology implementation and the multiplication of S&T field groups is a key challenge facing not only the AIPSN but also the DST. Documentation of the technology models and descriptions of the work of core groups supported by the SSD describe well both the achievements and the limitations of the spaces occupied by the S&T voluntary organizations. The space created by the PSMs is now occupied by even those S&T voluntary agencies that do not wish to get into entrepreneurship and are limiting their efforts to the development of technological alternatives (DST, 2008).

Although the PSM-initiated S&T voluntary organizations differ from the SSD-supported core organizations in their ethos with regard to dissemination of technology, the challenge of attracting younger members exists for all the S&T voluntary organizations working in the sphere of development action. The problem of how to retain the S&T volunteers is an important challenge because of the PSMs' insufficient access to financial resources. PSM organizations are clearly unable to offer remuneration at a reasonable level. As far as the PSMs are concerned, they are still trying to prove to the wider social movements that this experimental space is important and needs to be expanded through their intervention (Abrol, 2005). The PSMs are trying to consciously involve the wider social movements, the S&T community and interested policymakers in order to construct a broader pathway for inclusive innovation. In the PSM approach, the role of S&T-based voluntary organizations is critical to the nucleation and sustained functioning of the S&T field groups.

The PSM challenge is how to enrol more S&T personnel with appropriate thinking and commitment. Lessons from the experiments described above suggest that the S&T voluntary organizations need to have a mix of full-time and floating staff. Full-time staff normally include S&T activists with a background in system design, documentation, electronic data processing and information networking. Floating staff include visiting scientists and technologists, innovative technicians/ artisans, legal experts, social scientists and science popularizers. Activists should provide leadership to the programme of knowledge production, organizational development and diffusion of innovations from one area to other. They should provide an interface between different field groups and technology generators and undertake the task of training and orienting other activists for networked forms of group entrepreneurship and participative management.

The PSM approach envisages the involvement of technology generators selected from the mainstream S&T institutions by PSM activists. The mainstream S&T institutions get involved in the activity at the point of field investigation and opportunity analysis. The technology generators get involved in the field work and help to guide the design of manuals, assistance in start-up and trouble-shooting, prototype design, pilot-scale demonstration, adaptive research and so forth. The process of technology implementation needs to begin at the stage of choice of technology itself, that is, the identification of existing technologies that can be transferred, either directly or by adaptation, and the identification of requirements for new technologies based on needs. Close collaboration exists between the technology-generating groups and the S&T field group working at the grassroots.

PSM activists have collaborated to establish – in the form of IRTC, CTD, COSTFORD, STD and CERD – their own system design groups to steer and involve the group enterprises formed by the S&T field groups and the technology-generating groups in efforts to formulate technology generation and implementation plans. The S&T field group, system design group and the technology-generating group jointly perform the functions of need specification, field-testing and demonstration, production and replication. Promotion of the activities of value addition, by-product utilization and co-product development has been an integral part of PSM activities, and the S&T intermediaries have been required to focus on the use of local resources, capabilities and markets to develop the local economic system.

The interventions of the PSMs focus on the simultaneous development of technological know-how and group enterprise formation. Thus, PSMs have targeted not only the cultivation of research and development activities but also feasibility studies, system design and development of prototypes of systems, processes and products, demonstration of technology models, establishment of pro-poor, environment-friendly business models and so on. In some places they have deliberately pursued the organization of labour collectives and women's self-help groups. As system design groups, the CTD, IRTC, COSTFORD, CERD, STD, MPVS, Nav Nirmati, Jodogyan and SOPPECOM are now known for the competences that they have developed for the establishment of technological alternatives and forms of organization.

The practitioners of AT assumed that appropriate technologies are readily transferrable on account of their associated positive values. Although this weakness of the AT movement is being intentionally overcome by the PSMs, their struggle to find appropriate partners has become far more difficult following the onset of neoliberal policy reforms. The challenges that are involved in the realization of the values of ecological and social justice are not easily overcome when the alternatives need to compete within the environment of a deregulated and open market economy. Debate within the PSMs continues as to what the strategy should be in respect of the creation of alternative technologies and what it means to be the alternative at the grassroots. The PSMs hold the view that there is no escape from the ups and downs, and that the closing and opening of spaces has its own dynamics.

Technologies capable of generating enhanced employment incomes and for shifting the small producers towards industrial forms and creating economically viable groups need directed efforts and the collaboration of PSMs with the wider movement. Alternative technologies are not and cannot be generated through a passive mode. Alternative forms of organization need the active collaboration of the grassroots with the PSMs and the publicly funded R&D organizations.

Further, as their transfer and implementation will require the establishment of production networks, efforts at network development on the ground have to integrate the production intra-sectorally and inter-sectorally into ever-widening economic organizations.

Solutions have to be identified, developed and implemented in a systemic way with the help of policymakers, local communities and wider social movements. The PSMs have been focused on the need to scale up the organizational apparatus for the implementation of technology models that are competitive, as well as embodying the values of ecological and social justice. The PSMs have tried dealing with the challenge of scaling up and of stretching the grassroots innovations for their wider diffusion by undertaking the challenge of development of a new type of S&T voluntary organization. While the PSMs understand that the construction of pathways in the local economic systems can be undertaken only with the help of wider social movements, the challenge of PSMs is how to continue to forge the necessary conditions for the development of a new set of social carriers of techniques.

Greater participation of wider social movements in the processes of local self-governance and planning is evident as a key factor in the state-wide reach of the KSSP. The ability to establish alternative forms of organization is a key factor in success at the area level. Dilemmas faced on how to scale up by simultaneously fitting and stretching the alternative technologies and forms of organization into the market economy pose the challenge of how to create democratic business organizations and networks of small producers and workers that are capable of competing with big business, which has deep pockets and the benefit of greater state support.

The PSMs have used their ability to undertake need assessment and develop viable technology implementation models. They have been trying to nurture a new set of alternative technologies that connect with the resources, capabilities and markets accessible to the poor, fulfil basic needs and sustainably support the livelihoods of the poor. The techniques involved have been capital saving and have helped to develop traditional occupations in an interlinked manner so as to allow them to collectively achieve economies of scale and scope.

The PSMs view their interventions for the development of alternative technologies and forms of organization as socio-technical experiments, which broader social and political movements need to use in order to convince the public that these alternatives, when widely diffused, would bring about structural transformation in rural areas and so should be given larger support (Abrol, 1998). Realization of the enormous diversity of perspectives and approaches used in practice, capabilities, areas of strength, technologies developed for rural areas and even methods of utilizing the DST's support grants have been seen by some as the strength and by others as also the limitation of the methodologies under development by the respective PSM constituents.

Attempts by the DST to restructure the schemes of the SSD (as well as shifting contexts that have made it more difficult for S&T voluntary organizations to take the model forward) have also led the PSMs to debate and reflect on how well the model of innovation has actually been implemented and replicated in practice. The DST report on *Technology for Rural Development* explicitly suggests that the PSM technology implementation model of grassroots innovation is an important model for funding rural innovation in India (DST, 2008). However, the new S&T policy leaders in the DST are now under pressure to allow the S&T institutions to directly submit proposals to the SSD, rather than the S&T voluntary organizations choosing the partners and technologies for implementation of the projects. This poses a new challenge for the PSM strategy of S&T voluntary organizations choosing the technologies, partners and sites for real-world experiments.

Most of the alternative technologies involve the establishment of 'disruptive' social relations among the poor. Strategies require the social carriers of grassroots innovation to practise user-capability development, continuous technology improvement and network development within the local economy. The positive role of both the capabilities of the PSM members and the nature of the support being provided by the wider social movements remains critical to the emergence of the PSMs' desired pathways. This is well illustrated by the evidence gathered from the experience of several states. Experience of the wider adoption of alternative technologies developed for use in the states of Kerala (KSSP) and Himachal Pradesh (STD) confirms the role of these two factors very well. Contrary experience in some other states also lends support to the critical role of the capabilities of the PSM members and the nature of support being provided to their efforts by wider social movements.

In particular, when the practical challenges of enterprise-system building had to be addressed without the support of wider social movements, and instead with the help of entrepreneurial leaders who had only limited capabilities, important weaknesses of the S&T voluntary organizations became evident. Lessons exist from the experience of PSM work around leather processing in Haryana on how the roles of both PSM and wider social movements can guard against the challenges facing local S&T field groups.

Development of the knowledge base that the PSMs have been able to foster by collaborating with the mainstream S&T institutions is certainly indicative of the wider significance of the PSM technology-implementation model. Through the efforts of PSMs, this model has enabled the rural poor to pursue the upgrading of rural non-farm systems, involving diverse sectors and regions in collaboration with the DST. Technology adaptation involving the PSM approach of systemic development of local resources, capabilities and markets has now been successfully undertaken in a number of areas of traditional manufacturing.

But more recent changes to DST policy (for example, routing funds to the projects through the mainstream S&T institutions, requiring core groups to have a critical number of trained S&T personnel on the staff and directing funds for national-level programmes on the basis of non-local priorities) are also playing a critical role in the diffusion of technological alternatives.

However, it also needs to be acknowledged that how well developed the capabilities of S&T voluntary agencies are remains a critical contributory factor in the diffusion of technological alternatives. Experience of uneven results obtaining from the states of Kerala, Tamil Nadu, Uttarakhand, Andhra Pradesh, Maharashtra, Orissa, Karnataka, West Bengal, Madhya Pradesh, Himachal Pradesh and Haryana confirms the importance of this factor.

The wider impacts of the efforts undertaken in technology implementation by the S&T-based voluntary organizations in the evolving political economy context are a moot point within the PSM. After the mid-1990s the collaboration of the PSMs with the national and state administration and all the other national-level agencies experienced a weakening of support. PSMs have had to rely far more on their own self-generated resources. During the 2000s they recalibrated the scale of their nation- and state-wide campaigns and had to choose their district sites far more realistically. Although the PSM efforts continue to flourish, it is at a slower pace. This is also due to reductions in the scale of national public investment in the spheres of economy, education and health. In respect of people's technology experiments, the breadth and depth of the PSM activity is certainly in need of wider support for increasing the pace of scaling up the efforts of PSMs.

While the importance of support from PSMs, voluntary organizations and wider civil society is evident from the numerous examples described above, a clear lesson is that the continued support of and positive engagement by the mainstream S&T institutions is required for the construction of alternative pathways. To achieve a wider structural transformation of the economy, experiments that can deliver desired system change at local levels require the continued support of both social movements and the state. While the wider left and democratic movement has been broadly supportive from outside its partnership with the PSMs, its direct support and efforts are still a key factor in the pace of the process of diffusing technological alternatives and forms of organization.

Notes

1 The state of Orissa was renamed Odisha in 2011.
2 The All India Peoples Science Network came into existence in 1987 at Kannur in the state of Kerala, after a year-long campaign undertaken for the campaign on 'Science for People', as a network of over forty member organizations now working in more than twenty states across India.
3 These groups also included the Society for Technology and Development (STD), Centre of Science and Technology of Rural Development (COSTFORD), Centre for Ecology and Rural Development (CERD), Forum of Scientists, Engineers and Technologists, Madhya Pradesh Vigyan Sabha (MPVS), Paschim Bengal Vigyan Manch and Haryana Vigyan Manch.
4 This included the Centre for Technology and Development (CTD), Society for Technology and Development (STD), Centre of Science and Technology of Rural Development (COSTFORD), Integrated Rural Technology Centre (IRTC), Centre for Ecology and Rural Development (CERD), Forum of Scientists, Engineers and Technologists, Lok Vigyan Sangthan and MPVS.
5 In Kerala the PSMs have also focused on the organization of urban poor and industrial workers.

6
HACKERSPACES, FABLABS AND MAKERSPACES

Over the decade since the early 2000s, open access, community-based design and fabrication workshops of diverse kinds have spread rapidly around the world. Variously called hackerspaces, fablabs and makerspaces, these workshops provide people with access to tools and resources for making almost anything they want. They are typically equipped with versatile digital fabrication technologies, microelectronics and design software as well as traditional machine tools and craft equipment. Many workshops are networked internationally, whether informally via forums for shared interests and projects or, in some cases, formally through organizing associations (e.g. the Fab Foundation for fablabs). Networking allows participants to identify with a bigger movement in hacking, making and fixing as well as enabling users to share designs, machining instructions and practical help for using and running workshops.

Workshop organizers, participants and supporters share a commitment to the open use of widely accessible technologies, and to the personal and social emancipatory possibilities of giving tools to people. We conceive hackerspaces, fablabs and makerspaces as a grassroots innovation movement because there is considerable activity outside formal institutions and because their networks are committed to exploring the social possibilities of bringing tools to people. Motivations for associating with the movement are many. Interest can rest in personalized fabrication and the creation of objects, usually in a fun and convivial way. Interest might be motivated by the pursuit of innovative ideas and the use of workshops as an incubator for entrepreneurial prototyping. Others are interested in opening up (increasingly seamless) technologies to scrutiny, sometimes out of mere curiosity, sometimes for fixing and repurposing and in other cases as an overtly political act of technological citizenship. Interest can also rest in the social possibilities that workshops and projects imply for decentralized production and various models of economic regeneration and sustainable developments that these decentralized facilities might fit into.

Sustainability is glimpsed through very practical possibilities – the relocation of tools for making, repairing and repurposing durable goods and services in circular economies – as well as more sociological consequences, such as imaginaries and alliances forming around reconfigured relations of production, consumption and sociability. Overarching these associations is a sense that workshops are emblematic of deeper shifts in society that affect the ways things are made, exchanged and consumed; shifts that remain inchoate, and where workshops offer spaces for exploring new framings through hands-on participation.

Such aspirations echo a tradition of thought in modern environmentalism and development concerning accessible tools for local, sustainable developments. It is a tradition that includes the social ecology of Murray Bookchin, Stewart Brand and the Whole Earth project, Fritz Schumacher's appropriate technology, Ivan Illich's convivial tools, alternative technologists such as Peter Harper and Godfrey Boyle and ideas by Mike Cooley and others concerning socially useful production (see Chapter 3). While 'liberatory technologies' were important elements in earlier movements, many were aware that the kinds of tool available, and the purposes to which they might be put, are shaped by a complex variety of social, economic, cultural and political relations (Bookchin, 1967). Broader social visions underlay these earlier, tools-based agendas (see Smith, 2005, 2014b).

Currently, such sustainable developments are marginal to the practices of many hackerspaces, fablabs and makerspaces. Emphasis rests more in playing with technologies, doing cool projects and being creative. Nevertheless, the possibilities of rapidly and freely sharing designs, templates and code for fabrication inspire visions for global knowledge linking to locally distributed production. New flows of goods, ideas and value may arise (Birtchnell and Urry, 2012). Hackerspaces, fablabs and makerspaces are popping up in long-derelict industrial districts of cities such as Manchester, Barcelona, Detroit and Buenos Aires. Elites get excited about these creative enclaves cultivating a new entrepreneurial spirit in their cities and nations. Even President Obama has hosted Maker Faires at the White House. Enthusiasts see this as opening new spaces for connecting entrepreneurial creativity and rescaling and relocating production. Institutional interest tends to focus on the cultivation of entrepreneurship, skills and creativity for business, manufacture and economic growth (Dougherty, 2012; Stangler and Maxwell, 2012). As such, alignments between the movement's tools for people agenda and pathways for sustainable developments are far from assured: tooling-up could reinforce unsustainable developments. Much depends upon whether, why and how people associate with workshops, and what roles they come to play in social changes.

This chapter introduces the global growth, since the early 2000s, in hackerspaces, fablabs and makerspaces and discusses their potential roles in pathways for sustainable developments. After looking at the background to the emergence of hackerspaces, fablabs and makerspaces, the next section analyses the different framings associated with these workshops. We then consider the spaces where support and development of the workshops has been obtained, followed by three illustrative examples of workshops. The penultimate section discusses pathway dilemmas confronting this movement and the last section draws some conclusions.

Background

The rapid spread of workshops occurs at the same time as related growth in a variety of maker, hacker and fixer movements globally. All are interested in the myriad possibilities of people's creating, adapting, repairing and producing things with technology. Neither hacking, nor making nor fixing is exclusive to workshops. People hack, make and fix in other sites too, including at home, in workplaces or at temporary meet-ups. There are considerable affinities and intersections. Activities include large gatherings at Maker Faires, meet-ups at repair cafés and Restart Projects, hackathons, specialist open hardware networks, citizen science initiatives and grassroots smart urbanism.

Illustrative of some of the intersections between workshops and movements globally is Las Barracas Hacklab in Buenos Aires. The hacklab is a self-organized workshop situated in an autonomous social centre in the post-industrial Barracas district of Buenos Aires. Among the projects at Las Barracas is a do-it-yourself (DIY) book scanner. An online, open hardware community has been developing book scanners for several years, committed to sharing designs, improvements and instructions. The result is a machine for automatically photographing book pages and free software to process the images into a computer file. Digitizing books in this way, and making them freely available over the internet, sits well with the free culture and anarchist ethos at Las Barracas. It is typical of many projects at the hacklab, which always try to enable people to access and contribute freely to a knowledge commons and develop capabilities for personal and social development through self-directed and collaborative projects.

The book-scanner network is one of a variety of open hardware communities online that are providing low-cost design and fabrication capabilities to people. A wide range of socially oriented tools are being developed, including initiatives in developing low-cost prostheses, community Wi-Fi networks, environmental monitoring kits, street furniture, housing, vehicles and so forth (e.g. the Open Source Ecology initiative). While these activities are not exclusive to hackerspaces, fablabs and makerspaces, workshops do provide an important facility and focus for such activity. Workshops allow people to work together and share tacit knowledge about hacking and making, feel part of a community, demonstrate virtuosity and attain kudos, and educate and support one another, as well as expressing values and commitments to free culture and, in some cases, criticism of dominant patterns of ownership and control in design and production.

A high-profile project undertaken in many workshops is the RepRap 3D printer. The RepRap community develops designs and online support for people to make increasingly sophisticated tools for additive manufacturing, including making further RepRap 3D printers (Söderberg, 2013). Interestingly, the free evolution of RepRap took a controversial turn when members of the Resistor hackerspace in New York decided to commercialize their version of the RepRap and protect aspects of their modified design through intellectual property. Their Makerbot business was subsequently bought for $400 million by industrial 3D-printer manufacturer Stratosys. This enclosure attracted considerable criticism from hackerspace communities because it was seen to contradict the radical roots of these workshops in free software and free culture movements (Maxigas, 2012), although such controversies are typical to the free software movement too.

There are thousands of hackerspaces and makerspaces globally (see hacker spaces.org). Membership of these workshops runs from the low tens to the hundreds. Intensity of involvement varies considerably, whether it be attending open evenings or informal training courses, becoming involved in the development of projects or helping in the management of the workshop. The characteristics and aims of workshops vary: some are very outwards-oriented community hubs, such as MadLab in Manchester, while others are more like a club.

A parallel area of growth for workshops has been in fablabs (short for fabrication laboratories). These too are (more or less) open access workshops that are intended to provide rapid prototyping tools for people. However, fablabs were spun off from an outreach initiative of the Centre for Bits and Atoms at the Massachusetts Institute of Technology (MIT) (Gershenfeld, 2005). Each fablab has the same suite of digital design and fabrication equipment, so that designs in one workshop can be made readily in another on the other side of the world, and so that collaborative projects are possible. Courses are possible in a Fab Academy that MIT operates across this network. However, what was intended initially as a fairly coordinated roll-out soon took on a life of its own as groups decided to set up their own fablabs independently of MIT. At September 2015 there were 565 fablabs globally, with numbers growing.

A particularly ambitious project example coming from the international network of fablabs is developing designs and plans for a floating fablab. Equipped with advanced tools, FabLab Flotante will navigate the rivers of the Peruvian Amazon, bringing advanced prototyping capabilities to riparian communities. This physical and digital resource is intended to connect local communities, their knowledge, aspirations and experiences with the world of digital fabrication and its international platforms, designs and possibilities. The creative flows, exchanges and synthesis arising are intended to enhance sustainable development possibilities in the Amazon, and also elsewhere. The intention is for FabLab Flotante to incorporate the latest in ecological design and bio-mimicry, and by blending high-tech tools with traditional practices to arrive at designs respectful to the cultural diversity of the region. The insights and experience generated by this cosmopolitan agenda are intended to inspire communities elsewhere.

At least, that is the plan (FabLab Flotante had not sailed at the time of writing, February 2016). Each of the participating fablabs is involved in developing different modules for FabLab Flotante. Member labs include Buenos Aires, Cochabamba, Loja, California, Vancouver, Cali, San Salvador, Barcelona, San

Jose, Boston and São Paolo, with the project led by Beno Juarez from FabLab Lima. The MIT-based Fab Foundation connects these developers with interest and funds from governments, business and international agencies, excited by the prospects of locally rooted (or floating) workshops sharing ideas and designs internationally, yet with the tools to adapt collaborations to place specific developments. Sensitivity towards the Amazonian communities will be vital if FabLab Flotante is to succeed. After all, local communities have not asked for fablabs, so they may choose not to embrace the tools on offer. It would be unfortunate if enthusiasm for tools among advocates eclipsed attentiveness and respect for the needs, aspirations and social relations in the target local communities. Whether this project idea floats or not, it will still have served an important purpose, which is to help promote the fablab concept and cultivate a degree of fascination (and perhaps scepticism too) in digital fabrication futures.

These examples illustrate the diversity of workshop activities. However, all follow principles based in popular access to design and fabrication technologies, openness and collaboration, freedom to pursue projects so long as they do not harm others and helping others to learn. Hackerspaces are, arguably, more strongly committed to autonomist sensibilities, but, as with much about these spaces, there are no categorical boundaries. The degree and forms of grassroots involvement in workshops varies. Many workshops are membership-based clubs open to all-comers and that put on events in the wider community. Some workshops (fablabs in particular) also support commercial endeavours. Business services, including consulting support and rapid prototyping, help to cross-subsidize community activity, which typically occurs over weekends and evenings. In other instances, publicly funded services, such as popular education, are provided by workshops, and associations with institutions such as libraries, universities and local authorities enable some grassroots access.

Intersecting technological, social and economic changes in societies are opening up workshop possibilities. Growth in workshops is both a response and a contribution to these changes. In their varied ways, workshops give practical and symbolic shape to a number of broad, inchoate and ill-defined developments. Digital design and fabrication technologies have, for example, been falling in cost, reducing in size, expanding in flexibility and application and becoming increasingly accessible. As we have seen, some workshops also build tools for themselves using open hardware designs, and all offer either informal or formal training in the use of these tools, or both. Access is reinforced by online provision of freely available open software and instructions and guidance on how to do projects, including videos and discussion groups on social media. All these technological developments render these tools available in terms of people being able to try them out, seeing others using the tools and becoming interested in having a go.

Technological appropriation has been facilitated by the cultural saliency of technology, hacking and making. Hacking and making simultaneously involve processes of learning, revision and repurposing, as well as kudos in the demonstration of these abilities and connecting with like-minded people (Gauntlett, 2013; Jordan, 2008). Activists and practitioners experiment with ideas for free culture and open knowledge through open hardware and ideas around commons-based peer production, open source and open design principles, the collaborative economy and the democratization of material activity (Benkler and Nissenbaum, 2006; Kostakis and Bauwens, 2015). Cultural movements for free and open knowledge confront the institutions of intellectual property and the means of production (Maxigas and Troxler, 2014).

The burgeoning of workshops arises in this context of novel and unfamiliar social relationships in production and consumption. Freelance employment patterns that involve people working precariously on projects create a need for workshop facilities to do this kind of work. While such changes are typically cast in light of the new work informalities of the global North, possibilities are also glimpsed for workshops in the creative milieu of the global South, where informal economies imply different kinds of precariousness. Positioned against this background of livelihoods and accessible technologies, there are those who celebrate a kind of Silicon Valley entrepreneurialism and see workshops as incubating creative livelihoods. The figure of the design-savvy and networked (social) entrepreneur looms large here. In other instances, workshops are seen as boosting resilient, cooperative local economic activity based in grassroots initiative, collaboration, control and development. The figure of the community activist has a presence here.

However, ideas and practices in open and collaborative innovation have also filtered into business practices (Chesbrough et al., 2006). Rather than seeing openness as a threat, firms are becoming familiar with ways of engaging and appropriating the fruits of collective, alternative or deviant prototyping and learning how to enclose designs, control marketing and benefit from the diffusion of the resulting products and services (Flowers, 2008; Scholz, 2013). Moreover, it is striking how the digital design and fabrication tools now acclaimed for personal and social creativity in workshops have genealogies that go back to the automation of manufacturing, and to fears over deskilling and workplace struggle that were brought about by computer-integrated manufacturing (Noble, 1984; Söderberg, 2012; see also Chapter 3 in this book). Earlier versions of these tools threatened skills, livelihoods and identities in manufacturing communities – while today they are celebrated as enabling agency, identities and communities for makers. This says much for the transformed social settings in which these technologies are now experienced. Critics argue that the new settings, including workshops, simply open up new modes of exploitation, as ideas, design and research efforts are effectively outsourced to 'free labour' in workshops, but with capital retaining the power to appropriate, enclose and commercialize the most promising fruits of that common endeavour (Morozov, 2014; Scholz, 2013; Söderberg, 2013).

It is out of this ambivalent background that hackerspaces, fablabs and makerspaces are emerging, and the same is influencing the different framings being advanced for workshops.

Framings of hackerspaces, fablabs and makerspaces

It is clear already that while an access-to-tools agenda underpins workshops, the purpose to which they are put is framed in various ways. Some see workshops as heralding a new industrial revolution, or democratizing technology, or enabling greater grassroots innovation, or providing tools for more sustainable developments. These framings have a mobilizing effect and draw people into the workshops movement (Hielscher and Smith, 2014).

Free software, free hardware and peer production

An important framing for workshops is commitment to principles of free software, hardware and peer production. Fundamentally, this is a practice in which all code, designs and instructions in the making and repairing of something are made freely available for people to access, adopt and modify, so long as the source is acknowledged and any modifications also become freely available. These ideas are evident in hackerspaces, fablabs and makerspaces. Many workshops have a policy (not always implemented) that member projects should be documented and posted online in a project repository, so that others can share them (Wolf et al., 2014).

Associated with this framing are ideas for commons-based peer production, defined as 'decentralized, collaborative, and non-proprietary; based on sharing resources and outputs among widely distributed, loosely connected individuals who cooperate with each other without relying on either market signals or managerial commands' (Benkler, 2006, p. 60). Mimicking practices from software development, activities are organized for modularity, such that people can work with different elements of the project. Such framing has two important characteristics. First, rather than starting off with specialized teams, projects draw together people with diverse resources, skills and knowledge, and self-organize the most suitable teams to work on different aspects of the project. Second, activities are not managed through a centralized source. Decision-making processes rely on the collaboration of volunteers and work because individuals buy into the values of the project (Benkler and Nissenbaum, 2006).

Personalized manufacturing, mass customization and a new industrial revolution

Another framing sees workshops at the experimental forefront of a revolution brought about by digital fabrication. As user interfaces become easier and more intuitive, so some commentators envisage design and production reconfiguring and reducing in scale (Birtchnell and Urry, 2012). It will be easier to access designs, adapt and modify them and fabricate personalized products digitally. Crowd-funding and other social media sites will make it easier for makers to go into production and marketing. A new economic paradigm of digital fabrication entrepreneurship is anticipated (Anderson, 2012). Workshops are framed as opening up manufacturing and enabling unconventional entrepreneurs to participate in infrastructures supportive of personal productive activity (Mota, 2011). While widespread self-provision may be overstated, the possibility of a new set of 'service' activities enabling people to have a greater role in design and production is an area where entrepreneurs are working. The basis for this framing draws upon the transformation that ICT has facilitated in the production and consumption of cultural products, and extends it to material production through connections between digital platforms and physical fabrication (Gershenfeld, 2005). Fablabs, hackerspaces and makerspaces are consequently framed as places where new design, production and consumption practices can be incubated.

Democratizing power of technological citizenship

Increasing access to versatile technologies prompts some observers to claim that in this way technology can be democratized. Hackerspaces, fablabs and makerspaces are framed as enabling people to engage more directly and actively in technology politics (Carstensen, 2013; Gauntlett, 2013). So, this framing sees a form of technological citizenship arising from the affordances that workshop tools have with respect to access, learning, participation and control. Workshops help to blur the boundaries between expert and non-expert, professional and amateur, business and hobbyist, production and consumption. Widespread access to the means of production comes to be seen as a right. Commons-based peer production opens up manufacture to more democratic involvements: something that troubles institutions of property, ownership and control. Gauntlett claims that making encompasses

> critiques of the capitalist relations of production, the distribution of power over technology, of excessive affluence, of global division of labour, and so on . . . and dovetails with political visions of . . . local production and of shifting the division between production and consumption.
> *(Gauntlett, 2013, p. 233)*

As fixers are finding, the ability to repair products is constrained and complicated by producers whose goods are designed more for manufacturing and marketing, and less for disassembly, repair and reuse. Communities such as the Restart Project are encouraging people to become involved in fixing through meet-up events, where people are helped not only to fix broken electronics goods but also to reflect on the way they are made and the relationships people have with their stuff. As direct experience grows about these issues, so alliances for reforms in production and consumption can be built, including requirements to design for repair. As such, workshops are framed as sites for cultivating technological citizenship.

Unlocking grassroots innovation

Another framing conceives workshops providing infrastructure for grassroots innovation (Smith et al., 2013). '[E]xperimentation with new technologies and new social modes of coordination lead[s] to niche forms of technical and social innovations' (Dickel et al., 2014, p. 7). Workshops are conceived of not so much as heralding an industrial transformation or wave of democratization, but rather as places where ideas relevant to local communities can be explored in practice. New forms of access, training and skill swapping are emphasized, as well as processes for learning and reflection. Formal and informal networks between workshops are seen not only as platforms for sharing experiences but also as means to linking to investment in the wider development and diffusion of innovations. The point with this framing is to view workshops not as a new model for transforming production and consumption but, rather, as a real-life laboratory experimenting with grassroots fabrication possibilities in terms of objects, practices and ideas. The question, then, is how these workshops facilitate the sharing, collaboration and grounding of general digital fabrication possibilities in particular communities (Birtchnell and Hoyle, 2014).

Sustainable developments

Some envisage workshops as playing key roles in sustainable developments (Schor, 2010). The open, collaborative ethos towards technology and production is considered to have an affinity with social goals such as sustainability (Bauwens, 2006). A sustainability framing points to examples of workshops:

- prototyping sustainable designs and systems;
- exploring issues of sustainable energy through hacking solar panels and building DIY home energy systems;
- incubating up-cycling businesses and furnishing creative hubs for closed-loop materials cycles;
- hosting repair cafés and Restart Projects;
- building communities interested in making, repair, repurpose and sustainability;
- critical making that connects people to the political economies and material realities of production and consumption, and that explores alternative, more desirable futures;
- organizing workshops for the social innovation of local sustainability;
- outreach activities that connect other sustainable development groups, and mobilizing new thinking/action about technologies, sustainability and people;
- cultivating post-consumer identities, values and material cultures.

It is the development of new ideas and patterns for using tools in altered relations of production and new forms of consumption that intrigues those interested in sustainability. So, for example, in making things people become more connected with objects, which might provide a lever for post-consumerist values and material culture. As Ann Thorpe puts it:

> FabLabs and related activities also emphasize the craft of the user, but in this model it is the process design and fabrication that paces reward and stimulation. In addition, the quality of stimulation is shifted from the thing to the process. This holds true not only for making new things, but also for hacking and remaking 'old' things. Approaches that consider the craft of the user may have other benefits as well. The process of collaborating, working together to fabricate, and sharing skills and knowledge each relate to . . . wellbeing.
> *(Thorpe, 2012, p. 85)*

Some workshops have adopted sustainability as a central theme, such as workshops at Valldaura, Amersfoort, Cloughjordan and Incite Focus in Detroit.

Spaces for grassroots digital fabrication

Spaces supportive of workshops, and where resources and opportunities for development are provided, are found in grassroots movements, educational institutions and interest from business and government.

Maker movements and grassroots groups

Enthusiasm and voluntary commitment provide important spaces where workshops can be established and run by their membership, remain open to the community and are self-funded. Here, the maker movement, open hardware movement and movements interested in commons-based peer production provide a space in which workshops are set up and grow. These movements generate interest, and hence visitors and members, but they also constitute an infrastructure for sharing information and contribute to the culture of hacking, making and fixing. Stories about workshops feature in movement media, such as *Make* magazine or the Makery website, while simultaneously generating phenomena that attract mainstream media interest also.

Networking is informal among hackerspaces. There are online mail lists and platforms for sharing ideas and insights, and people can exchange experience with similar projects. Fablabs have more formal networks based around the Fab Foundation. The latter embraces regional networks and platforms focused on specific issues, such as Fab Economy, dedicated to a new economic paradigm of open digital fabrication, or Fab Share, which seeks to disseminate designs and projects, and the Fab Academy, which provides training courses networked across core workshops.

Educational outreach and skills provision

Fablabs arose through educational outreach. The US National Science Foundation funded the first FabLab in Boston in 2003. FabLabs in Costa Rica, Norway and Ghana soon followed. Most subsequent labs obtained their own funds for development from a variety of sources, including international development aid programmes in some cases. As the idea caught on, others opened fablabs, sometimes in consultation with MIT and sometimes independently, including grassroots initiatives. Growth took on a life of its own. Fablab growth has been facilitated by a cadre of alumni from the Fab Academy, which was launched in 2009. Fab Academy provides project-oriented training in all FabLab technologies, and where students come together through a combination of groups based physically at FabLabs, interacting with student groups at other labs via distance learning and collaboration. Graduates have helped to establish labs in Europe, Latin America and Asia.

Educational institutions have become interested in the possibilities that workshops provide for hands-on learning. Schools, colleges and universities have been opening makerspaces. Makerspaces and hackerspaces have also been looking to education services as a basis for their activities. Workshops run day courses in certain technologies, such as Arduino and electronics, laser-cutting or clothing. Unlike in conventional training centres, participants in workshop-run courses are usually welcomed as members who can then continue to pursue their projects. Libraries are opening workshop rooms. So, in a variety of ways, workshops are able to obtain finance, memberships and other resources by strategically positioning themselves in a space dedicated to education and training.

Business and state interest

Some governments have become interested in community-based workshops. The White House has even hosted Maker Faires. Public money is committed to establishing and supporting workshops, whether for training and education, or for promoting entrepreneurship and innovation, or out of a desire for citizens to experience these new technological possibilities. Iceland has opened nine fablabs around the country. Local authorities in Barcelona have been committed to opening a workshop in every neighbourhood of the city (see below).

Business associations welcome the way workshops cultivate enthusiasm for technology and entrepreneurship. Justification as well as pressure for the Fab Foundation to maintain its coordinating position comes from interest from large industrial, governmental and multilateral donors seeking a contact point for negotiating and distributing support for the creation of fablabs. As a peak association, the Fab Foundation can negotiate deals for labs. So, for example, Solidworks is promoting its computer-aided design package to all labs, Chevron has donated $10 million to help the Foundation promote and establish more fablabs in the USA, and there have been talks with the World Bank and others interested in developing country possibilities. Even the US government's Defense Advance Research Projects Agency (DARPA) has partnered with *Make* magazine and proposed funding makerspaces in US schools. These corporate approaches from the 'closed' economy are controversial (Finley, 2012; Hertz, 2012).

Some entrepreneurs have opened fee-paying workshops as a business venture (e.g. TechShops in the USA). Others offer rapid prototyping services for businesses and developers. Individuals also use workshops to prototype ideas that they subsequently develop entrepreneurially into commercial products. Commercial activity is criticized by some activists, particularly in spaces committed to free culture and more political ideals for alternative economic activity and pathways.

Illustrative examples

So far, we have seen how workshops are framed in a variety of ways and operate across different spaces. Some of the strategic issues this raises are illustrated in the following three cases. Each has been chosen for differences in relations with grassroots sustainable developments. Build Brighton is illustrative for many local, membership-based hackerspaces and makerspaces, and where projects are personal to participants. Amersfoort FabLab is also a grassroots, membership-based initiative, but with explicit commitment to sustainable developments. Such commitment does not pervade all member projects. Rather, it is through links with community groups and projects in the city that sustainable developments are realized. The third example, the Ateneus programme in Barcelona, is an ambitious initiative of the municipal authorities, borne of a vision for smart sustainability in the city. It illustrates the challenges and possibilities for engaging the grassroots in such visions.

Build Brighton

Build Brighton was among the first hackerspaces to open in the UK in June 2009. There are over 100 hackerspaces and makerspaces in the UK now (Sleigh et al., 2015), where the term 'hackspace' has been adopted by some, including Build Brighton. In this chapter, however, we continue to refer to the more generic term 'hackerspace'. UK hackerspaces network informally online in discussion forums and social media, and physically by meeting regularly at events such as camps, hackdays and Maker Faires. Members drop into one another's workshops when visiting other towns – including internationally. In this way ideas and issues are discussed, whether they be for projects or the day-to-day challenges of organizing and running a workshop voluntarily. People feel part of a scene.

Like many UK hackerspaces, Build Brighton emerged out of an international initiative to promote hackerspaces. It began with the US group Hackers on a Plane visiting Germany in 2007 to visit hacklabs and hackerspaces there. They returned to the USA and, through prominent hackerspaces such as Noisebridge in San Francisco, Resistor in New York, they began promoting the idea of people opening a hackerspace in every town. Jens Ohlig and Lars Weiler posted a hackerspace design guide on the internet for the Hackers on a Plane visit, which they had already presented at the Chaos Computer Camp that year. It too went on to inspire hackerspaces around the world. The initiative was motivated by the politics of hacking technology and sharing knowledge freely.

Mitch Altman, from Noisebridge in San Francisco, began promoting hackerspaces during his international travels. He subsequently visited Build Brighton twice, and encouraged a local robotics group, plus friends working in the digital and design sector, to form the Build Brighton hackspace. It began in a small room rented from a co-working space. The group met every Thursday to hack together and slowly accumulated electronics equipment, a laser cutter and other tools. Membership was around thirty people. In 2010 Build Brighton entered the Global Hackerspace Challenge. It was runner-up with a prototype toy owl that helped kids to spell phonetically. Its prize was electronics equipment and it received kudos and publicity.

Like all hackerspaces, Build Brighton's founding principles are that the space is organized and run by the membership, not for profit and open to the public. These have become the criteria for affiliating to the UK Hackspace Foundation, which helps to share advice and information about running a hackerspace. At Build Brighton, Thursday evenings are open to the public – anyone can drop by with questions, seek help or get involved. Access at other times is for members only. Members pay what they can to cover running costs and also contribute supplies of materials, equipment and components. Volunteers keep the space going, maintain the equipment and deal with organizational, legal and membership issues. A core group of volunteer directors facilitates and cajoles members to help with these tasks. The group moved to a bigger, dedicated space in September 2011 that allows access around the clock. Around the same time, Build Brighton helped to organize the first independent Maker Faire in the UK, inviting other hackerspaces, specialist groups and individual makers to run exhibits and workshops. Thousands of visitors attended. Membership of Build Brighton grew to over 100 people.

Members tend to do their own personal projects. Training on equipment works informally, with members showing one another how tools work, and helped through online tutorials and trial and error. Founding organizers talk about building a community through Build Brighton. Students and some local makers use the workshop for study or entrepreneurial reasons. Many members are simply interested in hacking electronics, technology and (increasingly) learning traditional crafts and sharing their enthusiasm for making with others. Members voluntarily run public workshops in these activities, with revenue from fees going to Build Brighton and the purchase of more equipment.

Like many UK hackerspaces, Build Brighton is not as overtly political as earlier hackerspaces, notably in Germany: some of the political motivations and ideals of workshops elsewhere, concerning knowledge commons, free culture and democratizing technology, are not a defining mission for Build Brighton. Which is not to say that people are unsympathetic; rather, that there is more of a pragmatic ethos towards making and being part of a supportive community where members develop skills for themselves. The real grassroots innovation in hackerspaces such as Build Brighton therefore rests in their being spaces that promote a community ethos towards inquisitiveness, knowledge and capabilities with technologies. In these more modest ways, technology becomes demystified.

There is hope and interest in being part of something bigger. According to one Build Brighton director:

> Hackspaces are still fairly new . . . We're still trying to find our feet. So our activities are limited at the moment to our own members and the surrounding local community that can sort of pop into the space. What I would like to see is there are lots of hackspaces, they all know what they're doing. They all have enough resources, enough people and enough money to be self-sufficient. And they start directing their energy outwards, towards a wider community, and sort of implementing projects that spread all of this knowledge that is available within the hackspace to a wider audience of people. Or alternatively, for developing these relationships with other institutions at a higher level to be able to output our knowledge and skills in a way that they can use and spread.
>
> *(Interview with Build Brighton director, 5 December 2014)*

But, like other hackerspaces, Build Brighton is busy enough being a workshop for members. There are limited time and resources to be able to work strategically for bigger possibilities. Other spaces in the UK have been able to secure resources to step up and into broader roles. MAKLab in Scotland and MadLab in Manchester, for example, have both attracted external funding for running courses, training and opening facilities for community projects. And others are seeking to emulate their example.

FabLab Amersfoort

FabLab Amersfoort in the Netherlands created one of the first 'grassroots' FabLabs (Troxler, 2014). Its self-organized, self-financed workshop instantly attracted interest from groups wishing to emulate it. What is interesting in this example is how the workshop facility extended community-based projects that the founding group was already pursuing. FabLab Amersfoort was opened in 2010 by activist artists in the De War collective (*in de war* is Dutch for 'confused'). De War operates in an abandoned dye factory that it has occupied since 2002. From this base it organizes and tour public events, exhibits and workshops on themes connecting art, technology, sustainability and science. It was through this activity that Diana Wildschut and Harmen Zijp from De War first heard of the FabLab concept and became interested in possibilities complementary to their collective.

De War had a Tweak Show exhibition that it had been developing and touring since 2007. The show is 'a labyrinth full of interactive installations that give the audience an intuitive understanding of the complex systems in science, the environment and society' (Wildschut, 2014, quoted in Hielscher, 2015, p. 8). The Braindetector exhibit, for example, converts brain activity into electricity and lights a bulb worn on the head. Developing Braindetector required knowledge that Diana and Harmen did not have. So they convened a group of friends, and friends of friends, who met up at De War to research neurology, electronics and sensors for the exhibit. The method worked so well that De War turned it into a regular event called Open Toko (*toko* is Indonesian for shop). At Open Toko people collaborated on group-selected topics involving electronics, coding and making things. 'We discovered that there's lots of people who have little blocks of knowledge . . . and if you combine all that, suddenly everybody has a quick start initiative in a certain topic' (Diana Wildschut, quoted in Hielscher, 2015, p. 8).

In 2009, a FabLab regional networker participated in an Open Toko. He told De War, 'listen guys, what you are doing is called a FabLab, you just don't know it yet and should get some machines' (Zijp, 2013). So Harmen read about FabLabs and liked the idea. Reading further into commons-based peer production (Bauwens, 2006), Harmen found resonance with ideas and practices at De War. They decided to set up a FabLab. However, the MIT model involved tools costing $100,000. De War approached the local chamber of commerce, the local innovation centre and the municipality for help. After long discussions, no assistance materialized. Unperturbed, De War took matters into its own hands, as with its other activities. It bought a second-hand laser cutter for €3,000 and, with help, made its own 3D printer and began accumulating a growing suite of tools. With these tools it opened its FabLab in 2010.

Membership has grown ever since. Members pay €50 to join, which they earn back by helping to run the FabLab, or by sharing project reports on the Amersfoort website. People are encouraged to take responsibility for the space. There are workshop cleaning days, tool maintenance and joint projects. Visitors have to be self-initiators. Learning to work with the tools, proposing projects or joining projects is all self-directed. Volunteers are on hand to give guidance where necessary. In this respect, FabLab Amersfoort is like many hackerspaces in its informal and self-organized approach.

Right from the start, De War has connected the workshop to sustainability initiatives in the city. Working with the local Transition Town group, it set up a Transitielab. Here tools are put to use in prototyping sustainability devices, repairing and up-cycling objects and experimenting with peer-production ideas and practices. The FabLab also hosts a Repair Café, where people meet and use the tools to bring new life to broken and discarded objects. De War is trying to link its FabLab facilities to the infrastructure requirements of urban farming and energy projects in the city. FabLab Amersfoort has been building monitoring systems for beehives, for example, and promoting their construction in the city. De War has also connected the FabLab to citizen science initiatives. Participants build their own environmental monitoring systems and share analysis. An international network called Public Laboratory – an international network sharing designs for

DIY environmental sensors, monitoring and reporting – has been an inspiration. There is a strong commitment to people's producing their own environmental knowledge, which is key for ideas about tool-based community empowerment. At Amersfoort discussions developed with the municipal council to run courses for citizens to build environmental monitoring networks. Other FabLabs have been doing similar work. Indeed, in the case of Barcelona, the FabLab has developed and hosts the Smart Citizen initiative: a sensor kit using an Arduino micro-controller platform connecting and comparing measurements globally via a web platform. Smart Citizen developed through crowd-funding and FabLab networks.

A grassroots approach focused on sustainability remains relatively unusual within community workshops internationally. When the annual international gathering of FabLabs came to Amsterdam in 2010, De War presented its grassroots approach as a method to 'hack systems' of production, consumption and economy, thereby contributing to new, resilient and sustainable communities. Groups from around the world have subsequently contacted FabLab Amersfoort for advice and to learn more. In response, De War developed *The Grassroots FabLab Instructable* manual and began hosting an annual conference for grassroots labs called FabFuse. According to Peter Troxler, De War was instrumental in a grassroots 'insurgency' and appropriation of MIT's FabLab model (Troxler, 2014). What enabled De War to do this was its collective's ethos of just getting on and doing projects with the resources available, without seeking permission or funding.

Nevertheless, De War recognizes that people arrive at workshops with different motivations. Some share commitments towards peer production, sustainability and collaboration, whereas others are more interested in pursuing personal projects unconnected with sustainability. The challenge of fusing workshop ideals further into member practice continues. De War plans to expand the old factory site, including the FabLab, into a hub for local social change networks. To do this, its occupancy of the site under squatting arrangements needs to be formalized and secured. It has constituted itself into a cooperative, and it has developed a business plan for purchasing the site with the support of banks. However, at the time of writing (February 2016), the future is uncertain. De War's request to buy the site from the municipality has been rejected, amid rumours that real estate developers are interested in the land. Undeterred, the group continues to organize its FabFuse activities and promote sustainability locally.

Ateneus de Fabricació Digital

Unlike the council in Amersfoort, public authorities in Barcelona have committed to a visionary aspiration for workshops. As part of a vision for a smart, self-sufficient city by 2040, city leaders announced plans to open public workshops across different city districts. The municipality has funded a network of Ateneus de Fabricació Digital, which is envisaged to spread to every neighbourhood as part of the public infrastructure for a sustainable city that, within thirty years, will manufacture half of its material needs locally. Workshop managers have access to funds and outreach possibilities that directors at Build Brighton dream of. Barcelona is not alone. In February 2015, city authorities in São Paulo announced plans to open a network of twelve public FabLabs in an initiative conceived to bring the tools of digital fabrication to the people, equipping them for a fuller role in a revolution towards decentralized and democratized production and consumption. Iceland has also opened public workshops, and other public authorities are casting an eye over the – potentially – empowering possibilities of public workshops.

At the Ateneus in Barcelona, it is envisaged that citizens will appropriate digital fabrication in ways analogous to earlier adoption of ICT, and create socially innovative ways to develop livelihoods and improve their neighbourhoods. Interest in community workshops began in Barcelona with its first FabLab at the Institute of Advanced Architecture Catalunya (IAAC) in 2006. Originally intended for relatively closed use – for student prototyping and architectural commissions – the lab garnered global attention for its pioneering vision for 'fab cities' and urban governance (Diez, 2012). More than simply making new widgets, IAAC founder – and subsequently City Architect – Vicente Guallart envisioned maker-citizens using new tools such as 3D printers and open source designs as a means of taking an active, material role in city development. This image of the technologically empowered citizen appealed, and FabLab Barcelona's model went on to provide the template for the Ateneus programme as part of the vision of the Mayor of Barcelona, Xavier Trias, for transforming Barcelona into a smart, self-sufficient city.

Supported by Barcelona's civic leaders, each Ateneu receives public funds to run popular local events: family days and school visits; training courses and social innovation programmes: everything necessary to equip citizens with the digital fabrication nous necessary to 'materialise their ideas and create their worlds' (according to the Ateneus slogan). By this vision, high-tech public infrastructure will make it easier for Barcelona's citizens to lock into a global 'maker' network – uploading designs that people in, say, Singapore, might use; or collaborating in prototyping with FabLabs in São Paulo, adapting ideas produced globally to fit their own local needs.

The first Ateneu opened in July 2013, in an abandoned silk ribbon factory in the Les Corts district. A further twenty workshops were planned to some degree for later down the line. The Ateneus network director stresses how embryonic and exploratory the programme is. A community workshop for digital fabrication is a strange concept for public administrators to get their heads around. Councils traditionally provide conventional public services for people to receive and consume; conversely, Ateneus offer a space where citizens do the producing. Simply convincing city bureaucracies to experiment with this concept is already an achievement.

Setting up the workshops – installing machinery, running courses – proved relatively straightforward; the real challenges come in weaving the workshops into the everyday fabric of the local community. It takes time to build familiarity, confidence and commitment among local people, and considerable resources and patience on the part of the city authorities before the possibilities loaded onto

Ateneus can be realized. The experiences around the second Ateneu in Ciutat Meridiana highlight these tensions. Ciutat Meridiana is the poorest neighbourhood in Barcelona – unemployment exceeds 20 per cent and family incomes are one-third of city averages. The neighbourhood association is constantly in battle with the council over changes to social services and resisting evictions from mortgage lenders. People in Ciutat Meridiana needed food, not 3D printers. The Ateneus project did not help itself by siting the workshop in a building that local people were already using as a food bank. (The mayor's support for Ateneus also counted for little in a neighbourhood that felt ambivalently towards him.) Rather than embracing the project, locals were alienated and occupied the Ateneu in protest. Negotiations ensued, eventually leading to two conditions of agreement – the food bank was re-established, albeit elsewhere in the neighbourhood; and the Ateneu would emphasize training and work for young people.

Ciutat Meridiana shines a light on the tension between what citizens wanted from their city now, and what city leaders envisaged for future citizens. Even if local stakeholders are engaged beforehand, as happened with the first Ateneu in Les Corts, opening up a workshop is the easiest part of the project. Embedding the facility into community life is far more challenging. While the Ateneus programme was being rolled out, other self-organized and spontaneous workshops were also flourishing across the city. Over in Ciutat Vella, the Maker Convent offers open and informal training programmes for their machinery. Vailets Hacklab runs courses for children in a variety of locations, now including the Ateneus. Similarly, the Fab Café, run by the Makers of Barcelona, offers workshop space, education and tools for anyone walking in off the streets. The ethos of these spaces borrows heavily from a Silicon Valley 'can do' form of urban entrepreneurship, in which people happily share enthusiasm for digital fabrication and explore new forms of collaboration together.

Whether citizens suffering precarious employment and other economic hardships wish to embrace this form of citizenship is a moot point. Despite the public imaginary of makerspaces as user-led spaces, neither the Ateneus nor these other workshops are especially grassroots phenomena. One test of whether the civic vision for workshops can coexist with grassroots activities comes with Can Batlló, a massive disused textile mill proposed as a potential site for an Ateneus workshop. Can Batlló is in the Sants district of Barcelona, and working-class Sants has a long tradition of political and community organization – including many squats and social centres – and a history of its own autonomist and cooperative activities. In response to the economic crisis, Sants activists occupied and renovated Block 11 of Can Batlló. The building was converted into an autonomous, self-organized community centre and cooperative working space, housing a library, carpentry workshop, bar and urban gardening space; and the Sants activists have aspirations to seed local, cooperative economic activity for the neighbourhood through the centre. If grassroots activists are already involved in this type of community building, does a project like Ateneus offer anything more than a shiny technological patina to the process? Or could an Ateneu provide useful tools that unlock wider possibilities and plug the district into a global community of design activists experimenting in digital fabrication for DIY urbanism and commons-based economic development? The association of Ateneus with Mayor Trias's smart city vision was seen by critics to be the latest in a series of city makeovers, prioritizing international capital markets and speculative investments in the city over the real needs and aspirations of its residents. According to Ivan Miró, an activist from the Ciutat Invisible cooperative, the smart city is merely a different brand of the same neoliberal model of urban regeneration whose democratic and local economic credentials are deeply suspect. In Barcelona, the council's (sometimes violent) evictions of long-established squatted social centres have deepened suspicions and heightened antagonism with the city's grassroots activists.

The Ateneus programme, with city leaders' notions of an orderly cultivation of technological citizenship, has encountered very different forms of citizenship in action. Ateneus are trying to establish themselves in a context where people feel the strain of economic crisis, and increasingly question whose interests are truly being served by future visions of their city. Such contexts influence the relative ease and kinds of support available for putting tools to particular purposes. If communities such as those in Barcelona are truly to be liberated to debate, use and resist tools in ways that they see as appropriate (rather than those encapsulated in elite visions), then the politics of these contexts will need engaging. Deployed sensitively, the Ateneus programme could provide important spaces for exploring technology, citizenship and urban governance in very practical ways that are supportive of diverse forms of neighbourhood-led development. The programme is still young, and patience is required.

Interesting possibilities might arise from a shift in political leadership in Barcelona following elections in May 2015. Mayor Trias's centre-right Catalan nationalists lost control of the council to a new party, Barcelona en Comú, that had emerged from grassroots opposition to austerity. The council is now under the leadership of Ada Colau, who rose to prominence organizing effective resistance to housing evictions. The Ateneus programme continues. It remains to be seen how the Colau administration will develop its support, but it is convening groups to explore the possibilities for more cooperative and solidary forms of economic development in the city, including digital platform cooperativism. Whatever their eventual framing, any longer-term promise, as with community workshops elsewhere, rests with workshops becoming a community resource owned by the neighbourhoods in which they sit, rather than tied up with the patronage of local politicians.

Workshops building pathways for sustainable developments

Bringing tools to people requires skilful community development as well as skills in design and fabrication. Hackerspaces, fablabs and makerspaces have gone through a period of impressive growth. A diversity of workshop forms, locations and practices are being explored. It is important to remember that for most participants, voluntary involvement is born of a sense of curiosity, enjoyment and community through engaging with technology creatively. People learn skills, have fun, become frustrated and inspired by turns, and along the way they gain recreational, developmental and socializing experiences. Such seems to be the main dynamic of activities in workshops like Build Brighton.

Central to workshops are ideas that people have a right to tools. The unstructured possibilities that this offers to participants for experimentation are significant. An impressive and inspiring flow of designs, prototypes and objects is being generated in these workshops, whether it is the development of low-cost prosthetic limbs, monitoring equipment, games, buildings, furniture and so on. An ethic towards openness and collaboration further develops and disseminates these devices through global collaboration. In addition to prototyping objects, new identities are being innovated (e.g. makers, fixers, hackers), and new ideas are being articulated (e.g. commons-based peer production). There is a lot of energy and hope amid these open, collaborative, playful developments.

Conviction in the emancipatory power of giving tools to people leads some advocates to resist attempts to further direct the purposes towards which these tools might be put. Workshops encourage people to be open, collaborative and imaginative – to 'be awesome', as a slogan popular among hackerspaces puts it. Directing people along certain pathways consequently contradicts the cherished spirit of openness, access, participation and autonomy. The goal is merely to make the tools as widely accessible as possible, to the extent that, in the view of Tomas Diez from FabLab Barcelona, workshops eventually disappear because personalized design and fabrication becomes all pervasive (Diez, 2012).

However, even the most personal projects, in aggregate, have social consequences. The social meaning of this activity is something participants should be encouraged to think about reflexively. To the extent that workshop members are taking advantage of deeper-seated changes in society – be they the emerging social movements, new technologies, shifting cultures or restructuring economies discussed earlier – workshops provide an arena for reflection on these changes. This suggests that the more transformative aspects to workshops rest in the kinds of technological citizenship that are forming. Moreover, as our framings indicate, various social agents already have designs on these workshops. Claims are already being made concerning workshop potential; expectations and indicators are forming for evaluating workshops; surveys and research are being commissioned with particular questions in mind; and funding and investment are offered with certain assumptions and agendas built into their criteria. Workshops need to figure out how to respond to these developments. One strategy is to ignore these framings of their futures, and to continue along a path of autonomous spaces for hacking technologies.

However, if workshops are to genuinely realize the transformative potential of their framings, they will have to engage with these wider interests. Doing so non-strategically risks becoming pulled into the institutional logics of those wider interests, and that could force design and fabrication activities back onto dominant development pathways. While this may be acceptable for some, it leaves little space for more transformational pathways to flourish (Maxigas and Troxler, 2014). FabLabs in particular are located within or financed by host organizations that expect them to deliver certain objectives after a period of time. Some workshops are required or encouraged to increase their income through facilitating commercial activities or aligning with conventional training institutions. Outside institutions welcome particular forms of activity and seek to harness workshops to wider ambitions, such as education institutions tapping into enthusiasm in these spaces for technology and entrepreneurship. None of this is necessarily wrong. It is simply to point out why a desire for autonomy can jar with institutionalization, and why a lack of strategy for institutional transformation can constrain workshop aspirations. Unstructured, open-ended and flexible activities are something that increasingly audited and instrumentally driven institutions find tricky to comprehend and support.

We live in a structured world. Vested economic interests, positions of political authority, cultural privileges, social norms, technological infrastructures and research agendas selectively appropriate the innovative ideas and practices emerging from community workshops. At the moment, a kind of crowd-funded, Silicon Valley social entrepreneurship predominates in workshops, and that frames developments accordingly. This runs the risk that workshop contributions are reduced to specific design issues, seen as providing tractable solutions involving the production of discrete objects, and addressed in a modular way to facilitate collaboration and openness, without attention to the wider causes and consequences of alternative development pathways.

The question is, can the workshop movement move beyond its demonstrated possibilities for prototyping and become involved in processes for catalysing deep-seated transformations? Workshops are riding on the possibilities presented by structural changes, but can they assert influence over which social directions are taken, and really open up alternative pathways? Where workshops try to connect with community activism for social change, as with the Ateneus in Barcelona, or with FabLab Amersfoort, effort is required to make design, prototyping and fabrication tools meaningful for the grassroots activists and their causes. Relevance needs to be demonstrated, and not assumed. Workshop possibilities have to be seen in terms of helping alliances to convene and collaborate. FabLab Amersfoort has been exploring this through its links to Transition Town activities and citizen science projects in the city.

The ability for workshops to tap into international networks simultaneously to being locally rooted is where much potential might be found. Workshops also need to recognize that they generate important critical awareness (Ratto and Boler, 2014). Workshop activities can prompt reflection on the limitations currently constraining the development and diffusion of some of their open designs and fabrications. These limitations are not necessarily failings on the part of workshop designs and participants. They may point usefully to complementary areas of work. Low-cost eco-houses developed in workshops may, for example, prompt participants to consider wider issues of land tenure, finance and urban planning, say, where workshops in themselves do not have the means to resolve these issues.

This is not a criticism. It merely recognizes a limiting point for tools-based grassroots innovation, a point where alliances need to be forged with other agents and forms of social change capable of transforming wider institutions, such as reformed urban governance in the case of housing initiatives.

If workshops are to realize alternative development pathways, activists and sponsors will require strategies to counter inhibiting structures, retain autonomy from some institutions and influence the shape of new institutional forms. There is a long way to go in order for the socially transformational aspirations to materialize in practice. The ideas and experiments are there in workshops, and they point to inspiring possibilities for anyone pushing for wider changes in economy, society, politics and culture.

Conclusions

In many respects, hackerspaces, fablabs and makerspaces involve uneasy convergences. Wider developments are drawn into the world of workshops, whether developments in thinking, in technology, in society, in economies, in politics or in the values and interests concerning production and consumption. What we see is various groups involved in a figuring out and sifting through of different practical possibilities arising from this convergence. Excited claims are made. A variety of agendas are drawn up. Different models and strategies are experimented with. Spaces for further development (or long-term survival) are sought by positioning workshops variously as incubators for design, innovation and entrepreneurship, as engaging and effective means for educating and training people in digital fabrication possibilities and as a resource for communities and social development.

Perhaps the chief dilemma for this movement is to manage expectations regarding tool-based approaches to development. It is misplaced to insist that workshops substitute wholesale for the existing regimes in design, manufacturing and consumption. No matter how much enthusiasts might wish for such a transition, it would be misguided to seek agency in workshops alone. Rather, the unusual possibilities being experimented with in workshops point to possibilities; and the challenges in realizing those possibilities in an everyday sense point as much to the structural inability of incumbent regimes of design and fabrication to respond to demands for sustainability, community involvement, democratization and convivial forms of production and consumption as they do to the limited agency of community workshops.

At the heart of the workshops movement is a familiar dilemma. Structural change opens up opportunities for people to access technology and explore new social possibilities with those tools; but any changes are not decisive enough to enable the more radical possibilities to be realized on a wide scale. Prevailing institutions still privilege conventional forms of appropriation and control, and of production and consumption. Whether grassroots experimentation in workshops wants to connect with programmes for further structural change, and how it might do that, is a moot point. Many novel uses of tools in these spaces are susceptible to being developed into more muted forms for commercialization, which might be construed as a sensible means for sustaining the activity (and livelihoods) for participants. For many enthusiasts, this is acceptable; they are not interested in social transformation so much as in the pursuit of particular projects in rewarding ways within their communities. But it signals disappointing co-option for others.

It is important not to underestimate the significance of what people are doing in community workshops. For many of us, technology development has been, and is increasingly, proceeding in a direction of ever-seamless interfaces and hidden workings. To hack open a device designed for obsolescence, and to repair it and upgrade it and then to share freely that knowledge about the device and its workings is a deviant act within the logics of cognitive capitalism. To question why it is deviant behaviour, rather than everyday practice, is to practise a critical reasoning. Workshops are already working against the grain. The question is whether these initiatives, such as the Restart Project, can connect to movements that are seeking pathways organized to alternative logics of sustainability and social justice. These constructively critical activities are an important reminder that framings for participation and democracy need to move beyond a kind of Silicon Valley entrepreneurialism, where anyone can make it so long as they raise enough money through crowd-funding.

7
THE SOCIAL TECHNOLOGY NETWORK

In July 2004, a heterogeneous group of institutions, led by the Bank of Brazil Foundation and including several national ministries such as the Ministry of Science and Technology and the Ministry of Social Development, together with semi-public companies such as Petrobras, met numerous representatives of non-governmental organizations (NGOs), social movements and universities to discuss policies for social and technological development. This meeting led to the creation of the Social Technology Network (STN; Rede de Tecnologia Social [RTS] in Portuguese), a hybrid experiment to promote grassroots innovation in Brazil and seeking to combine the participation and empowerment of civil society actors in technological development with the design of large-scale public policies for social development and poverty reduction.

Created just after the beginning of the administration of President Luiz Inácio Lula da Silva, the STN embodied much of the aims and hopes of the new political scenario of the early 2000s in Brazil. This scenario combined the long-term rise of social movements such as the Landless Movement and the recently created World Social Forum with some restoration of the role of the state and a broad commitment to redistribution of income. The emergence of the STN coincided with a propitious time to experiment with alternative frames of development and new ideas in public policies, such as solidarity economy, fair trade and sustainable development.

From its origins in 2004 until its suspension in 2012, the STN reached more than 900 members, involving a wide range of participants, from academics to activists, trade unions, government representatives, funding agencies and, especially, NGOs, community representatives and social movements.

Over a seven-year trajectory, the STN documented hundreds of grassroots technological developments and selected dozens to be reapplied by the thousands in other communities, through collaboration with funders, technicians, academics, policymakers and civil society organizations. Innovative initiatives were evident in areas such as water and sanitation, agroecological production, social housing and solid waste recycling. Through these actions STN also fostered a debate, in Brazil and elsewhere, about the need to combine technological development with social inclusion and the democratization of knowledge: a vision that became acknowledged and incorporated among social movements, NGOs and policymakers. However, the network itself was suspended in 2012, owing to irreconcilable differences between civil society organizations and funders over its formal structure, funding and pace of development.

The short story of Brazil's STN raises questions about the best strategies in the pursuit of grassroots innovation, the role of the state, funders and civil society actors, and how to combine the urge to scale up solutions to poverty situations with the aim of empowering marginalized social actors.

In order to understand these issues, this chapter will try to answer the following:

- how and why the STN was created;
- how social technology advocates mobilized support and activities in grassroots innovation;
- what challenges and dilemmas the STN faced.

This work is based on a qualitative approach that benefits from the great amount of documentation and interest around the STN, along with a set of interviews with relevant actors in this process. The chapter is organized as follows. The first section explores the origins and background of the STN, including some considerations of the political landscape in the 2000s. The second section analyses the diverse framings of social technology (ST). The next section describes the main spaces where ST was able to develop, followed by a section providing some relevant examples of reapplied technologies. The following section discusses some results and lessons that can be learnt for path construction from the history of the STN. The chapter concludes with some final remarks on the contribution of the STN to understanding grassroots innovation in Latin America.

Origins and background

In 2002 Luiz Inácio Lula da Silva and the Workers' Party (PT) won the Brazilian presidential election in what was regarded as a watershed moment for the country. After three consecutive defeats, the PT's rise to government represented a change of political tone, as compared to the neoliberal policies prevalent among governments in the region, and signalled a shift towards more socially inclusive policies oriented towards fighting poverty, inequality and exclusion. Furthermore, the PT, the largest left-wing party of Latin America, would finally have an opportunity to implement, on a national scale, what it was doing locally in several cities and states and what was being called PT's 'way of government' ('*modo petista de governar*'). This involved the commitment to redistributive policies in favour of the poorest part of the population and the 'democratization of the state' through increasing forms of participation in setting public agendas including, for instance, participatory budget schemes (Hochstetler, 2004; Paes de Barros and Carvalho, 2003; Samuels, 2004).

In this political scenario, the construction of new public policies that could target social development and at the same time build bridges with social movements was keenly favoured by the government. As Hochstetler argues, there was a genuine effort to include social movements and NGOs in some areas and initiatives of the government. This involved the inclusion of several activists among its staff and the call to support government social programmes (Hochstetler, 2004). In this sense, the changes that the PT was implementing in Brazil signalled a shift from a state-centred managerial approach to a different one, more permeable to public participation and social movements, in particular regarding areas of social assistance. This scenario thus combined the aim of implementing new policies of poverty alleviation with the commitment to public participation. It also provided the opportunity to experiment with innovative policies of social inclusion and science and technology development at a national scale.

However, the PT faced huge challenges in translating the experiences of some pioneering local policies to the national level. In part, the PT was tied to alliances with other political parties, and it also needed to deal with a looming debt crisis, all of which left little space for radical policies and constrained the simultaneous implementation of the goals of inclusion and democratization. The PT government did indeed privilege the construction of massive social inclusion programmes, such as Bolsa Familia, a social security programme of direct cash transfer based on existing initiatives of the previous administration that was inspired by the United Nations Millennium Goals and later received worldwide recognition (Graziano da Silva, 2009; Hall, 2006).

However, there was also room for more experimental policies on public participation and social inclusion, such as the creation of the Solidarity Economy Secretariat (SENAES) within the Ministry of Employment in 2003. One of those initiatives was the Social Technology Network.

Early antecedents of social technology

The drive towards ST started at the end of the 1990s and beginning of the 2000s. In the beginning it involved a diverse set of public and semi-public institutions that were experimenting with different concepts and visions of technology for social development.

In the early 2000s a small group of people at the Ministry of Science and Technology started to explore the possibility of launching a revamped version of the old appropriate technology programmes that were implemented by the National Council of Science and Technology Development (CNPq) during the late 1970s through to the 1990s. Having reconsidered ideas and experiences underpinning appropriate technologies, they later joined and contributed to the discussion of the concept of social technology.

The Bank of Brazil Foundation (BBF) is the private foundation of the flagship bank and one of the largest in Brazil. Its interest in ST arose from recognition of the limits that its own social development programmes faced and its acknowledgement of the need to include technological solutions in the fight against poverty (de Olivera Pena and Mello, 2004; Fonseca, 2011). As a result, in 2001 the BBF created the National Prize on Social Technology, with the aim of publicizing the then fairly unknown technological solutions for social demands in themes such as water supply and sanitation, food production, energy, education, income generation, health, social housing and environment (de Olivera Pena and Mello, 2004).

Another important actor at the beginning was the Institute of Social Technology (ITS – Instituto de Tecnología Social), created in 2001 and aimed towards linking social needs with the scientific knowledge available in the country. Between 2001 and 2004, the ITS developed a series of workshops and debates on how to build bridges between the third sector and public science, technology and innovations institutions that led to the first discussions of the concept of ST (Instituto de Tecnología Social, 2004).

On a smaller scale, the STN's early setting also involved a small number of academics directly involved with earlier research on appropriate technologies and other complementary themes, such as solidarity economy, agroecology and permaculture and Freire's 'pedagogy of the oppressed'.[1]

From the beginning the STN was also supported by several social movements and NGOs, such as the Semi-Arid Association (Articulação no Semiárido Brasileiro), the Amazonian Working Group (Grupo de Trabalho Amazônico), the Brazilian Association of NGOs, Abong (Associação Brasileira de Organizações Não Governamentais). Therefore, to help the creation of this network along with public institutions was advantageous for the new government, not only because it would aid in the empowerment of its own political base, but also because of its potential creation of challenges for the incumbent monopolies in public policy (Hochstetler, 2004). The alliance between social movements, public and semi-public institutions also proved to be fruitful, helping to install the idea of social technologies at the national level and to promote support for social technologies programmes. The network organization helped to create spaces for the flourishing of ST.

However, as with other initiatives involving civil society organizations in the Lula administration,[2] these heterogeneous institutions were not easy to coordinate. The actors and institutions in Brazil's STN comprised very different knowledge and practices, as well as aims and spaces of intervention that represented an institutional challenge for every participant and ultimately turned into a limitation for some of its members.

Framing for social technologies

At the beginning of the new century, some Brazilian institutions and social movements realized the need not only to challenge market-driven strategies of economic growth but also to search for new approaches to tackling poverty and social inequality.

The work of framing and the vision of the STN resulted from the encounter between these different actors. It was an explicit attempt to bridge the role of the state and its public policies with the mobilization of social movements and NGOs. Acknowledging previous experiences and debates (such as earlier ideas about appropriate technologies and discussions about science, technology and innovations policies for social inclusion), the framing of the STN included concerns and aims from different positions including: (a) the new drive to redirect resources from public and semi-public institutions towards inclusive social development in conjunction with social movements; (b) social movements' and NGOs' previous experience in programmes and approaches in the fight against poverty and exclusion; and (c) the aim to engage with scientific institutions in a different arena, that of social development problems and policies.

Between 2000 and 2004, these actors held a series of debates that would result in a definition of ST: 'Social Technology comprises products, techniques and/or re-applicable methodologies developed in the interaction with the community and that must represent effective solution in terms of social transformation' (RTS, 2014).

'Reapplication' is arguably the main idea present in this concept. It implies that successful experiences and technologies should be multiplied, but in a way that allows them to connect properly to the local contexts in which they would be implemented. Thus, for the STN, scale-building was just as important as respect for the local culture, economy and environment. Therefore, the mandate of the STN was as follows.

The STN has the aim of fostering:
- the adoption of Social Technology as public policies;
- the re-appropriation by the communities' stakeholders of re-applied Social Technologies;
- the development of new Social Technology in those cases where there is not Social Technology for its re-application.

(RTS, 2014)

Although these concerns were complementary, they were not always coherent and tensions between different frames sometimes remained. In this section we explore the framings of social technology, focusing on the following issues: public policies; income generation, empowering and public participation; and the interpellation involved in the creation of a network that ultimately led to a process of identification with ST.

An alternative strategy of development

The framing of ST offered a fresh view into the demanding problems of inequality and poverty. In that sense, the basic framing of ST attempted to bridge some ideas that, although related, were not explicitly connected, such as social inclusion, income generation and sustainability and social empowerment, with long-term goals of structural transformation. Two themes in particular that were supported by actors would become very relevant for ST: solidarity economy and sustainable development.

Advocates of solidarity economy[3] participated from the beginning in the debate about ST. For solidarity economy advocates, ST initiatives were important in order to upgrade and adapt technologies used in cooperatives or occupied factories in areas such as urban disposal recycling, renewable energies, sustainable food production and open software for social inclusion (Alves da Silva and Sardá de Faria, 2010, p. 70).

Similarly, sustainable development was very much present in the imaginary and practices of ST's actors and institutions. Ecological ideas were used to challenge the advance of agribusiness, which involved massive monoculture, with heavy use of agrochemicals, and displaced local farmers. Since the bulk of stakeholders and experiences that were promoted by the STN were mostly rural, it was not surprising that there were clear affinities with sustainable methods of production and development. Moreover, in the long term, the STN's vision was keen to create a whole strategy of development that was 'more sustainable' than available technological systems (RTS, 2005).

Beyond mainstream notions of science and technology (S&T)

In the early 2000s an incipient counter-hegemonic discourse sought to modify the Brazilian S&T orientation from market-driven innovation to the resolution of pressing problems of poverty, hunger and inequalities (Dias, 2011). This diagnostic was based on two main issues. First, ST advocates claimed that S&T in Brazil had achieved a high level of development and expertise that was oriented by the international scientific agenda and thus was unable to attend to local problems (Suarez Maciel and Castilhos Fernandez, 2011). Second, there was an untapped reservoir of technological and knowledge solutions to social problems developed by publicly funded institutions such as Embrapa (the Brazilian Agricultural Research Corporation),[4] or by federal universities, which had generally lain idle on the shelf of these institutions. So, there was a feeling of 'why didn't we think of social technologies before?' (Lassance Jr. and Pedreira, 2004, p. 65). There were two issues that differentiated ST from the frame of mainstream science, technology and innovation: juxtaposing ST with conventional technology, and creating knowledge and technology from the grassroots.

The idea of ST was built upon previous debates about appropriate technology (Dagnino et al., 2004). In particular, ST was opposed to what were regarded as conventional technologies, namely those artefacts and innovations that were designed for maximizing profit, assuring control over production and limiting social participation. It was claimed that conventional technologies not only did not attend to the social needs of the poorest population or environmental problems but also largely increased them (Dagnino, 2004).

At the same time, this critique had further ideological implications, since the rejection of conventional technology implied a critique of the market-driven vision of S&T where public knowledge and technologies were privatized through commercial innovation. Challenging conventional innovation implied changing focus, away from firms as exclusive innovators (and profiteers) and towards the grassroots via a more open participatory model.

Thus, instead of talking about innovation, ST members stressed the idea of technological development, public access to knowledge and technology and the possibility of reapplication of technology by the communities without the constraints of commercial patents. Avoiding paying fees or licences helped, in turn, to lower the cost of devising and implementing public policies on a large scale.

A second, interrelated element was the idea that local knowledge was key to the development of suitable social technologies:

> The principal aspect is that this change [i.e. sustainable development] is produced by a solution generated from the alliance between local knowledge and scientific knowledge; that is why it is acknowledged and appropriated by the communities. Therefore, this is an endogenous solution, one of the key elements of any process of local development.
>
> *(RTS, 2011, p. 6; our translation)*

By highlighting the local dimension of knowledge creation, the STN not only challenged conventional ideas about innovation but also made an explicit call to democratize access to technology design, technological evaluation and policy-making of S&T.

Empowerment and participation

From the beginning, the definition of ST was based on the recognition of the new role that third sector organizations could play in the development of technological solutions for their own problems (Baumgarten, 2006).[5] Giving voice to third sector organizations also implied the recognition of other forms of knowledge, such as popular knowledge, indigenous knowledge and visions of technological development alternative to those most predominant in the mainstream science, technology and innovation system (Instituto de Tecnología Social, 2004).

The goal of ST was to empower people and seed wider social transformation through the capabilities acquired during a particular project, and then drive initiative in subsequent projects in the locality. Therefore, the STN advocated a complex vision of participation that rejected an a priori division between technology developers and users. Stakeholders such as local communities, NGOs, cooperatives and social movements had a central role in the process of replication of technology. It was assumed that they should intervene in the design and implementation, but they should also have a voice in the process of policymaking. In practice, the partnerships that were formed were about making sure that immediate solutions were locally fitting, but also about empowerment in the process of the development of technology. However, aspirations for grassroots influence over broader technology policy agendas proved elusive.

A second aspect to participation in the technological process was that of appropriation of technologies in a double sense. On one side, it implied the ability of local communities to control their technological solutions as a key element of autonomy and self-management. On the other side, the same process of participation and autonomous technological development was assumed to guarantee the adaptation of technologies to local context, allowing redevelopments to include local and traditional knowledge in a sensible way. In contrast to market-based understanding of the term, appropriation for ST did not mean exclusive ownership but, rather, the ability to build capabilities and learn from others (technicians, scientists, neighbours and politicians) in a process of cooperative development.

Finally, social technology was also intended to improve the ability of the community to organize and solve further problems, develop and exploit economic opportunities and create the capacity to mobilize resources from others. Grassroots innovation capabilities were seen as requiring political and economic capabilities whose capacity increases through successions and networks of projects. Therefore, each project needs innovations to adapt to local contexts and hence build innovative capabilities that help to create a voice for these communities in larger debates on S&T agendas and economic development (Instituto de Tecnología Social, 2007).

Social technologies as public policy

The STN frame on public policy was based on lessons about the problems that appropriate technologies faced in Brazil. The 'isolated' character of appropriate technology solutions was particularly highlighted. To avoid this, the STN aimed to connect particular social technologies with public funding in order to gain national-scale reapplication (RTS, 2010).

The strategy to transform ST into public policies involved the mobilization of important state resources (from knowledge to funding and public procurement) but also required some degree of institutionalization in order to achieve stability or even irreversibility for long-term policies. So it was important to identify and connect the diversity of ST initiatives around Brazil and to select certain experiences that could be scaled up (Instituto de Tecnología Social, 2004). Central to this vision was the concept of reapplication that was aimed to promote certain technologies and artefacts at a large scale. According to Fonseca (2011), the reapplication of technologies implies: (a) reproduction adequate for the local space, (b) appropriation by the local population and (c) assessment of results for new reapplications.

Driving S&T capabilities towards the solution of social and environmental problems was one of the ideas for public policy, but it was not the only one. Grassroots innovations were considered as a creative force based on local solutions, sometimes retrieving knowledge in ways that contrasted with expectations arising from linear conceptions of R&D. Thus, the STN aimed to provide recognition, support and technical validation to grassroots initiatives, and to translate those initiatives into systematic schemes or models that could be reapplied later elsewhere.

The complex challenge of how to translate known ST into public policies and how to develop new solutions required a strong effort of coordination and advocacy. It also required network members and activists to challenge incumbent policies and practices in S&T institutions and state bureaucracies that were not used to negotiating knowledge with local actors or were reluctant to assume the risks of unproved technologies (Lassance Jr and Pedreira, 2004). In order to achieve that, the strategy of the STN was to create a powerful and hybrid network between semi-public companies, public institutions, universities, social movement and NGOs.

Spaces for social technologies

From the beginning, the STN involved a heterogeneous mixture of civil society organizations and public and semi-public institutions. The spaces of ST constituted an effort to mobilize social actors and communities, fostering participation in grassroots innovation while at the same time requiring the protection of the public policy umbrella. In this section we describe how the construction of these spaces helped to expand the STN, and how this expansion also took the STN to its institutional limits.

Building the STN

Following a call from Luiz Gushiken, the then head of the Social Communication Office of the Lula administration, a group of public and semi-public institutions (including the Bank of Brazil Foundation; the State Oil company Petrobras; the Financing Agency for Studies and Projects (FINEP), a state S&T funding agency; the Ministry of Science and Technology; the Brazilian Service of Assistance to Micro and Small Enterprises (SEBRAE); and the Secretary of Communication and Strategic Management of the Presidency of the Republic) started to organize a series of meetings that would eventually lead to the creation of the STN.

The first of these meetings was held in July 2004 in Brasilia and was attended by thirty participants. These included NGOs from the Northeast region of Brazil (RTS, 2005). This meeting revisited the discussion on the concept of social technology and began a debate about the possibility of devising alternative strategies of development. At the same time it was argued that the network would not get legal status as an institution (this was a decision that would have further consequences for the management of the STN). Thus the network was proposed as open, democratic, dialogic and inclusive in order to encourage the participation and collaboration of heterogeneous actors (RTS, 2011). After a series of further meetings (including the First International Conference of Social Technologies) the STN was created in January 2005 with 100 participants (RTS, 2005).

The structure of the STN consisted of an Executive Secretary with a staff of five and a Coordinating Committee, which included representatives from the STN's funders, up to four network enablers from NGOs and social movements and a representative from academia.[6] The Committee's main tasks were to select and coordinate the reapplication of technologies, assess its implementation and set goals for the communication and dissemination of the STN. A further layer of decision making was the forum of the STN, which involved all the other members and participants and had a consultative role.

From the beginning it was established that the STN would not limit its task only to the communication and dissemination of ideas but would also implement actions and develop social technology programmes. Its aim was also to coordinate the capacities of state institutions (i.e. large-scale projects and funding) and NGOs and social movements (i.e. creativity, plurality, local knowledge and implementing capacity) (RTS, 2005). These requirements called for a very delicate balance and coordination between 'social diversity' of grassroots and the 'need for scale', as well as between funders, network coordinators and stakeholders (all of which have, in fact, very different backgrounds).

From 2005 until 2012 the network reached out to other actors and really spread the idea of social technology, thus extending the original frame of knowledge and allowing new ideas and problems to be included. Over its seven-year trajectory, the STN incorporated a total of 928 institutional affiliations, of which a large majority were NGOs and social organizations (546), followed by private foundations (110), while there were only sixty-three public research institutions and universities. By 2012 the STN had reached institutions from Peru, Colombia and Venezuela and its ideas had triggered discussions in Argentina and Uruguay. Activities of the STN included the promotion of major events, such as international conferences on ST and two national forums (2006 and 2009) in which issues were discussed such as agroecology and food security and sustainable development (RTS, 2011). At the time, the STN had constant participation in other forums and activities including S&T meetings, university extension and outreach, solidarity economy meetings and a presentation at the World Social Forum in 2010.

As a result, civil society organizations and public institutions in Brazil started to reflect upon and to experiment with ST's ideas and frames. These 'network effects' seemed to indicate that the STN managed to spread beyond its original institutional arrangement. As Larissa Barros, the former Chair of the STN, argued, the STN had succeeded in creating a debate around S&T and social development that included actors traditionally regarded as outsiders; for example, NGOs and social movements such as agroecology and solidarity economy.

On the other hand, the relationship with mainstream S&T institutions remained ambivalent. While ST was enthusiastically adopted by knowledge extension units at federal universities, attempts to introduce the debate into S&T forums such as the National Week on Science and Technology received lukewarm responses. And despite the fact that the term 'social technology' has appeared in a few documents released by state organizations such as the National Secretary of Science and

Technology for Social Inclusion, there was never a clear federal policy for promoting ST in Brazil.

Social technology and public policies

From the beginning, both public institutions and social actors were keen to promote new public policies on ST. The construction of ST as public policy was assumed to guarantee continuity of efforts and to avoid isolated initiatives, and it was aligned with the aim of promoting alternative forms of sustainable development. There was, therefore, a conscious effort first to identify experiences and problems and then to translate grassroots initiatives into reapplying technologies that were able to gain scale.

At the same time, through debates at the STN, it was decided to prioritize ST projects that favoured income generation among beneficiaries, an issue that coincided with the overall aim of social policies in Brazil. The STN also selected as priorities the semi-arid and Amazônia Legal regions and urban peripheries. At the same time, the STN selected a wide range of technologies for its reapplication. These included water collection, solid recycling, small agroecological farm methods, forestry techniques, fish farming, cashew nut-processing plants, small oil-processing plants, social housing techniques, platforms for cooperative incubation and pedagogical techniques. Some of these projects, such as the water-collection systems that came to be a core aspect of the One Million Cisterns Programme (P1MC), grew to quite a large scale and became a national endeavour for social development state agencies. During its existence the STN helped to manage funds for developing social technology experiences amounting to more than R$440 million (approximately US$200 million) (RTS, 2011, p. 3).

One of the particularities of the hybrid institutional arrangement of the STN was that, since it did not have legal status, it did not fund any projects (or events) directly. There was no central management and instead it was the responsibility of funding institutions to implement the projects in collaboration with the social organizations and NGOs. Thus, for example, some smaller programmes such as Basic Sanitation Technology for Rural Areas were funded by only one institution, the BBF. However, more complex and larger programmes were generally funded complementarily by several different institutions. For instance, the total investment in the Sustainable and Integrated Agro-Ecological Production (PAIS) Programme for agroecological small farms, of approximately R$113 million (approximately US$50 million), was jointly funded by the BBF, SEBRAE, Petrobras, the Ministry of National Integration, the Ministry of Social Development and the Ministry of Science and Technology (RTS, 2011, p. 16). Coordination between different funders was not easy to achieve and there were questions of which institutions enjoyed most the symbolic benefits of their association with each project. Other difficulties of coordination involved different expectations around results and what the pace of the implementation of technologies should be. In a general sense this was a product of the clash of different rationales and organizational cultures, mainly between the more rigid public structures (i.e. the national ministries) and the more fluid patterns of the emerging social organizations.

At face value, during its existence, the STN had a huge success in mobilizing public funds for technology and social development. Nevertheless, to what extent the goal of building long-term public policies was achieved remains a matter of debate. Since the funding was obtained on a project basis, ultimately the STN was caught, as were other grassroots innovation movements, in the dilemma of working on project-based solutions to situations that ultimately required more structural answers, that is, public policies (Costa and Dias, 2013).

As will be shown in the next section, attempts to overcome these issues through the construction of long-term public policies within the national government were caught between the limitations of the institutional structure of the STN and the inertia of incumbent elites in the state.

Illustrative examples

In a similar way to other examples of grassroots innovation networks and movements, STN started by surveying and acknowledging a wide reservoir of local ingenuity. Grassroots technologies were mainly mapped by the BBF and documented at the Bank of Social Technologies. In 2013 the Bank of Social Technologies recorded 696 examples (Interview with Jefferson D'Avila de Oliveira, Brasilia, 13 November 2013). However, only a handful of these technologies were selected for reapplication and funding by the STN. From those cases we analyse two of the most representative cases: the agroecological production method known as the PAIS Programme and the P1MC. These cases are relevant not only due to their scale of implementation but also because they show alternative forms of linking grassroots participation, poverty reduction and technology to mainstream science, technology and innovation institutions.

The PAIS Programme

The STN has supported a wide variety of agroecological farming and food production methods (Faria et al., 2011). However, one of the best-known and most widespread examples of ST has been the PAIS Programme. The PAIS Programme is a low-cost technology designed to be implemented on small farms (up to 2ha) and favours the use of local materials and knowledge, while avoiding the use of pesticides and external inputs. As the programme's description highlights, PAIS

> Is a solution for the production of healthy food that seeks the achievement of food security and the generation of a marketable surplus capable of ensuring a supplementary income. This is a sustainable model of production that combines the creation of small animal farms, cultivation of short-cycle

vegetable species and cultivation of agroecological gardens with long-cycle or permanent vegetable species. The model also seeks the production and use of local materials and recycling of available biomass.

(RTS, 2009a, p. 9)

The design of PAIS was based on a previous project, named Mandalla due to its shape of concentric rings. Based on that design, the technology was then upgraded through the use of localized drip-irrigation and the incorporation of a central henhouse. Farmers who use the technology receive a kit for reapplication that includes components of a water irrigation system, wire fences, seed, small plants and even hens, along with a user's manual and a training course. The idea is that the design of the garden allowed farmers a simple routine of circulation from the henhouse through the rest of the crops, while also promoting a rational use of land, water and organic fertilizers. The design also sought to promote diversity of crops, including the possibility of selecting those vegetables that were best adapted to the soil or had better prospects for commercialization. In 2004, PAIS was selected by BBF, SEBRAE and the Ministry of Integration for reapplication in twelve states. While BBF funded the reapplication kits, SEBRAE and the Ministry of Integration, along with municipalities, funded the training and the creation of networks of technical assistance (Faria et al., 2011). Later, other funders such as Petrobras, Banco Nacional do Desenvolvimento and the Ministry of Science and Technology were also included. In 2011 the STN affirmed that the general investment in PAIS was over R$113 million, with an approximate unit cost of R$10,000 (RTS, 2011).[7]

PAIS was praised as a 'silent revolution' in sustainable farming on the cover of the magazine *SEBRAE Agronegocios* and regarded as a tool that combined simple technology with direct results and had the potential to be included in the rising market of organic products in Brazil (*SEBRAE Agronegocios*, 2007). Today PAIS units are often found on small rural properties in several regions of Brazil. The strong point of the technology lies in its capacity to promote income generation and foster association between farmers. As some authors have described (de Olivera Pena, 2009; Souza Costa et al., 2013), a family could make a surplus of between US$200 and US$400 by selling at local fairs or through public procurement schemes, such as the National Fund for Education Development within the National Programme of Food for Education (Fundação Banco do Brasil, 2013). This represents a significant increase in family income. However, at the same time, PAIS was regarded as a 'static' technology, with enough flexibility to allow a choice of crops, but not too much, in the different components of the kit (Faria et al., 2011). In this sense, PAIS was very different from other, much more dynamic technologies that were focused on empowerment, such as P1MC.

The One Million Cisterns Programme

A second illustrative technology supported by the STN is the P1MC. P1MC aimed to build a massive number of water cisterns in a large, semi-arid region in Northeast

Brazil with a population of around 25 million. This region is characterized by low rainfall and scarce groundwater sources. Water scarcity and poverty were usually attended by an instrumental state approach that favoured huge infrastructure projects for massive agriculture schemes combined with aid solutions, such as water-tank trucks (*caminhões-pipa*), for the poor. These aid schemes ultimately reinforced local patronage and increased inequalities (Alves da Silva, 2003), since water, food and money have traditionally been used to buy votes for politicians.

The programme was originally devised by the Semi-Arid Association as an answer to these practices, known as the 'industry of drought' (*indústria da seca*). The Semi-Arid Association, a network of more than 700 institutions, social movements, NGOs and farmers' groups, has its origins in popular mobilization against the 'industry of drought' and later become an important actor of the STN. Instead of relying on water supplied by water tanks, the Semi-Arid Association proposed to build simple, cement-layered containers that collected rainwater from the roof, with a capacity of around 16,000 litres, enough to sustain a family's needs through the region's drought season. This proposal was part of a significant change in how these organizations approached one of the region's core problems: instead of seeking ways to 'fight' or even 'eliminate' the drought, they began designing strategies for living with the drought. This shift in the rationale created a whole new tranche of possible actions that could be implemented.

With the start of the Lula administration in 2003, the Semi-Arid Association found an opportunity to insert this programme into national development policies, to be funded by the Ministry of Social Development. Later, in 2005, the programme also became part of the reapplied technologies of the STN.

From its start in 2003 to 2015 almost 590,000 water cisterns were built and put in place by local inhabitants with the support of the STN and the Ministry of Social Development (Ministério do Desenvolvimento Social e Combate à Fome, 2015). The main feature of the technology is that it is built by its 'users'. The self-building aspect of the cisterns is intended to foster relationship building in the community through the process of learning to build, use and modify the technology, indicating a strong link with the empowering and participatory framing. The water system empowers local people in the building process, while also providing autonomy from local governments and water suppliers.

P1MC was one of the most successful experiences with which the STN was involved, particularly in terms of scale. It was paradigmatic in the way that most of the ST framing in terms of participation and negotiations of knowledge between local people and technicians was embodied in it. The model of horizontal participation in the construction of the cistern was explicitly positioned as an alternative to aid schemes and big infrastructure programmes, both of which excluded poor farmers from the decision-making process. Participation empowered the people and strengthened the link with the mobilization of the Semi-Arid Association in the search for alternative forms of development. Furthermore, this participation shaped a learning process that led to the creation of technological variants such as the Uma Terra e Duas Águas (one land and two waters) project, a scaling up of the cistern that seeks to collect water for farming production and combines with other technologies such as PAIS (Barbosa, 2010).

However, the insertion of this model into a government programme became problematic in early 2012, when the Brazilian government announced a plan to speed up the implementation of the programme through the purchase of 300,000 plastic water cisterns at almost twice the price of the original cement scheme. Focused on outcomes, this policy change disregarded the process of participation and empowerment that was central to the design of the programme. Private, profit-oriented firms displaced social movements and NGOs as the main partner of the Brazilian federal government in this programme (Dias, 2012).

The narrowing of the model's scope by the Brazilian government led, on 20 December 2011, to a public rally of about 15,000 farmers in the city of Petrolina in Pernambuco, marching against the plastic cistern initiative (Passos, 2011). Protestors claimed that changes in management disempowered people from participation in the construction. Another element of the controversy included concern that introduction of the plastic cisterns would enable the local political elites to regain power over the control of water, by controlling the market in water cisterns. By the time this occurred, however, the seed of empowerment had already been planted. Banners waved at the rally contained phrases such as 'We do not want water at any price. We want to participate.' While the government's approach was built around the artefact and the accomplishment of policy goals, the users' approach was mostly concerned with the process and the inclusive dynamics it generated. In the end, access to clean water seemed to be tightly interwoven with empowerment and the strengthening of community bonds.

The cistern example shows how the Semi-Arid Association and the STN managed to draw power from mobilization in order to renegotiate a model of innovation and social inclusion. For almost a decade this model was very successful in building several hundreds of thousands of cisterns and empowering the population of the semi-arid region. However, as the government attempted to strip the programme of its empowerment element and focus instead on inclusion as the outcome, the mobilizations by the movement pushed the government to reinstate the self-build cistern programme. Though they continued to install some plastic cisterns for some time, in the end the P1MC was transformed into a national public policy through the programme Water for Everyone of the Ministry for Social Development (Costa and Dias, 2013).

Path construction and the Social Technology Network

In less than a decade the STN was able to put the idea of social technologies onto the public agenda in Brazil. Social movements and NGOs around the country appropriated the ideas and values of the STN and started to discuss social technologies. The STN was able to recognize hundreds of STs and to support experimentation in the reapplication of a few of them at a massive scale, covering the huge territory of Brazil. In the universities, 250 research groups have stated that they work with ST and related themes.[8]

More importantly, the debate around ST went well beyond the original extension of the STN and is still strong in 2014, reaching other networks and movements such as the Agroecology Movement and the Network of Extension Units in federal universities in Brazil. In that sense, the STN was able to create a specific framework of knowledge around ST, a sense of identity and a long-lasting debate that goes beyond the network itself. But what does the demise of the STN mean in terms of strategies for grassroots innovation movements and alternative pathways of development? In this section we explore this question, focusing on the issue of public policies, the politics of knowledge and forms of social inclusion.

The limits of the network strategy

In 2009, about five years after its creation, the STN held its Second National Forum of Social Technology and the Second International Conference on Social Technology in Brasilia. This was an opportunity to discuss the achievements of the STN so far and to look at the challenges it now faced (Barros, 2009). For example De Paulo (2009) stated that the STN had already developed an identity, received significant support from funders and was able to introduce ST into the public agenda. According to de Paulo, it was now time to forge new alliances with local development and sustainable movements and to focus on the construction of a new agenda of development. This was a question of how to gain momentum and strengthen the influence of the STN by extending the scale of experimentation and transforming its projects into long-term public policies. However, this was not an easy task, since, as the STN grew, the complexity of the network also increased, leading to further requirements in terms of communication, participation and funding (RTS, 2009b).

As a result of these debates, at least three courses of action were outlined. First, the network widened its focus from income generation to a set of goals around sustainability, including: sustainable food production; sustainable water and forestry management; clean energy production; sustainable social housing; income generation through sustainable business schemes; and learning and education (RTS 2011, p. 10). Second, there was a clear aim to create a regional space for STN, especially with regard to the Mercosur.[9] By 2009 the STN had already gained members from other South American countries such as Colombia and Venezuela. Attempts to include the STN debate into the regional agendas of South American blocks included a discussion about STN at the Social Mercosur meeting in 2010 and a series of meetings held along with academic supporters in Argentina and Uruguay.

A third strategy was aimed at the institutionalization of ST in order to consolidate its experience into public policies. One such initiative was the proposal of a National Law for Social Technologies in 2008. The proposed law aimed at the creation of a national policy of social technologies and the creation of a national institute of social technology.[10] In 2011, some of the funders within the Coordinating Committee aimed at the creation of a national inter-ministry panel of public policies on ST which would include open public participation.

Plans for the expansion of the STN showed that the maturity and strength of the idea and vision of the ST was not matched by the formal structure of the network and its level of insertion into the state. Some actors in the STN became aware that the expansion of the network and the creation of new spaces for ST depended on the integration of projects and the creation of national public policies (*SEBRAE Agronegocios*, 2007; Suarez Maciel and Castilhos Fernandez, 2011). Meanwhile, the policy of increasing the scale of experiences required further funds, and also more coordination, technical support and so on. All of this has put some extra pressure on funders and implementing institutions in terms of assessment and has raised the issue of who got the symbolic rewards.

As the STN grew in partners and experiences it was increasingly clear that the original informal arrangement between NGOs, social movements and funders was becoming inadequate. There was tension between the need for insertion into the public agenda and the will to maintain mobilization capabilities. However, it was not clear how to solve the institutional challenge. Ultimately, differences about how to formalize the hybrid structure of the STN and how to give the network a more stable form of governance were impossible to overcome, and in 2012 the STN was suspended by its Coordinating Committee.

From network to public policies

The question of how to build public polices for STs was an early goal of the STN and remains an issue of discussion to this day. In a broader context, this was a question of how to challenge monopolies of public policy that were colonized by a market-driven agenda during the 1990s in Latin America. To challenge incumbent bureaucracies was regarded as instrumental in order to create an incipient alternative frame of development. This idea was present in the Workers Party's vision for 2003 (Samuels, 2004), and also in social movements such as the Landless Workers Movement and the Social World Forum.

The alliance between social movements, NGOs and state agencies was a hybrid institutional experiment that sought to create new public polices of social development and new forms of knowledge democratization. In that sense, the success of the STN depended on two linked goals: the aim to mobilize and empower social organization to participate in social technology and the subsequent drive to create long-term public policies. For a while, this alliance had great success in the diffusion of the frame of ST to almost a thousand organizations and the mobilization of more than R$440 million in resources for the reapplication of technologies. But, as the STN started to grow it also faced the limits of its own institutional arrangement and increasing resistance to its policy demands and other activities by incumbent actors.

The loose, informal structure of the STN started to crumble under crossed pressures, different expectations and different forms of assessment. Since the STN lacked any formal capacity to manage projects, this tension grew with the increment in scale of the projects it proposed. Furthermore, as the P1MC example showed, this tension quickly became a clash between claims of participation and network creation and claims of accountability and efficient ways of delivering technological solutions. The broad framework and ideas and wide array of institutions that had once allowed the STN to grow rapidly shaped the network in an arena where different interests, rationales and political projects frequently clashed.

At the same time, the dispersal of funding from donors and the fact that these funds were provided on a programme-by-programme basis conspired against the early goal of avoiding partial solutions and seeking long-term public policies. Overall, the suspension of the STN by the Coordinating Committee came at the moment when the debate around ST was growing and including more and more organizations and the idea of ST was becoming widespread among social movements. However, just when the debate started to heat up, funders and civil society representatives were unable to get a suitable institutional arrangement and, as a result, the STN was suspended in 2012. As Larissa Barros put it, 'it failed because it got it right' (Personal interview with L. Barros, November 2013). Meanwhile, the strategy of institutionalization and creation of long-term public policies of ST has also not been successful.

It is interesting to note that, despite the suspension of the STN, many of the projects, including the P1MC and PAIS Programme, continued to receive funding through the different supporting institutions. Furthermore, Banco do Brazil continues to support the Social Technology Prize and the database of ST and has started to build centres of demonstration for ST, partnering with a few universities and municipalities.

As the momentum of the STN seems to be lost, there remains the question of whether the STN has been able to overcome the tension between insertion and mobilization, while at the same time promoting long-term public policies.

Questioning S&T and creating a new politics of knowledge

A second space where the STN achieved mixed results was around the issue of democratization of knowledge. From the beginning, the debate about ST focused on the need to reorient domestic S&T capabilities and put them to better use for the resolution of local social needs. At the same time, the STN seeks the empowerment of social movements as active agents in the development of technologies and S&T policies. Both actions combined represented a powerful critique of the political economy of S&T. However, this process of questioning incumbent elites also presented the dilemma of how to engage with the institutions and actors of mainstream S&T while criticizing its goals, practices and values.

The STN was able to enrol the network of federal universities with extension activities and received significant support from the Ministry of Science and Technology and the entrepreneur funding agency FINEP. These institutions carved out a small niche for ST that nevertheless represented an intense experiment in grassroots participation and technological creativity that led to the implementation of huge social programmes.

However, the amount of funding was very small when compared with funding for mainstream S&T.[11] It was mostly used for low-tech initiatives and did not require important R&D capabilities. Neither did it interest mainstream scientific groups. Thus the amount of support from universities and R&D groups was small, leading to the disconnection of ST from mainstream S&T agenda and capabilities. Ultimately, ST as a policy was insulated from mainstream S&T, thus reaching a position very similar to the place that previous appropriate technologies had occupied in Brazil (Brandão, 2001). For STN advocates, 'future expansion of ST is, in part, related with the chance of altering the incumbent policies of S&T in the country and turning [ST] into public policies' (Castilhos Fernandez and Suarez Maciel, 2011, p. 40; our translation).

Indeed, the challenge to enrol S&T actors raised further questions about institutional change, such as how to create an endogenous agenda of S&T for social inclusion, how to balance the requirements of scientific relevance with those of local social needs and how to enable social organizations to engage with the restricted areas of expertise of S&T. Some of these issues were already present in the debate of the STN, but during its short life the practicalities of this sea change had not even begun to be considered.

What kind of social inclusion?

From the beginning, the goal of the STN was to combine concrete technological solutions to tackle issues of poverty with democratic participation and autonomous management of the initiatives. In this context, the question of social inclusion was deeply embedded in the constitution and framing of the STN. But what kind of inclusion was promoted by the STN? In order to tackle this issue, the STN experimented with at least three framings of inclusion (Smith et al., 2014): (a) inclusion as ingenuity through the acknowledgement and assessment of grassroots technological solutions; (b) inclusion as empowerment by encouraging participation and appropriation of technologies in the field; and (c) inclusion as structural transformation by fostering the debate on alternative forms of development. At the same time, these framings had been built as part of a hybrid alliance whose actors attributed different meanings to inclusion over time. During the first years there was a general consensus that inclusion needed to be framed as outcome, for instance in the form of income generation, and also as a process in terms of empowerment, capacity building and strengthening communication and learning through the network. However, as the network grew and new challenges of insertion into public policies were presented, this accord shifted over time.

As we have seen in the case of P1MC, when public institutions pushed for an increment of scale in the reapplication of technologies they faced tensions with civil society organizations and stakeholders in the field that resisted this reduced form of implementation. As Costa and Dias (2013, p. 237) pointed out, to scale up initiatives in a very short time risked harming the process of mobilization and disrupting the characteristics of social technology, transforming the original vision into a much simpler scheme of 'simple implementation' of technologies. The issue of scaling up not only divided different interests and goals within the STN, but was also symptomatic of the difficulties in transforming incumbent elites within the state. This was a problem that ST advocates had envisioned from the beginning, and yet they struggled to find alternatives. Thus, like the larger tensions between commitments towards democratization and economic redistribution within the PT government, and public institutions, in the case of the STN, advocates were tempted to favour inclusion as an outcome over empowerment and participation through process. It was only when social movements and NGOs committed to the aim of inclusion as empowerment that they could resist the tendency to simplify the idea of inclusion.

Conclusions

Born at the beginning of the Lula administration, the STN carried many of the expectations and challenges of the new government about social inclusion and participation that were mixed with a long-standing practice of mobilization and a will to experiment with alternative models of development. The STN was in that sense an interesting example of hybrid networks that combined a new direction in public and semi-public institutions with the capacity of NGOs and social movements to translate new ideas and vision about technology and social development (Ely et al., 2013).

For a while, the STN was very successful in creating a large network of support and reapplication of technologies that tapped into new public resources. It also helped to create an alternative framing of sustainable development and social inclusion that highlighted the role of technology. As a result, social movements, NGOs and practitioners realized that they could also be part of the discussions about pathways of development, while at the same time experimenting with their own solutions. However, at the same time STN faced at least two challenges that have resulted from its very achievements.

The first challenge was related to the difficulties in widening the space for engagement with S&T mainstream institutions. After a decade of S&T and market-driven innovation, the STN again managed to place technology and participation on the agenda of development. This action helped to open up a new debate on the directions of S&T research and innovation. However, this movement was not enough to mobilize further support from public laboratories and universities beyond extension activities. Thus, the process of learning and tinkering with scientific knowledge was limited and remained marginal in relation to mainstream activities of S&T.

The second challenge points to internal tensions in the network and beyond in terms of mobilization and inclusion in public policies. As the STN grew and some of its projects gained visibility, differences between scaling up and empowerment also increased. Some projects, such as P1MC, resisted a reduced inclusion into public policies and gained more space as a result of mobilization. However, this was not the case for the rest of the STN, where tensions between the plurality of civil society actors and the constraints of public policy eroded the structure of the network.

The suspension of the STN showed the difficulties and the limits of this kind of strategy and the problems that alternative grassroots innovation faces when dealing with mainstream institutions. Even with the support of powerful institutions within the government and a wide array of NGOs and social movements, the STN struggled to overcome these challenges. This difficulty highlights that the underlying differential of power between grassroots movements and incumbent elites in Brazil (and South America in general) is still huge.

And yet, despite these shortcomings, what the STN achieved is huge, not only in terms of reapplication of technologies but fundamentally by opening the space for a new debate on the democratization of technological development in at least two ways. First, by expanding the limits of social development to include the technological dimension, and second, by questioning pristine notions of conventional technological change and innovation and proposing social technology as a new agenda for science, technology and development. Overall, these ideas contributed to redrawing the debate about science, technology, democracy and development. Whether new social movements pick up the baton and develop these ideas further, only time will tell.

Notes

1 Some researchers involved with these early efforts were professors Renato Dagnino (UNICAMP), Paul Singer (University of São Paulo and then National Secretary for Solidarity Economy), Ladislau Dowbor (Catholic University of São Paulo), Jacqueline Rutkowski (Federal University of Ouro Preto) and Sidney Lianza (Federal University of Rio de Janeiro).
2 PT's strategy of including civil society organizations did not always work so well. Some initiatives sponsored by the government, such as the Economic and Social Development Council, were embraced eagerly at the beginning by civil society organizations, only for them to wonder later if this kind of space was suitable for their demands (Hochstetler, 2004).
3 The concept of solidarity economy includes issues in areas such as economic and solidarity relations, work economy and alternative economic arrangements in civil society. There is some consensus among groups and movements that a solidarity economy entails the search for economic alternatives to a full-fledged capitalist market economy.
4 Embrapa is linked to the Ministry of Agriculture and probably one of the bigger research institutions in Brazil.
5 As Baumgarten (2006) describes, the reconsideration of the role of the third sector, in particular NGOs, was already debated during the 1990s in Brazil and was included in White Paper on Science, Technology and Innovation (Ministério da Ciência e Tecnologia, 2002).
6 In its last annual report (RTS, 2011) funders included Caixa Económica, BBF, Petrobras, FINEP, SEBRAE and four national ministries: Science and Technology, Social Development and Fight Against Hunger, National Integration, and Employment. The social organizations were the Semi-Arid Association, Abong, the Amazonia Task Group and Cerrado Network. Finally, the academy was represented by the Forum of Deans of Extension Activities at Public Universities in Brazil and communication was under the charge of the Secretary of Social Communication of the Republic.

7 It is estimated that there may be as many as 10,000 PAIS units in eighteen states in Brazil (CIAAT, 2015).
8 See http://dgp.cnpq.br.
9 Mercosur refers to the community of nations of South America including Argentina, Brazil, Uruguay and Paraguay.
10 The law was proposed by Rodrigo Rollemberg of the Brazilian Socialist Party in 2008 in the Chamber of Representatives but was never approved. A second presentation was made, now in the Senate House, in 2011 but its approval was still pending at the time of writing.
11 For instance, the funding allocated to social inclusion in the Ministry of Science and Technology (where ST was included along with other programmes) was only 2 per cent of its budget (Brito Cruz and Chaimovich, 2010).

8
THE HONEY BEE NETWORK

Scholarly attention to the contribution of the Honey Bee Network (HBN) has evolved fairly rapidly both in India and abroad in response to growing interest in how to promote the diffusion of inclusive and environmentally friendly innovations in developing and emerging economies (Abrar and Nair, 2011; Bhaduri and Kumar, 2011; de Beer et al., 2013; De Keersmaecker et al., 2011; Pansera and Owen, 2014; Shivarajan and Srinivasan, 2013). A leading scholar of innovation studies has even suggested that the notion of grassroots innovation developed by Anil Gupta should be considered as the endogenous, intrinsic version of Prahalad's external, top-down version of bottom-of-the-pyramid (BoP) innovation (Soete, 2013).[1] Some already see this also as a pathway through which the incentive of intellectual property rights (IPRs) protection has been productively used to enhance the diffusion of alternative technology in respect of emerging economies and the developing world (Greenhalgh, 2014).

In the field of grassroots innovation the place of the HBN is seemingly distinct, since it focuses on the contributions of non-formal, uneducated innovators. For the HBN, grassroots innovation is the innovation of uneducated people (without a professional degree) who are self-employed outside the formal sector and develop their innovation without any outside help from formal institutions and organizations. The HBN considers the exclusion of these innovators from the formal sector to be the main characteristic of grassroots innovation.

The HBN displays a number of unique features in comparison to other grassroots innovation movements. In contrast with the People's Science Movements (see Chapter 5), a distinctive aspect of the HBN is its advocacy of the use of IPRs protection to promote grassroots innovation efforts. The HBN uses this protection strategy to recognize, respect, protect and financially reward non-formal grassroots innovators, and as an instrument to facilitate fair collaboration among non-formal innovators, formal sector science and technology (S&T) institutions and large private sector enterprises.

Focusing on this and other aspects of the case study, this chapter investigates the HBN from a historical and comparative perspective. We first outline the context and background of the network going back over thirty years to the mid-1980s. We then investigate the framings of grassroots innovation adopted by the network (as articulated by its key protagonists), the spaces and strategies adopted and occupied in order to further its goals and the ways in which the network's promotion of grassroots innovation has enabled the construction of pathways to sustainability and social justice. In order to do so, we draw on secondary documentation, textual and interview data and the personal experience of the primary author (Dinesh Abrol).

Context: origins and background of the HBN

The HBN was established in India by Professor Anil Kumar Gupta of the Indian Institute of Management Ahmedabad (IIM-A)[2] in 1988–89. At that time his key aim was to ensure the implementation of the idea that the documentation of any knowledge must refer to and acknowledge the knowledge holder. Anil Gupta was concerned that academics and consultants were becoming rich by writing about people's knowledge and that they were not sharing their wealth with the holders of traditional knowledge. In the words of Anil Gupta, the philosophy of the HBN has rested on four basic principles:

> Cross pollination of ideas in local languages, acknowledgement of individual and common creativity without making them anonymous, protecting their knowledge rights, and sharing the benefits in a fair and just manner accrued from value addition in the innovations or traditional knowledge.
>
> *(Gupta, 2014a)*

The social diffusion of grassroots innovation, encouraging grassroots innovators to practise knowledge sharing with people locally and globally through interaction with the scientific community, and the voluntary mobilization of people to use these innovations for community building were also the important aims of the HBN (Interview with Professor Kuldeep Mathur, Formerly Member of the Board of the National Innovation Foundation India, 11 February 2015).

In the case of the HBN the first formal step was taken when Anil Gupta started a newsletter at the IIM-A in 1990. To begin with he published it only in English and shared it with scientists, policymakers, conservationists and others. The newsletter set out the basic framework for a voluntary network where students, rural people, like-minded non-governmental organizations (NGOs) and others joined in to identify innovations and document them for publication. To date, the newsletter *Honey Bee* (in its English-language version) continues to be an important instrument for the volunteers of the HBN to publicize the innovative practices of rural people. In the first year, 1,613 innovations and traditional practices were identified and documented. Students and volunteers were initially asked to fan out individually in rural Gujarat, but from 1993 these individual efforts have been supplemented by collective journeys, known as Shodh Yatras, taken on foot through villages in different states.

The efforts of the HBN gained momentum with the establishment of the Society for Research and Initiatives for Sustainable Technologies and Institutions (SRISTI) in 1993. Innovations that were scouted required validation and verification. Initially SRISTI used only IIM-A facilities to set up a laboratory to perform the primary microbiological, entomological and chemical analysis of materials and products scouted by the HBN. The first model of cooperation with an educational institution was developed here. When more sophisticated equipment was needed for verification, SRISTI sent samples to the laboratories of other cooperating research agencies. For SRISTI, the first aim of the organization remains to help in the protection of the intellectual property of grassroots inventors and innovators. Scouted and patented grassroots innovations and grassroots innovation based on traditional knowledge have grown, in terms of the numbers of patents filed, from just two in 2001 to 557 in 2012 (Ustyuzhantseva, 2015).

The other important aim now is knowledge networking, and five main activities performed today by the HBN are: scouting and documentation; value addition and research and development; IPRs protection and licensing; information and communication technologies application and dissemination; and business development and micro-venture. The Grassroots Innovation Augmentation Network (GIAN) was set up by SRISTI in 1997. The GIAN helps to commercialize grassroots innovations. Innovators receive help from the GIAN to create its own companies to sell products. An innovator can create a joint company with an experienced entrepreneur and can also transfer technology for further commercialization by a third party.

The National Innovation Foundation (NIF) was set up in the year 2000. In 2006–7, the Department of Science and Technology (DST) scaled up its support to the NIF, which became an institution under the DST and has since then been receiving annual grants from the government of India. Today, the tasks of promoting and using the grassroots inventions identified by the volunteers of the HBN are implemented by the professional staff of the NIF and the GIAN. Currently the system of innovation includes the supporting organizations that have been established in the form of GIAN, NIF, the Micro Venture Innovation Fund (MVIF), the Grassroots Technological Innovation Acquisition Fund, Gandhian Young Technological Innovation Awards and Techpedia (connecting technology students with grassroots groups).

Anil Gupta characterizes innovations in three ways: *at, for* and *from* the grassroots. The HBN has collected from more than 500 districts throughout the country over 150,000 ideas and 10,000 examples of contemporary innovations and several outstanding examples of the use of traditional local knowledge in the sustainable management of natural resources. Information on these grassroots innovations is being shared with local communities and individuals in over seventy-five countries through the *Honey Bee* newsletter, which is now issued in eight languages (English, Spanish, Hindi, Gujarati, Tamil, Kannada, Pahari and Telugu) (Gupta, 2001a, 2014b; Ustyuzhantseva, 2015).

From its origins as a totally voluntary initiative, the HBN has become a distinct system of formal sector support for grassroots innovation via the NIF in India, an institution of the central government. The NIF is responsible for implementing the complete cycle of grassroots innovation augmentation and development and its professional staff are recruited with advice from the HBN. The HBN is free to choose partners from within both private and public sector organizations and to receive their help at all stages of the development of innovations. The NIF can decide on the nature of incentives for grassroots innovators to encourage them to participate in the process of innovation development.

In order to add value and disseminate grassroots innovations the HBN is making effective use of the facilities, recognition and public organization status of the NIF to collaborate with several public sector research organizations. The NIF also has an in-house innovation laboratory for developing grassroots innovations. The corporate sector is willing to collaborate with the HBN in the work of creating a marketplace for them.[3] Because the HBN has been given full freedom to construct the mechanisms of support for grassroots innovation and to supplement the resources available to the NIF from the central government[4] with those from private and public agencies, it seems to be free from the usual problem of bureaucratic hurdles preventing timely action.

The initiative that began in a small way in the state of Gujarat today has the recognition and support of central government for the organization of a separate mainstream system of innovation to promote grassroots innovators identified by the HBN from across all of India's states (Ustyuzhantseva, 2014). Initially, the institutional structure of SRISTI was motivated by the growing size of the database and an inability to handle it, and it was set up to provide an organizational base for the wider dissemination of traditional knowledge and uses of biodiversity in local languages, so as to allow the efforts of volunteers to spread as a social movement in all parts of the country (Gupta, 2000). Today, SRISTI's important emerging mission is knowledge networking for the benefit of grassroots innovators. Interestingly, its efforts also now contribute equally to the promotion of the grassroots innovations of students who are immersed in the sources of modern scientific and technological knowledge.

Shodh Yatras as the loci of voluntary mobilization

For a period of over two decades every summer and winter SRISTI has been organizing Shodh Yatras that celebrate creativity on its doorstep. These journeys are made to (a) explore creativity and knowledge systems at the grassroots; (b) honour innovators and traditional knowledge holders on their doorstep; (c) create awareness among both young and old of what others have done to solve problems without any external assistance, by sharing the multimedia, multi-language Honeybee database and initiating dialogue with innovators; (d) discover and elaborate the knowledge of women on local biodiversity and its rare uses; and (e) look for young geniuses who possess extraordinary sensitivity towards the environment. Shodh Yatras are also used to honour knowledge experts in order to convey the message that outstanding traditional knowledge matters as much as contemporary innovations. Volunteers receive the blessings of centenarians on the way and try to learn from their lives.

The HBN's strength in voluntary mobilization

Even today the main strength in the HBN comes from the fact that informal and voluntary mobilization is thriving and has continued to do so through the gradual process of institutionalizing the network. The credit course that Anil Gupta developed at the IIM-A, whose students have been volunteers for the HBN, including in Shodh Yatra, has enabled the HBN to keep its voluntary character intact. Professor Kuldeep Mathur, a former member of the Board of NIF observes that Shodh Yatra and the credit course started at the IIM-A are the strengths of the HBN. Shodh Yatra provide the NIF with its close link to the voluntary character of the HBN. Even since the year 2000 and the constitution of the NIF, when the institutionalization phase of the HBN can be said to have taken off, neither the students nor the grassroots inventors are known to have faced any problems in working with Anil Gupta in this previously informal space. The leadership of the NIF has been developed by him and it mostly shares his values. The voluntary spirit continues to thrive under this leadership and the dedicated and committed voluntary system remains intact within the HBN and its affiliates (Interview with Professor Kuldeep Mathur, 11 February 2015).

HBN's framings

The motivations that initially moved Anil Gupta and the student volunteers of the HBN – namely, conservation of biodiversity and respect, recognition and reward for indigenous or traditional knowledge, wider social diffusion of traditional and local knowledge, redeeming the self-confidence of the local talent and community building through its use – received the attention of many other radical figures of the day. During the 1980s several governmental and non-governmental bodies were engaged in this field, telling policymakers how they should be using traditional knowledge in the process of development in India. Within civil society, also active in the field, with their own initiatives on traditional knowledge, were Suman Sahai of Gene Campaign, Vandana Shiva of Navdanya, Claude Alvares, Smitu Kothari, Ramchander Guha, Shiv Visvanathan and Ashis Nandy of Lokayan and the Centre for Developing Societies, and Ashish Kothari of Kalpavriksha and People's Science Movements.

All of them shared the broad framing that traditional knowledge was being undervalued and needed to be supported for its potential contribution to social and environmental goals. A number of these individuals and organizations actively engaged with the public on the issue of how the question of IPRs should be tackled by policymakers in order to achieve the objectives of conserving biodiversity and promoting traditional knowledge in India.[5] But among them only the HBN chose to use the institution of IPRs as a means to bring the contribution of grassroots innovators into the mainstream.

During the 1980s, advocacy of several environmental groups was framed in terms of the ideology of 'environmentalism of the poor' (Alier, 2002). This framing included a belief in traditional communities as the social carriers of environmentally relevant knowledge and innovation.[6] The protection of biodiversity and traditional knowledge were an integral part of this framing. Although the efforts of the HBN were co-evolving amid the contestations that were ongoing in the sphere of where and how to use traditional knowledge, the HBN's emphasis on the contribution of individual grassroots innovators to traditional knowledge, the use of a competitive spirit and the element of market competition made an important difference. This emphasis gained for the HBN the influence that it received among the policymakers of the day. Anil Gupta clearly preferred to align with those policymakers who were supportive of market liberalization and IPRs protection for traditional knowledge. The idea of sourcing innovative solutions from the individual grassroots innovators for the benefit of the emerging market economy was a key move on the part of the HBN.

In the late 1980s, Anil Gupta was actively associated with the activities of the Patriotic and People-oriented Science and Technology Group (PPST), which advocated the development of the community dimension of traditional knowledge and saw it as the basis for the development of alternative sciences and technologies. During the 1980s, the PPST had emerged in India as a radical social movement in the area of cognitive justice for traditional knowledge, which was also aligned with the ideology of 'cultural nationalism', which is known to be embraced by both Hindu nationalists and secularists. When the first Traditional Science and Technology Congress at the Indian Institute of Technology (IIT) Mumbai was organized by the PPST in 1994, Anil Gupta was closely associated with the group. Discussions with Navjyoti Singh of the PPST suggest that the HBN deliberately chose to promote the strategy of making individual grassroots innovators competitive. It is notable that, in spite of his active association with the efforts of PPST, Anil Gupta chose not to frame the promotion of indigenous knowledge by the HBN as a challenge of developing local communities more broadly. The option to frame the challenge of promoting traditional knowledge mainly as a problem of strengthening individual innovators (rather than emphasizing the community origins of traditional/indigenous knowledge) was deliberately chosen to suit the changing times.[7]

Historically, at the beginning the core idea of the HBN had been to ensure the granting of respect, recognition and reward to grassroots inventors, and its framings revolved around the establishment of a mechanism of intellectual property protection for the conservation of biodiversity and traditional knowledge. The HBN supported the institution of stronger IPRs even though, according to many others, IPRs' adverse influence on access and innovation was an important concern in India.[8] During the early 1990s the problem of IPRs was turned into a question of recognition of the rights of farmers and local communities in agriculture by Anil

Gupta, along with others such as Suman Sahai and Vandana Shiva.[9] The National Working Group on Patent Laws (NWGPL) was also a key participant in the debate on IPRs, with a solution to the protection and promotion of traditional knowledge that was significantly different.[10]

At a time when the governments of the industrialized world and transnational corporations were describing the Indian inventors of process innovations as free riders and pirates (because the Indian Patent Act permitted patenting of process innovations in the pharmaceutical industry), a vast majority did not want the Indian government to accept the proposals of the TRIPS Agreement in the sphere of pharmaceuticals and agriculture. During the late 1980s and early 1990s most of the political and social movements in India were using the frame of neocolonialism to engage with the wider public on the question of IPRs. But Anil Gupta, in the case of traditional knowledge, chose to view the demand for stronger IPRs as an issue of cognitive justice for farmers and grassroots innovators.[11] He suggested that the Indian government should accept the principle that innovators (wherever and whoever they might be) must be protected and compensated through the institution of strong IPRs (Gupta, 1992). He argued that it was more important to allow the farmers and holders of traditional knowledge to gain from the IPR negotiations than to concentrate on the demands (from the governments of the industrialized world under TRIPS) for a stronger IPR system for medicines. Gupta argued that, by adopting his stance on the subject of IPRs in the *General Agreement on Tariffs and Trade* (GATT) and Convention on Biological Diversity negotiations, the developing world governments would be able to stake the right of their farmers to have a share in the global profits of multinational corporations.[12]

In September 2000, the World Intellectual Property Organization (WIPO) established the Intergovernmental Committee on Intellectual Property and Genetic Resources, Traditional Knowledge and Folklore to provide a forum for governments to discuss intellectual property matters with regard to access to genetic resources and benefit sharing and the protection of traditional knowledge, innovations and creativity and expressions of folklore. In India, the Biological Diversity Bill 2000, *vide* section 36 (IV) of chapter-IX, provides for the protection of the knowledge of local people relating to biodiversity through measures such as the registration of such knowledge and the development of a *sui generis* system. Sections 19 and 21 of chapter-V also stipulate prior approval of the National Biodiversity Authority before access and mutual benefit sharing. The HBN, through Anil Gupta, has been able to make a significant contribution to the issue of IPRs for traditional knowledge at both international and national levels.[13] Meanwhile, SRISTI is advocating for the establishment of an International Network for Sustainable Technological Applications and Registration.

The HBN deliberately chose the idea of individual grassroots innovators as knowledge-rich, economically poor individuals who were deprived of recognition, respect and reward. The HBN's idea that strong IPRs would enrich rural areas rather than exploit them was new (Dutfield, 2006). It is important to underscore the point that, until that time, environmental activists had mostly preferred to advocate for the ownership of biodiversity as resting at the level of local communities. The HBN chose to frame the challenge of knowledge networking as also providing for incubation and entrepreneurship support to individual grassroots innovators. Due to the efforts of the HBN, the institution of strong IPRs for traditional knowledge (whose carriers are now the individual grassroots innovators identified by the HBN) is the most important mechanism for the insertion of traditional knowledge into the mainstream development process in India.

The HBN has been able to provide legitimacy not only to the concept of individual innovators' ownership of traditional knowledge but also to the idea of how, by using the institution of IPRs, these individual innovators are now able to become competitive. More recently Anil Gupta has suggested the idea of creating a market for green grassroots frugal innovations, and that the innovations of poor people have substantial potential for green transformation. The frame of human survival in the age of climate change is also now added, so as to attract a contemporary motivating factor:

> At the time of the HBN organized biodiversity competitions the people from outside try those recipes that have some uncultivated plants as ingredients. In the wake of climate change we might need new sources of food if the present one succumbs to new diseases or pests, and we have started preparations for any such catastrophe in the foreseeable future. Many of the so-called weeds are actually a rich source of nutrition. The inquisitiveness and the survival instincts of poor people might actually hold the key to the survival of humanity in the future. Thus, attention to their knowledge need not only be justified only on its own account and for potential help to the poor, but also because it will provide ways of survival for the more privileged ones who have lost such an instinct.
>
> (Gupta, 2014a)

Another characteristic of the HBN's framing of grassroots innovation is the potential for (and importance of) blending different types of knowledge. Anil Gupta framed the issue of promoting traditional knowledge as a problem of ensuring access to the knowledge of other people, with institutions and knowledge systems in their own languages. Although traditional knowledge was cast by the HBN as an alternative and complementary knowledge, to be integrated into the process of 'modern development' in order to align this frame with the policy of economic liberalization (Gupta, 1990), it was conceived also as a problem of grassroots innovators not being given access to local or nearby scientific laboratories and workshops for validating and adding value to their knowledge of herbal healing (and other technological claims).

The HBN chose to actively access the institutions of modern S&T to provide hand-holding support on the doorstep to grassroots innovators who were pursuing creativity and innovation for survival, in order to convert their ideas into enterprises (see Gupta, 2009). The HBN focused on increasing its access to local-language multimedia tools and databases of traditional knowledge or grassroots innovations held by other communities in the region (or around the world). The HBN did not reject modern S&T as 'Western knowledge'. Like the People's Science Movements, Anil Gupta is in favour of the active blending of people's traditional or informal knowledge with modern scientific and technological knowledge. Vandana Shiva, Alvares, Nandy, Visvanathan and many others still promote the systems of traditional knowledge as alternative sciences and technologies. They have chosen not to accept the embrace of modern science and technology. The HBN, on the other hand, favours access to local or nearby labs and workshops so as to add value to such knowledge, to fabricate tools or to commercialize traditional knowledge-based innovation.

The HBN has been using the frame of celebrating cultural knowledge and creativity and has been linking the frame of cultural creativity and educational innovations so as to recognize the value of biodiversity during Shodh Yatras. Food recipes and ideas competitions in the villages have been used by the HBN in the course of Shodh Yatras to demonstrate the grassroots spirit in the spheres of the education of young children, the building of excellence and the development of collegiality (Gupta, 2014a).

The HBN has been able to address the challenge of simultaneously obtaining legitimacy both from the emerging policymaking apparatus and from the networks of activist groups who in the 1990s were aligning themselves with cultural nationalism and environmentalism of the poor. The HBN remains conscious that the framing of grassroots innovation combines its efforts only with the ideology of 'secular cultural nationalism'. Its strategic use of post-Nehruvian environmental, cognitive and social justice movements for the cause of grassroots innovation is evident.

The HBN has been continuously adding new frames to motivate both grassroots innovators and the policymaking apparatus to provide support to and participate in its initiatives. After starting with the original frame of recognition, respect and reward, Anil Gupta today uses the frames of sustainable livelihoods to motivate people to support the initiatives of the HBN. The sustainable livelihoods frame includes equity considerations, conservation concerns, the preservation of traditional practices and culture, preventing the appropriation by unauthorized parties of components of traditional knowledge and the promotion of the latter's use/importance in development.[14] The HBN's initiatives aim to foster creativity and upgrade the capabilities of people who lack a professional background. The HBN collaborates with them to commercialize solutions for sustainable development.

Promoting interactions between grassroots innovators and other regular entrepreneurs and supporting governmental institutions is today seen by the HBN as its key task. In the ongoing long evolutionary process of thinking on and learning from the role of people's knowledge in development in India, the efforts of the HBN represents a discontinuity, as compared to earlier attempts to articulate people's knowledge in development. Compared to these earlier approaches, the HBN's main framing fits in with the pathway of market liberalization, but the idea of scouting and documenting traditional knowledge, and of providing IPRs protection as an incentive to non-formal innovators, is still under test. Using the individual grassroots as social carriers of grassroots innovation is also a clever and risky step (see discussion on this issue in Dutfield, 2006).

Spaces and strategies of the HBN

The spaces and strategies of the HBN can be better understood when related to the outcomes of knowledge networking in practice in the form of encouraging student volunteering for the scouting and documentation of grassroots innovation, helping to build linkages between grassroots innovators and the publicly funded S&T institutions and private companies that are undertaking value addition, research and development, IPRs protection and licensing, and providing catalytic risk capital to grassroots innovators. In terms of the strategies used, the efforts of the HBN can be characterized as mainly informed by the frame of grassroots innovation movements using local ingenuity and their utilization in the process of mainstream development. Currently the spaces and strategies, in practice, largely reflect the desire of the HBN to help uneducated grassroots innovators to consolidate their monetary position. The HBN's frame of rewarding individual innovators so that they are able to compete in the market through their own strength is also firmly written into the spaces and strategies.

So far, altogether about 150,000 ideas, innovations and traditional knowledge practices (not all unique) have been mobilized from 545 districts of India through the efforts of the HBN. It is not a small achievement if one notes that more than 90 per cent have been collected by the volunteers of the HBN, while the remaining 10 per cent have come in response to advertisements issued by the NIF. It represents a significant contribution to the politics of innovation and intellectual property systems for the management of traditional knowledge.

The HBN has been using the faculty and students studying in engineering colleges, universities and national institutes of design as its collaborators. The HBN is implementing a strategy of providing recognition to university and college students through various award initiatives (IGNITE Awards, Techpedia and Gandhian Awards). While these efforts are seemingly still insufficient for the realization of effective collaborations between grassroots innovators and innovators from formal S&T institutions, the initiatives such as the various awards can help the HBN to tap from this pool a new generation of volunteers supporting grassroots innovation.

At a time when S&T institutions are being asked to adjust to the changing environment for research and technology development activities (due to the decline in public funding, market-led selection of research projects, greater collaboration with the private sector and generation of revenue from sponsored research, exclusive technology licensing and stronger IPRs), the HBN's strategies fit well with the developments taking place within the national innovation system. The NIF has become an apex institution of a system of grassroots innovation support in India. It has been able to involve organizations of the Indian Council of Medical

Research and the Council of Scientific and Industrial Research in its network that is under development to support the steps of innovation development from idea to product diffusion.

The use of micro-venture capital for the purpose of business development is an important HBN strategy. In 2003, the HBN was able to set up a Micro Venture Innovation Fund (MVIF) with the help of the Small Industries Development Bank of India (SIDBI). It has already invested more than Rs2.5 crores (Rs25 million) in the ideas and innovations of ordinary people without any collateral or guarantor.[15] The national MVIF is the principal financial source for the GIAN. This fund is being effectively used to support innovations which have market potential at the national and global levels. The MVIF provides risk capital support to only those entrepreneurs and companies that are interested in commercializing grassroots innovations. The MVIF is not a grant but a loan.

> Out of total four crore fund, till date, we have supported total 191 projects and the total sanctioned amount is Rs3,87,06,637 (Three Crores Eighty Seven Lakhs Six Thousand Six Hundred and Thirty Seven only), Disbursed Amount is Rs3,40,37,637 (Three Crores Fourty Lakhs Thirty Seven Thousand Six Hundred and Thirty Seven only) and the total repayment amount is Rs2,13,01,676 (Two Crore Thirteen Lakhs One Thousand Six Hundred and Seventy Six only).
>
> *(National Innovation Foundation, n.d.)*

Using the MVIF, the HBN has been able to extend risk capital to many successful ventures that would otherwise normally be considered as too risky for the regular commercial financial institutions to fund. The NIF supports grassroots innovations in many ways, including support for converting market-ready prototypes to the stage of manufacturing in small quantities based on the orders received by the innovators, and support for certification by regulatory authorities, field trials, market research and benchmarking. An example is the motorbike-polycultivator, invented by Mansukhbhai Jagani in a small village in Gujarat. The NIF requested the National Institute of Design to develop a product design. The Sloan School of Management at MIT developed the business plan. In May 2008, NIF and GIAN took the initiative to test and improve Jagani's design. About thirty innovators and another twenty stakeholders met to discuss ways and possibilities for design and functional improvement (Ustyuzhantseva, 2015).

The Grassroots Technological Innovation Acquisition Fund, established as recently as 2011, acquires rights to technologies from the innovators for the purpose of generating public goods. It undertakes the acquisition of grassroots technologies by the HBN so as to share them with other grassroots entrepreneurs. In 2012, twenty-four farmers from eight states, who had developed over thirty-nine improved varieties of fifteen crops (such as paddy, wheat, mustard and beans) received Rs120,000. In total, the NIF has acquired rights to seventy technologies at a cost of Rs275,000 (National Innovation Foundation, 2013).

The GIAN also accesses small sources of funding from the Gujarat government and the Department of Scientific and Industrial Research. Unlike many other grassroots initiatives that are still struggling to mobilize innovation finance, the HBN is receiving generous help from the central and state governments.

The commercialization of grassroots innovations is carried out through the GIAN. More than sixty technological licences have been given, mainly to small companies and individual entrepreneurs, with the benefits going back to the innovators. Small entrepreneurs have chosen to license technologies from the innovators in about two dozen cases. Initiatives have included: (1) establishment of an innovator-based incubator with financial support from NIF – GIAN extended support of Rs1,583,000 to six innovators from Gujarat under this programme; (2) tie-in with Reuters for technology diffusion to farmers through mobile (SMS) phone. Each innovator received about twenty calls per day on average; (3) GIAN West's market research on herbal formulations developed from the knowledge of traditional healers, namely Herbaglow, Pain Relief, MosqHit, Herboheal and Zematic; (4) GIAN's development of brands for two innovative products, launched at the annual SATVIK traditional food festival. Herbal practices and traditional food items are being marketed under a common brand name by SRISTI.

Value addition, business development and technology transfer are very important to the HBN's strategy of ultimately making the individual innovator 'economically rich' and 'competitive' in the market. The HBN started by collaborating with the publicly funded R&D system; today, with the help of the corporate sector (another space for collaboration), the HBN is moving forward to provide support to individual grassroots innovators. Within the corporate space, GIAN West has been able to rope in automobile manufacturers. Sunil Parekh (Cadila Ltd), Rahul Bajaj (Chairman, Bajaj Auto Ltd) and Sunil Munjal (Chairman, Hero Honda Ltd) have taken an interest in the automobile technologies developed by grassroots innovators. In the private sector, the NIF has started working with the Futures Group (owner of the largest retail space in India).

More recently, in terms of the linking of grassroots innovators with the formal sector for business development, more spaces are opening up for the HBN's grassroots innovation activity, with the support of the corporate sector.

Progress in path construction

Our investigations indicate that the goal of the HBN is at present mainly restricted to developing the ability to mainstream, insert and include the innovations of socially excluded, non-formal grassroots innovators into mainstream developmental processes. Its achievements can be seen mainly in respect of the insertion of non-formal grassroots innovators into conventional markets. In selected cases (with the help of the NIF) the HBN has been able to help grassroots innovators to go global and to create business. These examples have encouraged many others to contribute grassroots innovations to the HBN registry, thinking that they too can improve their financial position by getting support from the NIF.

However, it is also important to recognize that the product and technology commercialization strategy of HBN relies basically on the individual producer to mobilize the resources for the introduction and diffusion of innovations into the market. Lack of success with the diffusion of a pedal-operated washing machine in Kerala and a hand-pump installation encouraging local water storage for human and animal consumption indicates that community building, social diffusion and group enterprise are necessary for a higher level of success.

Success is not forthcoming in many cases because the individual producer is not able to compete successfully in the market, particularly where medium- and large-scale firms are already active with similar or alternative products. Even when the individual producer has been able to obtain the collaboration of big business he or she is being encouraged to grow without changing the organization of production. The HBN does not have yet the arrangements in place for the growth of group entrepreneurship and to act as a co-producer to address the social diffusion of grassroots innovation within the space of locally evolving economies.

It is quite likely that the successful introduction of grassroots innovations of high commercial impact will largely come from collaboration and cooperation with big business. However, there are as yet not many cases of successful technological collaborations that are led by big business. Innovations that are being introduced with the help of big business have yet to bear significant fruit even for business development. Of course, this leads us to question the idea of the HBN as the endogenous, intrinsic version of Prahalad's external, top-down version of BoP innovation (Prahalad, 2009).

Further, our discussions with some of the grassroots innovators and state-level coordinators and collaborators from within the S&T institutions and government also indicate that (a) identification and acceptance by the NIF of grassroots innovations needs to be undertaken with more clarity about the expectations that grassroots innovators hold with regard to awards and financial and knowledge-related intermediation; and (b) patent filing and prior art searches need to be undertaken with far more responsibility because the payment of maintenance fees will make sense only for those patents where the NIF's public investment in patenting grassroots innovations can be suitably recovered by the state from the returns to the NIF (either from fees received as lump sums and royalties or from revenue from sales of the grassroots innovation).

The HBN faces the challenge of ensuring that the spaces created fulfil the aspirations of non-formal grassroots innovators as well as its own expectations for the wider diffusion of grassroots innovations. Investigations show that grassroots innovators have a mixed experience regarding their interactions with the NIF (see Bhaduri and Kumar, 2011 for further discussion on the mismatch between individuals' motivations and community expectations). As things stand today, the NIF has been quite flexible and liberal with regard to accepting the grassroots innovations identified and submitted during Shodh Yatras. But when they have developed expectations and the NIF has not been able to meet their aspirations, the response of grassroots innovators has at times been one of frustration and disappointment.

The NIF is generating a lot of expectations among grassroots innovators, and many of them have opined that the NIF needs to be democratized. One possibility would be to have representation on the governing body and executive from other such initiatives.

The HBN also faces the unanticipated challenge of mobilizing those grassroots innovators who are knowledge rich but who are not necessarily demanding economic benefits for their knowledge or innovations. Many among them feel that what they possess is a God-given gift that should be shared among the members of the community. More importantly, making the transition to being an entrepreneur is not easy, even for a person who strives for it. Our analysis suggests that the desire to share and to help each and every one remains strong among non-formal grassroots innovators, without such a great need for individualized financial gain. The NIF could possibly look into how the identified grassroots innovators could realize far more from the diffusion of their own innovations through open modes, which seems to be the desire of many grassroots innovators (as observed from the stories being put out by the NIF) (Abrol and Gupta, 2014).

As the diffusion of grassroots innovations is an important challenge at the local market level, the capacity to empower communities cannot come without augmenting the intermediation arrangements away from a focus on each one being competitive as an individual producer. The NIF needs to work out appropriate strategies in order to exploit the potential to develop interrelations between selected grassroots innovations, and to develop synergies among the enterprises under development in order to realize the wider possibilities of local economic and social development. While it is true that affordable and accessible technologies can also be diffused through private retail chains, the social diffusion of open source technologies is an even more important potential contribution of the HBN.

Efforts towards the mobilization of grassroots innovators that are needed so as to realize the potential of green grassroots frugal innovations at the level of the development of the local markets are receiving insufficient attention. The HBN has been far more successful in bringing about a change in the level of support for grassroots innovators to commercialize grassroots innovations at the national and international levels. In many examples, it has been able to assist innovators to improve their individual incomes in a significant way. But the impact of these innovations on the improvement of rural economies is as yet quite limited.

Future challenges for the Honey Bee Network

Drawing on the analysis above, we next set out some of the main challenges that the HBN faces in constructing pathways to inclusion and sustainable development in India, and offer some suggestions for how this might be done.

During the two and half decades since 1990 this idea of including non-formal grassroots innovators has made important strides as a result of the efforts of the HBN and its affiliates in India. An important strength of the HBN's strategy seems to lie in the programmes for mobilizing students and scientists from within the formal sector S&T institutions. The HBN might achieve broader results if these voluntary S&T personnel were to support a model of group (rather than individual) entrepreneurship and promoted the social diffusion and use of grassroots innovations for community building.

Commercial organizations (which include large corporate organizations such as Tata Agrico, Hero Honda, Bajaj Auto, Kirloskar and Futures Group) and the formal sector institutions of S&T that retain their own culture and are joining hands for the promotion of innovation, incubation and entrepreneurship cannot be expected to change their own motivations in a spontaneous way in order to align with those of the innovators. Although the interaction of grassroots innovators with big business is giving traditional and local knowledge innovations much visibility, in the absence of strengthening rural communities and the local production and innovation capacity that communities need so as to upgrade their forward and backward linkages, the potential loss of creative spirit and autonomy is also a real possibility. Since interaction with big business is double-edged, with both advantages and challenges, the HBN also has a responsibility to safeguard the sources of local initiative and innovation for community building and social diffusion.

At the national level the HBN is clearly driven by a single leader. The leader, in the person of Anil Gupta, provides sustenance to the moral values of the network by recharging it through the personal example of thought and living. To some extent, in collaboration the team is also able to provide technocratic guidance and now possesses necessary capabilities in every component of professional activity. At the ground level, however, the grassroots innovator-turned-entrepreneur is still facing major problems and gaps.

The market demands the standardization and validation of products, the wherewithal to meet demand and the capacity to take risks. There are many professional activities that need to be undertaken before an innovation can enter the market as a commercial product. These activities take time and, in the process, a knowledge-rich person may lose patience and enthusiasm in pursuing the goal of becoming economically rich. At the level of business development, enterprise building and incubation, the gaps in state-level leadership are clearly evident. Furthermore, most grassroots innovators wish to obtain a reward for their contribution through the enhancement of livelihoods at the local level only. This is an important organizational challenge for the HBN.

Strategies devised for the recruitment of mainstream science, technology and innovation to the incubation of product and technology development efforts need to move away from the 'hand holding' of high-impact grassroots innovators. While a few have certainly found some success, the number of products introduced into the market by successful grassroots innovators is still not large enough to make an impact in the relevant market segment.

Further activities relating to the tasks of incubation and developing entrepreneurship also depend, in the case of the HBN, on the professionals who are being recruited on a formal basis by the leadership of the movement to pursue its goal of converting grassroots innovators into entrepreneurs. At the moment these professionals are working largely out of platforms operating at the national level from within the NIF and at the regional level from within the GIAN. At the local or project level some professionals have also now set up not-for-profit organizations in a few cases. Aakar is one such organization which has been set up by Joydeep Mondal, who previously worked as an intern at the NIF and the GIAN.

The 'missing middle' level of leadership arrangements is an important issue to be tackled within the network as represented by the HBN, SRISTI, NIF and GIAN. The problem exists at the level of the organization of innovation and enterprise building, and for the collective diffusion of innovations identified even within the same district or state. It is readily apparent that while today a small network of volunteers dedicated to the ethical values of the movement does seek to undertake efforts in scouting and documentation, recognition, respect and reward, it is the professional staff recruited on a formal basis that are pursuing the goals of converting grassroots innovators into entrepreneurs. The professional staff are working largely from the platforms operating at the national level within the NIF or at the regional level within the GIANs.[16] Although the interlocking relationship that the HBN has been able to develop among the units in place is the strength of the network, the management of such a relationship is not an ordinary challenge for the staff at the national and regional levels. In practical terms, the observations of Professor Kuldeep Mathur imply that there is also a huge challenge facing the network in terms of aligning the aspirations of the professionals who come to work in the areas of knowledge and finance at the formal sector institutions. Experience of the building of GIAN North and GIAN Northeast, which has its office IIT Guwahati, indicates that the development of middle-level leadership arrangements requires a concerted effort on the part of the HBN. Engineering design capabilities need strengthening and GIAN Northeast's experience needs to be reflected upon (Personal communication with Professor Kuldeep Mathur, 11 February 2015).

Many of the problems that are being encountered by grassroots innovators in the commercialization of products and technologies are in the field. Grassroots innovators face huge challenges in the marketplace, in their efforts at collaboration with the academic world and in the space of demand articulation for inclusive and green development. In the case of the students who are committed to scouting and documenting the innovative practices of rural people, they would like to see rural development as an outcome. Their attraction to the HBN relies on the assumption that the creative urges of individual grassroots inventors can be sustained and encouraged by them, and that these efforts will also ultimately help them to preserve biodiversity and traditional knowledge. The formal S&T institutions (which include non-governmental organizations) that support the grassroots innovators in the promotion and use of HBN-identified inventions have their own individual motivations. They would also like to take the collaboration with the NIF in directions that can contribute to their own S&T work and careers.

Related to motivations are expectations. The policymakers' expectations of wider economic development among grassroots inventors as a result of the implementation of the stated vision of the HBN may also call for changes in vision and strategy and in organizational development repertoires over time. Further, the HBN may also need to put in more effort to create a culture of cooperation among individual producers, all of which are today embedded in the vision and ideology of developing individual producers who are competing with each other in the market. Arrangements that are geared to keeping grassroots inventors as individual producers face many handicaps in practice.

Furthermore, experience tells us that policymakers should not expect broad, transformative outcomes to emerge spontaneously for the benefit of inclusive and green development. The HBN will have to demonstrate that grassroots innovators and innovations are in a position to implement and diffuse innovations suited for resource-constrained settings, and contribute to the agenda of inclusive growth and sustainable development in a significant way. Since the HBN has achieved a fair degree of legitimization for the idea that grassroots innovators matter, and exist in large numbers, it now needs to demonstrate that the idea of individual innovators can work well for the development of micro enterprises; and, finally, that it also works for the achievement of goals of ecologically sustainable development.

Conclusions

Important policymaking advances in India, in the case of the HBN, include the widening of the scope and spread of its activity, successful institutionalization of the activities of documentation and recognition, dissemination after incubation and value addition, promotion of entrepreneurship and the use of grassroots inventions in the processes of development at the state and national levels. And this is an important gain for the HBN's pathway of inclusion of uneducated grassroots innovators. The challenge is now for the HBN and others to learn from the implementation of the spaces and strategies in place, and to go ahead with the task of innovation using the resources that the HBN has been able to accumulate during three decades since the mid-1980s.

For the first time, the HBN and the organizations around it (SRISTI, GIAN, etc.) represent a grassroots initiative that has been given significant governmental support (through the NIF) in India, but that also retains a level of autonomy. As such, it is a unique example from which scholars, social movements and policymakers can learn a great deal. However, from the discussion above it should also be clear that concerns exist with regard to the promotion of biodiversity contests and the practice of giving awards when these become a source of jealousy. Because the HBN's framings include the idea of promoting competition and introduce unfair expectations that are now recognized to be emerging within the community of grassroots innovators, the introduction of competition and profit is certainly a source of anxiety and concern.

Further, it should be clear that the challenge of promoting green and inclusive innovation goes far beyond the framing of introducing discrete products and placing individual innovators who own them firmly in the marketplace. Social diffusion and community building, which were initially also key motivations, need to be given far more priority by the HBN. Anil Gupta has himself pointed out in his recent writings that, in order to achieve the objectives of frugal engineering, the HBN is faced with the challenge of how to promote place-based local economies as viable systems (Gupta, 2014b). However, it is also clear that the HBN cannot realize this goal without creating the necessary entrepreneurial leadership at the local level and the required intermediation arrangements. Such arrangements must link grassroots innovation to the design of local economic systems that are socially inclusive and sustainable.

Our analysis is that the HBN's framing of grassroots innovation can be characterized as a mixture of grassroots ingenuity and grassroots empowerment (Smith et al., 2014) for the inclusion of non-formal grassroots innovators into the mainstream of innovation. But inclusive innovation demands the development of new ways of producing and consuming resources by mixing up ideas or combining technologies, and – we would argue – some structural change.

Notes

1. Luc Soete (2013) suggests that the innovation process is now, in the true destructive creation sense, likely to be reversed, starting with the design phase that will be confronted directly with the need to find functional solutions to some of the particular BoP users' framework conditions. Spurring local reuse along the principles of cradle-to-cradle might well become a new form of sustainable grassroots innovation.
2. Dr Anil Kumar Gupta has been a professor at the Centre for Management in Agriculture, Indian Institute of Management, Ahmedabad, since 1981. Various positions held by him in IIM-A include Chairperson of Research and Publications, Chairperson of Ravi J. Matthai Centre for Educational Innovation and Kasturbhai Lalbhai Chair in Entrepreneurship. He is also now on the executive as a Vice Chair at the National Innovation Foundation.
3. In 2010 the Future Group, along with NIF and the DST, announced the formation of Khoj La, an innovation laboratory, to support grassroots innovations and create a marketplace. Future Group is an Indian privately held corporation that operates some of the most popular retail chains (such as Pantaloons, Big Bazaar, Food Bazzar, eZone and Home Town), in addition to other businesses.
4. Ustyuzhantseva suggests, on the basis of inputs from Anil Gupta, that these sums are definitely not enough for a country the size of India (Ustyuzhantseva, 2014).
5. During this period, policymakers were under pressure from big business and governments of the developed countries to accept a system of stronger intellectual property rights (exemplified by the World Trade Organization-administered Agreement on Trade-Related Aspects of Intellectual Property Rights (TRIPS) of 1994).
6. In the post-Nehruvian phase of economic development, local communities and the state had been the two main contending actors of choice for social activists in the development of new products, processes and practices in the domains of crop production, animal husbandry, food and health based on traditional or indigenous knowledge.
7. Discussions with Navjyoti Singh of PPST confirm that Anil Gupta deliberately did not conflate his decision with the PPST's overall understanding of the need to mobilize the holders of traditional knowledge as communities. This strategic move was important because many ideologues within the PPST were committed to the framing of

traditional knowledge as alternative sciences and technologies and were mobilizing communities of artisans and traditional practitioners (Telephone interview with Navjyoti Singh, July 2014).
8. While Anil Gupta differed at that time from many who opposed the demands for stronger IPRs, many of those who also wanted environmental and social justice to be respected did not think that stronger IPRs were a solution to the problem, in particular in the case of farmers' innovations. They were of the view that those who were promoting stronger IPRs would continue to erode and steal biodiversity from the developing world. They preferred open source-based approaches and more balanced IPRs to deal with the problem of knowledge misappropriation.
9. Anil Gupta argued that the technology gap in biotechnology was shorter to bridge, compared to most industrial technologies. He argued that, by compromising on the industrial front (read allowing stronger IPRs in pharmaceuticals), the country could gain a lot on the biotechnological front. He wrote (Gupta, 1992) that India should simultaneously refuse to accept the idea that biodiversity is the global heritage, and should document and patent various landraces and germplasm in the name of local communities.
10. The NWPGL considered the demand for stronger IPRs from transnational corporations to be causing much injury to the people as a whole and did not consider that the people's interest in Indian pharmaceuticals should be sacrificed. NWPGL also differed from Anil Gupta's arguments about the concerns of farmers in the debate on TRIPS. The NWPGL had prioritized the issue of farmers, access to seeds, and was opposed to the use of stronger IPRs for the protection of farmers' rights.
11. Anil Gupta (1992) wrote that the debate on protection of IPRs of the companies and scientific labs developing technologies through biotechnological means or otherwise had been highly surcharged with emotion, and got the policymakers to advocate farmers' rights and protection for traditional knowledge in the international negotiations on intellectual property.
12. The contrary view of the NWGPL was that the farmers would not gain much from the concept of farmers' rights. They wanted to strengthen the licensing regime within the legislation for the benefit of farmers as users of seeds from the private and public sector.
13. In a paper presented at a UNEP workshop in 2001, Anil Gupta (2001b) wrote that 'Intellectual property rights regimes used to be largely a domestic issue, but the forces of globalization have pushed it onto the world trade agenda, driven primarily by the rich developed nations whose companies hold the majority of the world's patents. This paper does not oppose a global patent regime as such, as one of the potential ways of dealing with rewards, but suggests it should be revised to fit more appropriately into the traditions and needs of developing countries, and operate alongside a portfolio approach to generating material and non-material incentives for individuals and communities for conservation.'
14. The contributions of Anil Gupta and the HBN made a distinct impact on the shaping of institutions of IPRs in respect of traditional knowledge. The operationalization of prior informed consent (see nifindia.org/pic.htm) in the NIF is a major effort which has never been tried on such a scale perhaps in any country. This has posed countless problems because people have never interacted with any institution that seeks their permission to decide how their knowledge should be shared with any third party and how it should be valorized or its benefits shared. This requires creating awareness about prior informed consent and it is a task that will take years.
15. Anil Gupta (2003) writes, 'On October 1, 2003, a small fund of about a million dollars has been set up at NIF with the help of SIDBI (Small Scale Industries Development Bank of India) for ten years to help convert innovations into enterprises. *An incubation fund to convert innovations to products remains to be set up.* With a corpus of about five million dollars, NIF has very limited degrees of freedom to operate with only interest income on the corpus. Declining interest rates and rising aspirations are bound to create problems of unmet expectations' (our italics).

16 The decision to keep only five professionals in the NIF besides a Chief Innovation Officer created a tremendous constraint on managing a national grassroots innovation movement. The need for networking was thus embedded in the structure of the organization, which would never have been able to achieve its goals without investing in strengthening the wider network. This is a lesson for designing lean organizations that draw their strength from networks of formal and informal volunteers, as well as professional mentors and other stakeholders (see indiainnovates.com).

9
GRASSROOTS INNOVATION MOVEMENTS

Lessons for theory and practice

Taking their periods of activity in sum, the case studies across the previous six chapters provide over a century of grassroots innovation experience. What can we learn from such experience? The aim in this chapter is to look across the case studies in order to identify recurring features and appreciate key differences that, amid the diversity and complexities of any particular movement, might nevertheless be instructive. Each of the case studies was motivated by the same three questions (Chapter 1).

1. Why did this grassroots innovation movement emerge?
2. How did activists mobilize support and activities in grassroots innovation?
3. What dilemmas confronted the movement when constructing alternative pathways, and how did it negotiate those dilemmas?

In Chapter 2 we suggested a framework for answering these questions based on an approach that looked at grassroots innovation as a technology-oriented social movement. We developed the concepts of contexts, framings, spaces and strategies, and pathways in order to help us look consistently at each case study while remaining open to its particularities. In this chapter we use the framework to analyse our grassroots innovation movements. Thus the chapter is structured in order to look in greater depth at framings, spaces and strategies, and pathways, and in so doing to provide answers to our research questions.

Each of the case studies demonstrates how the specific historical context is important to understanding the emergence of a grassroots innovation movement. Contexts were generative of each movement and provided opportunities for them, but contexts simultaneously presented limitations and challenges to movement developments. Emerging movements made sense of these contexts and sought to act in and upon them through the adoption and development of different framings.

All case studies saw movements opening up and occupying a variety of different spaces, and leveraging diverse strategies, in order to do innovation and contribute to sustainable developments. Dilemmas came in the form of strategic choices over what kinds of spaces to occupy and how to make most effective use of them.

What we find overall is that grassroots innovation movements emerge variously for the purposes of promoting grassroots ingenuity, empowering innovative communities and seeking to transform wider social structures. This proceeds through a variety of spaces supportive towards these aims and where resources can be furnished, but a major dilemma confronting movements is whether to realize their aims by trying to insert themselves into prevailing institutions for innovation, or to seek to mobilize support for transforming those institutions.

Framing grassroots innovation movements

In Chapter 2 we introduced the concept of framings in order to analyse how grassroots innovation movements form a collective self-understanding of their purposes and a coordinated interpretation of the worlds in which they act. Frames are seen as a fundamental part of the affirmation of collective identity, values, motivations and visions of change, and a reference point for action, as well as being shaped through action. Framing is understood to be a process negotiated among activists, in which commitments towards the promotion of grassroots innovation are given more specific form. Such negotiations seek to prioritize different motivating factors; suggest different roles for grassroots groups; guide activity towards different opportunities and possibilities in a society; emphasize different kinds of knowledge production and parts of innovation processes or expected outcomes; identify and promote certain exemplary artefacts and technologies; and manifest in contrasting strategies for promoting grassroots innovation.

The work of framing was usually triggered by contradictions in society on issues such as economic development, sustainability, employment and social inclusion or access to certain technologies, but also ideas and opportunities for overcoming these problems. With our case studies arising through different socio-historic conditions, cultural ideas and problems in a variety of locations, we expected each of our movements to frame its approach to innovation and mobilization in different ways. Moreover, Chapter 2 anticipated framings being under pressure to evolve over time, in the light of experience and social learning within a movement, and also in response to changing circumstances in the wider world.

Our case studies identified a need for flexibility in movement framings and a degree of plurality in order to accommodate heterogeneity of motivations, values and interests among the alliances making up the movements; but the flexibility and plurality of these framings had, at the same time, to retain sufficient coherence and consistency to hold movements together and keep them working effectively. Table 9.1 summarizes the contexts and framings for each of the grassroots innovation movements that we studied. While the comparison affirms some of the variety and context sensitivity of framing that we expected, there are also broad similarities

TABLE 9.1 A summary of the context and framings for grassroots innovation in each case study movement

Movement	Context	Framings
Socially useful production in the UK (mid-1970s to mid-1980s)	Manufacturing decline, new automating machine tools, job losses Restructuring and relocation of industrial capital in services, finance and overseas Grassroots socialism in trade unions, municipalities, communities and polytechnics New social movements for peace, environment and women Gradual rise and institutionalization of neoliberal ideology	Design, innovation and production for social purpose and environment rather than profit and military application Workplace democracy and skill-enhancing, worker-centred technologies Participatory design, community involvement, democratization of technology development Technological agitprop, alternative economic strategy, state support
Appropriate technology in South America (1970s and 1980s)	Political upheaval, social mobilization, state repression Structuralist ideas for autonomous development cede to neoliberal ideology Debt crises, economic restructuring, loss of industrial sectors Rise of development NGOs and environmental concerns Activism in social projects, in contrast to full-out political mobilizations	Technology of a form and scale appropriate as a tool for autonomous development by local communities Practical projects as site for developing social conscience and solidarity Community participation, traditional knowledge and indigenous rights Technology as a tool for development with attention to resource use/environmental impacts
People's Science Movement in India (1970s to present)	Indian freedom movements, Gandhian village self-sufficiency, Nehruvian heavy industrialization Science policy for 'weaker sections' in society Debates about opening Indian markets and introducing intellectual property regimes Social movements of urban and rural poor, environment	Enhancing indigenous resources and capabilities with introduction of appropriate science and technology Cooperatives and collective production systems at district scale Local area planning, organization and coordination Upgrading traditional production sectors and organizing their workers (e.g. food processing, handicrafts, construction, energy)

(continued)

TABLE 9.1 *(continued)*

Movement	Context	Framings
Hackerspaces, fablabs and makerspaces (2000s to present)	Free software movement and later, hacker and maker movements Accessible digital fabrication technologies Silicon Valley entrepreneurship and technological optimism Precarious employment, co-working, freelancing and social entrepreneurism Horizontality, peer-to-peer collaboration, openness	Open source, peer-to-peer collaborative design and fabrication Personalized manufacturing, mass customization, skills and entrepreneurship Democratizing technology and the right to hack, fix and repurpose Mobilizing for sustainable developments Decentralizing manufacturing
Social Technology Network in Brazil (2000s to 2010s)	Social movement links to Workers Party, Lula presidency from 2004, and ensuing state support for participatory development and solidarity economy Debt crises, uneven economic growth, persistent inequalities Corporate social responsibility funds and programmes Awareness of earlier generation of appropriate technologies	Moving beyond isolated appropriate technology projects Social technology as participatory process of empowering communities for local development Redesigning science policy agenda to include a programme for social technology Portfolio of specific social technologies suited for wide-scale replication and appropriation Democratizing technology and developing tools for solidarity
Honey Bee Network in India (1980s to present)	Inventiveness and wealth of traditional knowledge among India's grassroots Frustration with development professions appropriating knowledge from grassroots Neoliberal opening of India in 1990s and 2000s New innovation discourse and institutions in India	Giving due recognition to grassroots inventiveness and knowledge Prevailing innovations institutions repurposed for individual grassroots innovators Scouting for inventions, attribution of IPRs, resources for commercialization, support with marketing Fair and just rewards for grassroots inventiveness

in the extent to which framings address grassroots innovation as an act of ingenuity, empowerment or transformation.

We return to these common issues in framing later. Here we briefly summarize some of the more particular details of the framings in each case study. We do so in a way that highlights issues raised by the case studies and which those movements have to confront, including: the breadth and ambition of movement framings; whether to align with opportunities presented by institutional changes or to oppose their limitations; how movements reluctant to adopt explicit framings risk imposition of de facto framing; and how framings that may not achieve all their ambitions in practice nevertheless generate innovative practices that do endure, because they make sense to others beyond the movement. Framing issues are also important because they inform the choice of spaces and strategies pursued by movements for the development of grassroots innovation.

As explained below, movement framings went far beyond narrow and technical matters of grassroots innovation, and situated immediate and practical activities within broader visions for alternative pathways for economic and social development. While these gave purpose, meaning and motivation for supporting grassroots innovation, the realization of these broader visions involved an ambition and agency that was much harder for movements to attain. Movements contained both idealistic and pragmatic framings whose mutual accommodation was not easy.

Framing appropriate technology

The appropriate technology (AT) movement in South America illustrates how a narrow framing of technology development that had been circulating internationally was adopted and fleshed out within broader framings for social change in some contexts. While the framing of appropriate technologies as development interventions to be adopted by poor, rural communities existed, another of the AT frames (one of autonomy and economic self-reliance) resonated well with activists seeking to develop new forms of social activism that avoided a direct confrontation with the state. In this case, an international framework for technology and development resonated with the particular situation of networks of activists in the region; and then the domestication of these ideas led to a reframing that emphasized participation, autonomy and ideas of direct democracy, which were emerging among social movements in the region more generally under conditions of political and economic crisis. Moreover, many proponents of AT in South America sought to combine the rejection of mass industrialization as a pathway to development and the subsequent design of small, low-cost technologies with the need to retrieve indigenous knowledge in rural development. Largely operating away from urban centres, these framing ideas found particular expression in the development of agroecology, although housing and energy for rural communities were also foci of activity.

Some of the regionally inspired aspects to framings of AT have tended to be forgotten with time. What is recalled, if anything, is emblematic AT objects and guidebooks, and less the attempts at cultivating, say, participatory processes for empowering communities. There may be something in an easy caricature that casts appropriate technologists negatively, as seeing solutions to the complexities of development in simple technology fixes (Smith et al., 2014). But Chapter 4 also points to an overlooked aspect to the movement framing; one that sees grassroots innovation as requiring processes of community participation and empowerment to adapt tools and develop meaningful solutions locally, precisely because specific technology projects reveal and make tangible the complexities of development. This became increasingly apparent to many AT activists as the movement developed.

Framing social technologies

Attention to process and empowerment, as much as designed objects, is something the Social Technology Network (STN) picked up and tried to emphasize from the outset in its framing of grassroots innovation. Some proponents had direct experience from prior AT efforts. They were aware of the pressure to frame grassroots innovation as appropriate devices for diffusion among poorer communities, and they sought to resist this by emphasizing the social processes of building commitment, input and organization in each community where a social technology (ST) would be developed. Such a framing required a programmatic approach for publicly supporting grassroots innovation, rather than isolated development projects led by experts; which meant winning substantial backing and support from the state. For a period, during the early years of the Lula administration, this seemed possible. However, support did not extend as far as reorienting science, technology and innovation agendas and institutions towards the aims, approach and methods of the ST movement. A different framing for the STN became dominant, held by government and corporate associates, which saw ST as installing technologies for specific social development projects (rather like earlier international framings for AT). Tensions between these different framings led to the fragmentation of the network, and support for STs reduced to the development of devices, with much less emphasis on the social processes of community development and empowerment.

In neither the AT nor the ST cases were the broader, more radical framings of grassroots innovation able to hold. They mobilized insufficient power for instituting new social and economic relations in innovation. They were unable to garner support with sufficient reach and duration to change institutions. Rather, narrower framings that appealed to key financial backers, and which did not challenge or disrupt too much, were the ones that dominated in practice. That said, there was recognition of the more radical framings, and these did at least motivate considerable achievements of a more modest kind (such as helping to establish principles and practices for agroecology in the case of AT, or the adoption of participatory construction for rainwater harvesting in the case of social technologies).

The difficulties of finding autonomy from donor agencies in the case of AT, or state politics in the case of STs, ultimately meant that narrower framings had to be accepted as part of the conditions for supporting projects. Activists could still pursue their own framings within the scope permitted by support programmes, but the parameters were nevertheless defined for them and required negotiation and compromise. Putting into practice the more radical frames for grassroots innovation requires powerful allies, capable of restructuring the social, economic and political relations of innovation. Whether, as in some of the other cases, we are talking about collaborative peer production, more democratic control over technology development and use, or freely available goods and services for people to access and make livelihoods from – all these framings raise challenging questions about the ownership or control of critical resources, access to institutions, control over investment decisions and the ability to shape markets and distribute the value created in grassroots innovation.

Framing people's science

The framings for grassroots innovation in the People's Science Movement (PSM) emerged amid charged political debates about the directions of development in post-colonial India, as well as critical reflections among scientific activists upon the shortcomings of public programmes promoting both high- and low-technology pathways for development. Gandhian visions for village self-sufficiency contrasted with Nehruvian images of modernizing India through high-technology industrialization. Meanwhile, policy programmes for engaging science for poverty reduction were disappointing. Whether through knowledge to upgrade traditional village technologies or by cleverly downsizing industrial high technologies, science and technology programmes were finding the sustainable diffusion of innovations to be elusive. The PSM recognized a failure in both approaches to build the 'social carriers' for pro-poor technologies: the groups who would actually put technology designs to productive, sustainable use. It was this idea that informed the way it framed the articulation of science, technology and innovation with development. The viable practice of any innovative technique (upgraded, downsized or entirely new) simultaneously required a coordinated construction of local economic linkages upstream and downstream of the technique, in order to create a production system at district scale. And, given the social values of the activists, the organization of these necessary social carriers was sought through cooperation among workers in the districts that saw their future in such technology systems.

India has transformed dramatically in political and economic terms during the period in which the PSM has been active. Gradually, the hold of Gandhian and Nehruvian development models has given way to policies that align with the global rise of neoliberalism. The context for grassroots innovation has been changing. Markets for the kinds of goods and services provided by rural producers have become increasingly competitive. Foreign investment promotes more concentrated industrial production and services. Indian economic leaders look to develop activity overseas. And intellectual property regimes exist for knowledge production and use. Yet the issues motivating the PSM persist, whether in terms of continuing rural and urban poverty, insufficient attention to local development needs by science and technology institutions or environmentally destructive development pathways.

Persistent problems under changed circumstances raise the question of whether, deeper down, the surface changes are reinforcing the same old structural injustices and development traps. Unsurprisingly, the PSM is critical of the structural changes under neoliberalism. Nevertheless, its framings for cooperative organization in district-scale grassroots innovation have to address these changing circumstances (Kaplinsky, 2011). The PSM can draw on long periods of practical experience in working with grassroots innovation, yet the way it frames that work has to continually remain valid for the new realities and stay persuasive for the social movements, smaller-scale producers, political leaders, public administrators and scientists and technologists that the movement seeks as allies.

Framing honey bees

Experience in the contrasting framing of the Honey Bee Network (HBN) indicates different dilemmas in flexibility towards new contexts. India during the 1990s and early 2000s was not alone in experiencing cultural, political and economic disruption under the increasing reach of neoliberal ideology, which extended to ideas for commercially oriented science and technology in market-based developments (Moore et al., 2011). Institutions for patents, venture capital and commercial innovation gained broader recognition within science and technology institutions in many countries. Some grassroots innovation movements have seen opportunities in these transformations, such as in the case of the HBN, but also hackerspaces, fablabs and makerspaces. Ideas for socially entrepreneurial activity have emerged that emphasize the capacity (and the right) of the grassroots to secure ownership over their own innovations. Some grassroots innovation movements have framed themselves within the new institutions for science and technology and used the associated institutional legitimacy to demand recognition and space for grassroots innovation.

A key framing for the HBN, for example, has been to recognize the wealth of local and indigenous knowledge among even the poorest populations, which are capable of creating ingenious tools for improving their lives, and whose wider social and market value justifies an economic return to the innovator. A central thread in the network is to see grassroots entrepreneurship as boosting local development through fostering ingenuity, which can be supported by providing proper recognition to local inventions and by turning them into marketable innovations. The HBN created new possibilities by aligning with policy discourses favourable to innovation. Founder Anil Gupta saw new potential in the economic and institutional reforms of his country for realizing long-standing and deep-seated commitment to traditional knowledge communities and grassroots inventiveness in rural India. That potential meant reframing ideas for commercializing intellectual property, promoted by an emerging political and business establishment as something relevant for India's rural populations, and through which their rich knowledge base could prosper. In this view, the grassroots had a right to benefit from new innovation policy based in intellectual property, incubating innovation and marketing support.

The HBN made strenuous efforts to catalogue grassroots inventiveness and demonstrate the knowledge that pervades rural India, building impressive databases. Skilfully combining the extensiveness of this resource with inspiring individual examples, the network persuasively framed this activity in a way that gained institutional support for grassroots innovators. The National Innovation Foundation (NIF) and regional organizations aim to link promising grassroots innovators with the apparatus for securing intellectual property rights, incubating product development and expert help with marketing. This framing for grassroots innovation has proved popular with policymakers.

Yet research suggests that grassroots inventors are just as motivated by intrinsic concerns for self-realization and family and community well-being; they do not always wish to become entrepreneurs (Bhaduri and Kumar, 2011). Not all grassroots innovation is enclosed within utility-seeking motivation. Moreover, in going with the grain of prevailing innovation institutions, and undoubtedly winning extraordinary recognition for grassroots inventiveness, the framing is nevertheless susceptible to criticism similar to that attached to the institutional approaches with which it aligns. Questions exist about the extent to which any benefits trickle out to the wider community and just how socially inclusive the reliance is upon individual entrepreneurship. While the Honey Bee framing of grassroots innovation has unlocked the inventiveness of individuals, it is open to argument how this will lead to local development gains beyond the beneficiary innovators. The HBN recognizes the challenge. A more community-oriented framing of grassroots innovation also exists within the movement. The movement is trying to keep the collaborative and collective features of grassroots innovation in the frame also, by talking about peer-to-peer networking among innovators in some of its manifestos (Smith, 2013). However, this framing of innovation within the movement, seeing grassroots knowledge and creativity as a commons, sits awkwardly with the framing that is institutionalizing more conventional marketing activities through the supportive measures of the NIF and others.

Framing hackerspaces, fablabs and makerspaces

At the heart of the HBN is a quite straightforward, immediate and alluring idea: that there is a wealth of knowledge, creativity and inventiveness in rural India. The heterogeneous collection of hackerspaces, fablabs and makerspaces holds in common another straightforward, immediate and alluring idea. This time it is the idea that giving tools to people can unlock radical capabilities for self-development and social change, and especially the increasingly accessible and networked tools of digital design and fabrication. A variety of framings are brought to bear in trying to work out how to make the most of this potential. What is striking is how many of those framings take their point of departure from the same analogy, namely the origins of personal computing, free software and open, networked culture. Yet that common genesis in free software and open culture is framed in different ways and taken in different directions.

For some, the buzz about being able to make almost anything in these *unstructured* spaces, and getting involved in all sorts of fun projects that participants deem to be important, is the whole point. Any further framing of the purposes of these workshops, beyond their being open-ended spaces for experimentation, collaboration and prototyping, risks forcing them into particular moulds and pushes them in specific directions. Framing the purposes and potential of workshops too strongly imposes structure upon an unstructured space. There is much to this argument. Ironically, many of the framings of hacking, making and fixing identified in Chapter 6 depend on an ability to keep things open and free from structures. People need the freedom to play with issues, designs and technologies in order to be able to engage in the debating and doing of any further possibilities, whether those possibilities are framed as democratization of technology, peer-to-peer collaborative production, participatory design in digital futures, sustainable developments or becoming entrepreneurs and workers in new, decentralized webs of manufacturing.

Yet we live in a structured world. Inattention towards these 'external' social structures could mean that it is they that ultimately come to frame community-based workshops by default. Clearer, more articulate framings of grassroots innovation have the advantage of providing a measure against which to continually open up activities to critical reflection about possibilities, limitations and challenges. In the case of hackerspaces, fablabs and makerspaces, new-found popular accessibility to versatile design and fabrication technologies in societies has the feel of an answer looking for the right question. Access to these tools has historically been the privilege of manufacturing enterprises; and under circumstances where the terms of access to capital for development, the availability of infrastructure for prototyping, the ability to influence the forces that shape markets, the channels forming aesthetic sensibilities and so forth all present a highly uneven terrain whose structure is simultaneously cultural, organizational, economic, political and technological, and in which some innovating actors find themselves better positioned than others. Arguably, if the goal is transformative change, it is important for this grassroots innovation movement to better articulate framings that push against these structural conditions, and orient its activity towards broader purposes, such as democratizing technology and trying to insert the normative goals of cultivating sustainable developments, and to thereby structure workshop activities accordingly. Otherwise any potential in giving tools to people risks becoming just another consumption activity within the consumer societies where makerspaces are proving popular.

Putting the criticism crudely, people come to the workshops, adapt a design accessed freely over the web, use open hardware tools, but only to make a plastic object that essentially serves little purpose beyond being a memento of a fun afternoon in the workshop. Other makers are developing enterprising technologies and products, and workshops are cultivating grassroots ingenuity that could lead to economic activity – but it is viewed as entrepreneurship within a conventional start-up business frame. Many firms are noticing maker activity too and are marketing targeted materials, designs, guides and tools for that activity. Other firms seek to appropriate outputs by linking with more entrepreneurially inclined makers and helping them to get to market. There are also education and training institutions interested in adapting these workshops to training people for work and entrepreneurship. Seen in this light, framings for hackerspaces, fablabs and makerspaces appear really important because they situate access to tools within a social frame of reference. In Chapter 6 we saw examples that were trying to frame workshops in that way as hubs for cultivating sustainable developments locally – a framing relevant to this book. In trying to pursue their goals, however, these framings struggled to articulate the cultural, social, economic and political relations implied.

Framing socially useful production

The movement for socially useful production had a relatively strong framing of the structural issues it was addressing. Informed by the socialist political commitments of core activists, the grassroots innovations it promoted were framed within alternative industrial and economic strategy. The state was positioned as playing an active role, whether through legislating for workplace democracy, administering popular planning, socializing markets for products or instigating participatory design. At the municipal scale, sympathetic leaders at the Greater London Council (GLC) were able to implement these roles, most noticeably with the London Technology Networks and the Enterprise Board's commitment to cooperative enterprises. Movement framings were informed by an unusual amalgam of grassroots trade union activity, organizing the shop-floor insights of skilled manufacturing workers, and social demands from movements for peace, environment and community activism. The root causes to their varied problems were identified in capitalist economic relations, whose insatiable demand for accumulation did not appear to align with social good and environmental sustainability, alienated people from their own labour and were mired in a self-serving military–industrial complex that, in the context of the Cold War, had a self-interest in perpetuating insecurity through weapons development.

The technological agitprop of socially useful production rested in developing devices, practices and facilities that anticipated more directly democratic social, economic and political relations: popular prototyping, community workshops, cooperative enterprises and participatory economic planning. Realization of the broader, structurally aware framing required support, commitment and alignments from more powerful social actors in politics, the state and society. But sufficient support did not materialize. The Labour Party hierarchy, both when in government and in opposition, did not embrace the grassroots movement, neither did leaders in the established trade unions; and, ultimately, neither did the electoral system, which brought the Conservatives to power in the general election of 1979. Popular as the movement may have been, it was not powerful enough to shape political and economic transformations in the UK, which were eventually won by the forces of neoliberalism.

Despite being overwhelmed by wider social changes, the framings of socially useful production nevertheless contained very practical elements that enabled people to get on and do things and be innovative. There were tensions between those who were pragmatic towards the opportunities available (and which narrowed over time) and those who wanted to continue with a political programme of resistance to structural changes (see Eglash and Banks, 2014). Ultimately, however, the movement found itself exhausted by swimming against the political and economic tide. Activists moved on. The ideas, arguments and examples they provided – for participatory design, socially useful products and thinking about social questions of work, gender and environment in technology development – did not disappear. Rather, they dispersed and morphed into other spheres, whether in academia, community development, local economic development or elsewhere, and the earlier expression within socially useful production became a distant memory, forgotten and overlooked.

Framing grassroots innovation: ingenuity, empowerment, transformation

A remarkable and gratifying aspect of research on these diverse framings and histories of grassroots innovation has been the positive reception, whenever and wherever we presented the case studies, among audiences with different backgrounds, involvements and interests. Always the curiosity shown in the experiences we have reported from elsewhere has been heartening. We have publicized these cases in blogs, articles, presentations, events, radio interviews, talks and workshops and through social media. One particularly striking example has been the case of the movement for socially useful production, which seems to have struck a chord with hackers, makers and fixers today. We have received many invitations to talk about this history and it has been cited in articles about hackers, makers and fixers (e.g. Holman, 2015). Our impression is that the familiarity of the practices being pursued back then, as well as some shared ideals, albeit framed in different ways socially and politically speaking, all works to provide an enchanting and informative story. There is, simultaneously, recognition of shared struggles, connection with similar social roots and visions, interest in the differences, and also questions about what lessons diverse experiences hold for activities today. The same has been true for discussions about the AT movement in South America, and with the PSM and the HBN in India. Each provides beneficial vantage points from which people can take bearings and reflect on their own involvement in grassroots innovation (see also Chapter 10).

Part of this appetite, we think, derives from deep-seated features of framings that are common to all the grassroots innovation movements we have studied. Those features are the extent to which grassroots innovation activity is framed by a movement as a question of promoting ingenuity, community empowerment or structural transformation. That is to say, whether grassroots innovation is framed principally as the generation of novel initiatives, as a process for empowering local communities or as pointing to structural problems in conventional innovation institutions that require wider transformation. Drawing on our case studies, we finish our analysis of framings by elaborating these common fundamentals.

The *grassroots ingenuity* framing emphasizes processes that generate novel initiatives, products and services, and aims to develop and diffuse the objects produced. Support is framed and organized in a way that works to such ends. Grassroots innovation is seen mainly in a technical light, and the concern is with improving performance in such a way that the innovation can be rolled out and scaled up beyond the original grassroots setting, whether through commercialization in markets, as a good development practice in public programmes, or as an emblematic activity and symbol for social changes sought by social movements. Under the ingenuity framing, innovations move from inside grassroots activity outwards: it is in the ingenuity and knowledge of individuals and groups with respect to specific issues and solutions that the process begins; and support seeks to build on that ingenuity, improve the specific innovation and help it spread.

A *grassroots empowerment* framing is more interested in cultivating the enabling social relationships and material conditions in the local communities where grassroots innovation takes place. Innovation is seen as an opportunity for inducing a broader range of capability building among local communities that can be deployed for subsequent local development activities beyond the specific issue and innovation activity. With an emphasis on empowerment, so the framing may also draw in tools and resources whose origins may have begun outside a grassroots setting, but whose appropriation and adaptation is in the hands of local communities, and with those local communities retaining control over the process and decisions on how to distribute the benefits.

Framing grassroots innovation as *transformation* is borne of recognition that, in trying to do things differently, these activities actually confront and make visible structural issues of economic power, uneven development, political inequalities and social standing. The grassroots innovation activity is seen as pointing to alternative possibilities, were such structural limitations to be overcome. The grassroots innovation deliberately challenges norms and expectations. For example, there is resistance to the enclosure of the innovation through intellectual property, or its reduction to a good or service to be scaled up. Instead, there is an insistence upon the innovation, however imperfectly, to be an exploration in, say, a more democratic way of developing technology, or more inclusive innovation processes, or creating a knowledge commons that is accessible to everyone. Moreover, in pointing to limitations under conventional innovation institutions and incumbent development pathways, this framing emphasizes critical reflection with regard to the criteria against which good innovation performance is assessed, and the attribution of limitations to conditions in the wider institutional and social context rather than inherent to the grassroots innovation activity. Alternative institutional arrangements are informed and conceived by these wider transformational aspirations for the grassroots innovation that would enable it to flourish. This framing identifies the operation of power in setting the terms for innovation, and mobilizes alliances that contribute to transformational political programmes for structural change and that open up alternative development pathways of the kind that the more critical grassroots innovators anticipate.

Obviously, these three basic framings are elaborated, specified and expressed in different ways by each grassroots innovation movement. Each movement also has to negotiate how to balance its emphasis and focus between these basic framings. In principle, each complements the other. Empowered local communities ought to be better able to express their ingenuity and may seek to restructure institutions, while restructured innovation institutions responsive to grassroots criticism would be in better shape to support plural alternative development pathways. In practice, as we have seen in our case studies and in the discussion above, negotiating these framings in ways that build alliances and draw in institutions is not straightforward. We also see in the cases that science, technology and innovation institutions tend to have great affinity with the ingenuity framing, due to its greater interpretive flexibility, compared to the more demanding empowerment and transformation framings. The balance between these different framings will also influence where and how movements try to create spaces for practical activities, or the spaces into which they get invited. Business and policy spaces promoting inclusive innovation, for example, are likely to be much more open to movements that emphasize ingenuity, and even empowerment, compared to those seeking structural transformations. Movements that seek the latter are likely to look for spaces elsewhere. On this point, we now turn to consider the spaces and strategies that grassroots movements create and through which they seek to realize their framings.

Spaces and strategies for grassroots innovation

Spaces and strategies are those locations and coordinated actions that movements use to promote and cultivate grassroots innovation. While broader contexts were found to be generative of grassroots movements, in the sense that they were problematically failing to attend to some need or social value that grassroots innovators were addressing, our concept of spaces looks for situations conducive to the grassroots development of responses and solutions. In Chapter 2 we anticipated these situations arising across different physical, institutional and discursive spaces. We also considered the various kinds of action repertoires that might strategically open up and claim more space for practical grassroots innovation activity. Table 9.2 provides a summary of the various spaces and strategies we found in each of our case studies.

Obviously, an important space for all the case studies is the grassroots: the spaces that local communities inhabit and where activists operate. The grassroots spaces we came across included villages, factories, farms, neighbourhoods, community centres and street corners. These spaces are not simply physical, but are also social: the community relations and cultural resources that can be harnessed for the purposes of grassroots innovation, and through which supportive movements can find a base and develop. It is in these spaces that needs are identified and aspirations arise, but it

TABLE 9.2 Spaces and strategies for grassroots innovation

Movement	Spaces opened up	Strategic activities
Socially useful production in the UK (mid-1970s to mid-1980s)	Trade union facilities, events, organizational apparatus Factory shop floor – borrowing tools and resources Neighbourhoods Polytechnics – staff and buildings Local authorities – policies and funds Community workshops	Prototyping – technological agitprop, product banks, designs Media publicity – TV programmes, newspaper reports, books Trade union organization – motions, policies, conferences, visits, meetings Lobbying government and industrial action Linking to social movements and community activism Training people into new technologies, e.g. women into computing
Appropriate technology in South America (1970s and 1980s)	Dedicated development centres for appropriate technology Villages and field trials International development conferences, programmes and networks Support from public research institutes Links with university research groups	Prototyping Consultancy and production services Training appropriate technologists in the region Student research projects Community development initiatives Manuals and guidebooks Publishing magazines Grants from international development agencies Centre visits by high-profile national and international figures (Colombia)
People's Science Movement in India (1970s to present)	Research institutes and technology development centres Villages, field trials and cooperative systems Voluntary organizations Sympathetic governments and departments (e.g. programmes in Kerala) Annual conferences and regional meetings Processing facilities	Creating social carriers, e.g. through resource mapping, assessing village capabilities, organizing for cooperatives Project grants and public rural development programmes Consultancy and production services Product development and social marketing Science literacy campaigns

(continued)

TABLE 9.2 (continued)

Movement	Spaces opened up	Strategic activities
Hackerspaces, fablabs and makerspaces (2000s to present)	Community workshops Neighbourhoods Online networks of makers, hackers and geeks Education institutions – universities and schools Libraries and civic organizations Co-working spaces and innovation incubators Public programmes	Collaborative design and prototyping Meet-ups, conferences, events Training activities and networks Online networking, offline meet-ups Emblematic projects and specialist fields, e.g. open source furniture
Social Technology Network in Brazil (2000s to 2010s)	Villages Universities Local authority programmes Field trials and extension services Corporate social responsibility	Funding programmes from government and corporate foundations Awards and databases of social technologies Research, development and training in reapplication of technologies Emblematic initiatives (e.g. One Million Cisterns, PAIS) Meetings and conferences for network members
Honey Bee Network in India (1980s to present)	Villages Academia and student volunteers Research institutes International conferences and regional networks Business interested in licensing inventions and marketing products	Scouting and databases Product development and intellectual property provision Media publicity Challenges for engineering and science students Competitions and awards for innovations Micro–venture capital and business partnerships

is also where innovative ideas are discussed, and where initiatives develop through prototyping, field trials and the mobilization of results. Grassroots media for communicating and sharing knowledge and practices were important in all the cases, whether operating through newsletters, public meetings, noticeboards, meetings or internet-based social media.

We also saw protagonists in all the cases taking advantage of opportunities beyond the grassroots and seeking to open more space by forging alliances with sympathetic actors, whether working in research centres, trade unions, social movements, companies or local authorities, for example. The forms and level of supportive protection for grassroots innovation in these spaces are the result of the relationships negotiated with allies beyond the grassroots. Extra space for doing grassroots innovation was also sought by aligning activities with institutions in order to benefit from potential opportunities, such as positioning grassroots innovation as a worthy recipient of support through public policy programmes, or corporate social responsibility funds, or NGO campaigns, university research or business investment.

Each of these spaces was offered different kinds of resource and opportunity. The facilities made available at a research institute, for instance, are first and foremost dedicated to improving a prototype and validating its technical performance standards, but grassroots innovation groups also might reciprocally provide experimental spaces for student research and training (e.g. the case of the eco-community Gaviotas with various universities in Colombia). Innovation incubation centres provide services for developing business plans and marketing strategies. A local development programme might provide platforms for coordinating links with related economic sectors. The campaigns of social movement organizations provide a platform for advancing broader framings concerning, say, social inclusion, alternative economic development or democratization of technology (e.g. the motions at trade union conferences for industrial democracy framings of socially useful production). Social movement platforms provide political and social resources which are supportive towards grassroots innovation that is emblematic of the social values of concern, and which work to advance the social performance of grassroots innovation in ways quite different from the resources of, say, a research laboratory, which serve to validate and improve technical performance. It is the breadth and variety of resources that is important.

Rarely are the spaces for cultivating grassroots innovation found readily. They have to be actively opened up and occupied through negotiation, persuasion and validation. Some of the activities by which this is realized include prototyping; media campaigns; research, analysis and demonstration; scouting, documenting, awards schemes and other forms of recognition; community development and mobilization; education and awareness raising; and lobbying.

Such activities involve listening to needs, articulating ideas, mobilizing capabilities and resources, and spreading awareness about grassroots innovation. These activities work through networks of actors that seek to operate across these different spaces and that connect different actors. Indeed, it is this activity – pushing beyond the grassroots – that transforms isolated grassroots innovation initiatives into a movement for grassroots innovation. What we find across the cases is just how closely spaces and activities for the provision of material resources and opportunities for doing grassroots innovation are intertwined with arenas for promoting ideas, analysis and arguments about grassroots innovation. In this way, practical and symbolic commitments can be mobilized for working on grassroots innovation across a greater number of locations or to develop activities and processes for helping to spread grassroots innovation.

However, the activities listed in Table 9.2 do not really indicate their strategic *purposes* in terms of what precisely these strategic activities are seeking to achieve for grassroots innovation. Here the framings of the grassroots innovation movement are important – in giving purpose and direction. So, for example, a strategic activity that we see in some cases is to forge links with educational institutions and bring grassroots innovation into training activities. But strategies vary in terms of whether they furnish grassroots innovation as an ingenious project for learners in existing courses, or whether they are training to empower the community involved, or whether a framing is being followed that is trying to transform training for entirely different purposes and processes for training. Even prototyping, common to all grassroots innovation movements, is put to varied strategic purposes, and consequently takes on different forms. We have seen in the case of the HBN, for example, the development of sophisticated processes for taking an initial grassroots innovation from the field and through to product development. Prototyping here is informed by a grassroots ingenuity framing and consequently focused in product development for marketing. Activists in the movement for socially useful production, in contrast, included a technological agitprop strategy towards prototyping: in seeking technologies neglected by industry, activists were pointing to the deeper causes of that neglect, which they believed to derive from production for profit rather than social use. Technology network managers in the movement saw prototyping as much about building awareness and local alliances over social issues. They wanted to transform manufacturing as much as prototype the development of a physical artefact. The PSM similarly pursued more expansive prototyping strategies, in this case for developing regional systems and social carriers around the technology as part of local economic development. In both these cases, while the development of the prototype into a product remained a goal, activists saw prototyping more politically, as anticipating alternative production systems and building cooperative alliances for their realization.

The variety of strategies has implications for the kinds of spaces that movements seek out for grassroots innovation, and the ways they occupy those spaces effectively. As with framings, however, it is possible to discern across our cases some deeper patterns amid the diversity, and which underpin and give dynamism to that variety. We see the fundamental choice resting between the pursuit of deeper strategies of *insertion* within existing institutions of science, technology and innovation or strategies of *mobilization* to transform institutions (see also Fressoli et al., 2014). These two strategic orientations are contrasted in Table 9.3. In practice, all grassroots innovation

TABLE 9.3 Insertion and mobilization strategies for grassroots innovation movements

Salient features	Insertion	Mobilization
Relationship with institutions	Fit and conform to institutional requirements	Stretch and transform institutions for new goals
Core spaces for activity	Institutional spaces, e.g. laboratories, marketing, standards institutes	Activist spaces, e.g. social movement arenas, campaigns, community projects
Sources of validation	Performance to established innovation criteria, e.g. competitiveness, market diffusion, scale or even environmental impact	Demonstration for alternative criteria, e.g. social inclusion, community development, sustainability – as defined by a community
Kind of work emphasized	Technical work: improving conventional standards of performance, economic efficiency, codified knowledge, best practices	Political work: embodying social values in the innovation, building supportive alliances, articulating a social vision
Underlying logic	Proprietary: enclosure and attribution of innovation to a group or individual	Commons: cooperation and sharing of innovation through open networks
Expression and ordering of grassroots innovation framings	Ingenuity is embodied in individuals; empowerment through entrepreneurial activity; transformation of grassroots into something more formal and business-like	Transformation of institutions is the aim; empowerment works through collective and cooperative activity; ingenuity is distributed across networks

movements have to negotiate an uneasy combination of strategies of insertion and strategies for mobilization to varying degrees.

Strategies of insertion seek to make grassroots innovation legible, useful and appropriable for existing institutions. The aim is to align with dominant development paths. The strategic work rests in moving the outputs of grassroots innovation activity into existing innovation systems and product markets. That involves making grassroots innovations more like conventional innovations. Looking across the case studies, we find various strategic activities for doing this work; these include fitting into conventional innovation spaces and playing by the rules of dominant institutions, whether that is meeting the requirements of standards agencies, satisfying the expectations of investment, conforming to cultures of credibility, aligning to the demands of market consumers and so forth. Strategy brings the innovator into contact with more conventional development and technology institutions, where expertise helps to formalize the innovation into a product that can diffuse more readily, or to transform it into a scaled-up form.

Strategies for mobilization seek to use grassroots innovation in the cultivation of alternative institutions for innovation and the transformation of conventional ways of addressing experimentation in development. The aim is to develop alternative pathways. The strategic work rests in building influential alliances that are capable of challenging dominant technologies, innovation practices, power relations and discourses, and able to advance the grassroots alternatives. That involves making grassroots innovations meaningful to the agents pursuing alternative developments, whether in social movements, government, research, education or business. From the case studies we see that various strategic activities are open to doing this mobilization work. These include the promotion of specific innovations as emblematic for social values marginalized in existing institutions, engaging grassroots innovation in the transformational spaces where social movements operate, demanding a rethink and a reordering of criteria and processes for socially selecting and shaping innovation, questioning the assumptions within existing institutions for innovation, providing training materials in the new approaches or recruiting support from heterodox scientists and technologists.

What we find in the cases is that these broad strategies are fine-tuned and used dynamically, depending upon the degree of openness and risks of capture presented by mainstream science, technology and innovation institutions. These strategies are also used in combination and dynamically to different degrees in the light of experience. In practice, grassroots innovation movements navigate between the poles in Table 9.3. So, for example, the HBN worked for many years at the careful mobilization of interest, legitimacy and commitment towards grassroots innovation framed as grassroots ingenuity. Such mobilization challenged the norms of conventional institutions by arguing and demonstrating that innovation was not the exclusive preserve of the scientific establishment, and that creative solutions with immediate development benefits existed amid the wealth of overlooked knowledge in rural India. Having pursued its mobilization strategy successfully, the HBN was then able to strategically insert grassroots innovation into innovation institutions, through the creation of organizations that secure intellectual property, product development and help with marketing for specific grassroots innovators.

Similarly, hackerspaces, fablabs and makerspaces have mobilized around enthusiasm for digital fabrication and making, and the grassroots ingenuity so revealed has attracted considerable attention and interest. However, there is no clear strategy across the movement over where to take developments and interest, with some organizations, such as the Fab Foundation, following an insertion strategy, while others, such as hackerspace networks, are concerned to retain autonomy. There are groups and activities interested in the more transformational possibilities anticipated in community workshops and accessible design and fabrication tools, including the decentralization and democratization of design and production, but mobilization strategies for doing this remain underdeveloped. Indeed, the capacity for different currents of activity within movements to switch from mobilization to insertion, or to pursue combinations at the same time, even contradictorily, can be regarded as a deliberate attempt to retain autonomy yet progress activity. In the case of the One Million Cisterns Programme supported by the STN, for instance, earlier episodes of mobilization resurfaced when the insertion of rainwater harvesting into policy programmes threatened to close down community development features. This involved turning back to activist spaces in order that policy aspirations to accelerate roll-out did not come at the expense of local participation.

In the PSM and the movement for socially useful production we have cases that are attached strongly to transformation framings, and so more inclined towards strategies of mobilization than insertion. Nevertheless, when opportunities arise there is willingness to enter institutional spaces and use ambiguities and flexibilities in those programmes to pursue more transformational strategies, as the PSMs did with technology and rural development programmes in India, and as socially useful production activists did with links to polytechnics. However, strategic options and conducive spaces can and do close down at times. The AT movement in South America struggled to outlast the decline in international donor funding for its projects, centres and networks. Arguably, regional autonomy was won through dependency on international programmes and spaces, and an inability or unwillingness to become more inserted into regional institutions left the movement vulnerable. Wider social, economic and political forces eventually closed down spaces and strategic options for the movement for socially useful production too.

The fate of some of the case studies reminds us that both the ability to open spaces and the strategic choices available will always be constrained by wider developments as well as being shaped by the movement framings in play. Grassroots innovation movements exist in a dynamic and recursive relationship between contexts, framings, spaces and strategies. In the final section of this chapter we consider what this means for the kinds of development pathways that grassroots innovation movements are able to open up.

Pathways

The pathways concept recognizes that for any given situation there exist a plurality of directions in which sustainable developments can be pursued. There can be dominant development pathways, whose framings of the world and alignment with institutions give the pathway considerable momentum, and which tend to draw upon and reinforce wider power relations in societies. An example is the pursuit of a green economy led by business leaders and political elites and reliant upon market-based approaches and a neoliberal ideological apparatus (Scoones et al., 2015). As such, dominant pathways become locked in to certain directions of development (Leach et al., 2010). When confronted with pressures for change, such as demands for more sustainable developments, then incremental reforms along the historical pathway are usually easier, as compared to wholesale redirections of development. A corollary of this is that these widely institutionalized pathways tend to lock out other, more radically different pathway directions. These alternative pathways may be no less viable, perhaps even more viable under certain sustainability criteria, but they are at a structural disadvantage as compared to the privileges of dominant pathways. Concerted and enduring pressure for change can reorder these situations and open things up to alternatives by eroding the efficacy and legitimacy of the institutions and power relations reproducing dominant pathways.

We have seen in our case studies how grassroots innovation movements become involved in pathways in a number of ways. This may happen by their own design, or through other groups beyond the grassroots co-opting solutions for incremental repair work to dominant development pathways, or through groups committed to more radical pathways seeing in grassroots solutions an embodiment of social values that bolsters momentum for the development directions they seek. In Chapter 2 we explained how this pathways concept was useful for analysing the contributions of grassroots innovation movements to alternative directions for sustainable developments.

In the preceding sections of this chapter we considered the different framings held by grassroots innovation movements and how they informed the kinds of development activity towards which the movements considered their innovations to be contributing. We subsequently looked at movement spaces and strategies for realizing these framings in material activity that contributes to development pathways. Table 9.4 brings the analysis together by indicating the spaces and strategies most evident under different framings of grassroots innovation movements, as well as their primary focus and emphasis of pathway activity. These affordances are not deterministic: indeed the cases point to dynamic coexistence.

The final row in Table 9.4 considers how grassroots innovation movements contribute to development pathways. To an extent, the development pathways that the movements seek for themselves can be discerned in their core framings: for example, regional economic systems based in cooperative relations of production (PSM); autonomous local development (AT movement and STN in South America); recognition and reward for grassroots ingenuity (HBN); commons-based peer production of goods and services (hackerspaces, fablabs and makerspaces); workplace and community participation in technology development and production (movement for socially useful production). However, the plurality of framings evident in each movement also introduced ambiguity over the precise directions. This was perhaps most evident in the case of hackerspaces, fablabs and makerspaces, where considerable difference exists in the directions in which one can take the core idea of workshops for giving tools to people. Departing in a direction less

TABLE 9.4 Framings, spaces and strategies, and pathways for grassroots innovation movements

Framing	Grassroots ingenuity	Grassroots empowerment	Grassroots transformation
Focus	Objects	Communities	Structures
Spaces	Spaces for prototyping	Spaces for building social capabilities	Spaces for social change
Strategies	Insertion: fit and conform	Mobilization for insertion: fit and stretch	Mobilizing for change: stretch and transform
Pathway activity	Contributing specific grassroots innovations	Contributing skills and capabilities to innovative communities	Contributing critical awareness and social organization for alternatives

Lessons for theory and practice **187**

radically visionary than commons-based peer production were those makers, hackers and fixers using the facilities to kick-start their own enterprises, or to build alliances with educational institutions and training programmes, and so become inserted into supplying future technology workers into labour markets. Much more radical are those framings that envisaged a democratization of manufacturing; through tools that lowered entry barriers for debating, prototyping and participating in key design decisions, and more directly through decentralized, commons-based production facilities. Others envisage such restructuring becoming suffused with the principles of sustainable development. However, the alliances for mobilizing these framings in the wider social world, and for building a strong social and economic base, remain unclear. Ambiguity was also evident in the STN, this time between a pathway seeking to empower and equip communities with the tools for their own self-development and a pathway focused more in the development of pro-poor technologies. Alliances in social development were appreciative of the former, but alliances with actors in science and technology institutions looked more to the latter.

An important feature here is that ambiguity over framings, spaces and strategies also opens up interpretative flexibility and practical possibilities for groups beyond the grassroots movement. These other groups become interested in particular features of the grassroots innovation activities and consider forming alliances around those features and getting involved for their own purposes. They also can help to open up new spaces and build different pathways by making use of some of the contributions of grassroots innovation movements. Table 9.5 catalogues in more detail some of the different contributions coming from the grassroots innovation movements studied. What is important here is to acknowledge the varied knowledge, artefacts, methodologies, infrastructures, actors, alliances, concepts and ideas being created by grassroots innovation movements.

The extent to which grassroots innovation contributions are taken up and used in pathways depends on the nature of the alliances forged with others, and even on

TABLE 9.5 Contributions to development pathways coming from grassroots innovation movements

Pathway contribution	Description	Examples
Knowledge	A variety of relevant contextual and technological knowledge is created through grassroots innovation activity	Knowledge about community aspirations and social needs Know-how in providing solutions to problems Critical knowledge about socio-economic limitations on grassroots activity
Artefacts	The development of novel objects and services	Solar heaters, water collectors, non-toxic leather tanning, water-cooled refrigerator, open source book scanner

(continued)

TABLE 9.5 *(continued)*

Pathway contribution	Description	Examples
Methodologies	Procedures for involving people in knowledge production, design and developments	Participatory design, agroecological techniques, open and collaborative prototyping, grassroots entrepreneurship, scouting, prizes
Infrastructures	Facilities for people to access tools and enter into development spaces	Workshops, training centres, databases of open designs, shared tools, skill-swapping events, mentoring facilities, web platforms
Actors and alliances	New identities and social relations formed through grassroots innovation activity	Grassroots innovator, innovation scout, citizen scientist, empowered community, solidarity through prototyping, mutual awareness
Concepts and ideas	New ways of thinking and approaching innovation activities and their purposes	Appropriate and social technologies, commons-based peer production, grassroots ingenuity, empowerment, transformation, democratizing innovation, socially useful production
Capabilities	The development of different types of organizational, material and social capabilities	Technical and innovation capabilities (e.g. learning to build a cistern, or to teach others to build); capabilities to lobby for institutional change or to claim spaces

co-options by groups uninterested in actually working with grassroots movements. Much depends on the power relations in play. This was particularly evident for the STN, where the ability of sponsors to assert a 'pro-poor' technology framing (as distinct to pro-poor empowerment framing) led to the disintegration and eventual suspension of the network. But even highly sympathetic allies beyond the movement can find themselves constrained. The GLC simply did not have sufficient capital to invest in the manufacture of socially useful products, even though the resources given to its Technology Networks enabled very open and democratic prototyping. Going further required a more powerful social and economic base for challenging the wider political economy of production in the UK.

This is not a criticism but, rather, a description of the situation. Grassroots innovation movements find themselves working within alliances where even better-resourced partners can find themselves constrained. So, for instance, where grassroots innovation movements may struggle to obtain resources to boost activity in the spaces they occupy, so better-resourced actors embedded in more formal institutions are constrained in the way they can open up their institutional spaces towards the grassroots and the terms under which they can deploy the resources available there. A typical example is where there is institutional pressure to focus on only the artefacts generated by grassroots innovation movements, and to scale up and roll out versions of these artefacts. As a result, other contributions coming from the grassroots innovation activity become excluded from consideration, rendered illegible and invisible by the scaling-up process (cf. Scott, 1999). Some of the knowledge, actors, methodologies and ideas created by the grassroots innovation may point beyond scaling up, for example, to thinking about how to scale down or further open institutions to a deeper, fuller and more extensive contribution by grassroots and other actors, such as through, say, moves to decentralizing innovation systems (Smith, 2014a). After all, an important feature in grassroots innovation is context sensitivity; and going with the grain of grassroots situations when wanting to transform while remaining locally relevant is a perpetual dilemma for grassroots innovation movements. Any abstraction and relocation of innovations to other contexts should be done carefully, lest the recipient grassroots groups lose control and autonomy over the process. Losing sight of this feature can contradict much of what the grassroots innovation was originally about. Despite this, there is considerable pressure among funders, donors, investors, researchers and so forth to diffuse technological innovations widely and rapidly, with less consideration for context-sensitive and capabilities-building processes.

Allied actors can be constrained for institutional reasons. The constraints are thus different, but felt no less keenly. New spaces open up through alliance building, but their characteristics have an important bearing on the kind of development pathway that is possible and just how enduring it is. Much depends on building the social and economic base for the pathway. Where expanding that base proves elusive, so the pathway diminishes. Grassroots innovation movements can have transformational aspirations, and they can contribute to radical pathways for alternative sustainable developments, but their contributions to sustainable developments cannot be judged based solely on whether their sought pathway was realized. After all, such an achievement is beyond the agency of the insertion and mobilization strategies of grassroots innovation movements alone. Instead, it is important to acknowledge the rich and varied ways in which *all* grassroots innovation movements have contributed to opening up new pathway possibilities and that their experiences also help to identify limitations and challenges too. Such multidimensional contributions to opening development pathways can be harnessed by wider alliances and other social actors and, as such, provide an important resource for societies, regardless of the particular pathway dynamics into which they become enrolled.

Conclusions

The contributions that grassroots innovation movements make to development pathways, actual and potential, are much more varied and work more broadly than the provision of specific innovative artefacts or services. Indeed, it is such breadth of potential that creates the pitfall of misattributing limitations exclusively to the grassroots innovation movements, when some of these limitations rest just as much in societal inabilities to make more use of grassroots innovations. We hope that the frameworks and lessons we have developed in this chapter can helpfully inform greater appreciation and effective support for grassroots innovations and their movements in societies.

The picture that emerges across the case studies is much more complex than the distinction between grassroots innovation movements and the institutions of science, technology and innovation that we drew initially in Table 1.1 in Chapter 1. Support and opportunities for grassroots innovation open up through much more messy, compromised and hybrid spaces, strategies and pathways. Grassroots innovation movements can be framed as ingenuity, empowerment and transformation, although in reality advocates play off and move through more than one of these framings. Combinations of strategies develop that oscillate between inserting grassroots activity into existing institutions for innovation, or mobilizing to try to transform those institutions. The spaces where this work happens can involve material activity such as prototyping, skills development and marketing; but they can just as importantly be discursive spaces for debate and criticism, or network spaces for organizing autonomous action. What becomes clear, we think, is that approaching grassroots innovation too narrowly and too instrumentally, as the insertion of ingenuity, for example, fails to fully understand these movements and therefore make the most of their social potential. This is a point that we consider more fully in the final chapter.

10
CONCLUSIONS

We opened this book with the POC21 eco-hackers at their innovation camp on the outskirts of Paris in August 2015. POC21 was a practical counter-initiative to the high-level climate talks at COP21 (21st Conference of the Parties to the UN Framework Convention on Climate Change). As COP21 finally reached an agreement affirming social constraint in anthropogenic climate change, this deal will have profound implications for social, economic and technological transformations. In this context, the ingenuity and empowerment of civil society activities such as POC21 become even more relevant (Stirling, 2015); especially since government and business commitments to emissions reductions, while welcome and significant, appear insufficient in themselves. POC21 activists recognize this and speak of building a movement for open source, low-carbon, zero-waste living.

As we finish this book in January 2016, the open source designs prototyped at POC21 and posted to the Instructables website have attracted over 500,000 visitors – far more people than are likely to read this book. This amazing amount of interest and excitement achieved in such a short time highlights the potential of grassroots innovation to become a force for sustainable development and social inclusion at a global scale. Not all the visitors will adapt and make the POC21 designs, although some will and all visitors will have been exposed to the underlying ideas and vision and may tell others, as we are doing now. Those that do work on the prototypes may do so collaboratively across hackerspaces, fablabs and makerspaces, and perhaps even at future innovations camps. Their experiences, adjustments and improvements will feed back to the design commons. Meanwhile, three of the POC21 prototyping teams have already joined forces and raised funds through a crowd-funding website in order to develop a portable, solar-powered water filtration device. The ambition is to develop this at various scales, including as a village-scale technology.

One thing we have done in this book is to take seriously initiatives such as POC21 in their aspiration for building a movement. Indeed, we argued that movements for grassroots innovation already exist, and have existed for a long time. It is important to consider initiatives such as POC21 alongside similar initiatives, and to appreciate the connections between the ideas and practices that each of them adapts and reinforces. By working through case studies of six movements from different places and times in this book, we can draw some conclusions for supporting and harnessing grassroots innovation movements. Our conclusions emphasize activity *beneath* and *beyond* the development of specific artefacts, whether technological or service oriented. It means noticing and valuing the alternative forms of innovation activity (including but not limited to new organizational forms and novel social relations) beneath the generation of specific artefacts. And it means looking beyond the insertion of these artefacts into conventional innovation processes and taking seriously the social visions that motivate grassroots innovators.

Making the most of grassroots innovation requires concerted political pressure on those with power over conventional innovation agendas. All the case studies have wanted to contribute to an opening up of alternative pathways for sustainable developments and a transformation of the social structures shaping innovation activity. Transformative innovation has been the aim: simultaneously restructuring the conditions, supports and forms of innovation in societies, and in doing so enabling alternative, more socially just and environmentally sustainable development pathways to open up. However, we have seen repeatedly over the case studies just how challenging it is to realize these broader, longer-term and more transformative aspirations. Overcoming those challenges requires grassroots innovation initiatives to build upon their movement qualities and to make greater demands for social structures that support transformational innovation in society. Consequently, in this concluding chapter we argue the importance of grassroots innovation movements for:

- opening up alternative forms of innovation;
- resisting narrow interpretations and institutional insertion;
- mobilizing for alternative pathways.

We discuss each conclusion in turn below. They are interlinked: each implies the others. Overall, they suggest that a systemic programme perspective is required for supporting grassroots innovation – whether from policymakers, multilateral agencies or NGOs. Until such programmes are won, we hope that these conclusions will prove useful for people busy working in grassroots innovation.

Opening up alternative forms of innovation

Grassroots innovation is an alternative *form* of innovation. It is not simply another source of innovation. It is important to acknowledge the work needed to open up spaces for doing (grassroots) innovation differently, to understand and appreciate the wide variety of activities involved in the generation of grassroots innovations and to support the aims and purposes in grassroots innovation.

The case studies in chapters 3 to 8 demonstrate how grassroots innovation is underpinned by motivations, sets of practices, working relations and networks that constitute novel forms for doing innovation. These alternative forms seek to incorporate new or overlooked actors, issues, sites, networks, processes and purposes. Table 9.5 in Chapter 9 summarized constituent features in alternative forms of innovation. Those features included different combinations of knowledge and relationships, such as abstract engineering knowledge with situated community knowledge. Methodologies have been developed for helping people to articulate their ideas and experiences and participate in a collective innovation process. Open infrastructures were created, such as workshops that give people access to tools, prototypes, networks and platforms for sharing designs and lessons, and arenas for debating development challenges and responses. New actors were created and alliances forged. Different concepts and ideas were advanced and put to work. And, crucially, capabilities were developed and shared.

The cultivation of knowledge, skills, capabilities, working practices and community development was found to be simultaneously a requirement for grassroots innovation and a measure of successful outcomes. Finance, materials, tools, prototyping facilities, even markets, are an important part of the story, but so too are participants' imaginaries, values, skills and social relations, which animate these materials and motivate other people to join in and put their ingenuity into grassroots innovation for sustainable developments. Even where the focal technologies did not work out, more often than not the efforts nevertheless cultivated capabilities and lessons that had a more enduring value.

It is important not to let the more visible artefacts eclipse what else goes on. For all its hard-won success in crowd-funding the development of promising prototypes, POC21 was also emblematic of the (more) democratizing form in which it sought to demonstrate technological ideas. POC21 signalled a desire for alternative forms of innovation and development. In doing so, it drew upon novel organizational forms and working processes for open source, commons-based peer production that other groups and networks have been developing and working with over many years (Kostakis and Bauwens, 2015). Originating in the free software movement, and now developing in the open hardware movement, this is an alternative form of innovation that is being developed, and not simply novel artefacts.

Similarly, aspirations for collaboration in these open, commons-based organizational forms find relevant methodologies in participatory design that have also developed over many years. The incorporation of different ideas, with negotiations between different viewpoints, and always acknowledging diverse contributions in participatory design, was originally intended to help to democratize design and innovation and cultivate a form of technological citizenship (Ehn, 1988). However, the alternative form has also been selectively co-opted for corporate purposes and specific methodologies have been adapted into user-centred product designs for assuring sales and customer loyalty (Asaro, 2000). Under appropriate conditions, participatory practices are still capable of assisting the grassroots with transformative innovation (Ehn et al., 2014). The point is that it is the overall form, with all its underlying social relations, political-economic implications and motivations that needs to be recognized and supported, otherwise methodologies are at risk of being co-opted for tapping into the grassroots (or 'users') as a source and input into otherwise unchanged innovation processes and development pathways.

Over the course of this book, we have seen how important is the overall robustness of the alternative organizational form as a whole, in the face of pressure to conform. That robustness derives from the social framings motivating people and guiding activity, the material and social spaces for experimentation, the strategies for occupying spaces and securing resources and the ability to build momentum capable of transforming political and economic relations such that truly participatory, collaborative and democratic forms of innovation can flourish.

Resisting narrow interpretations and institutional insertion

Throughout the book, we have noted periods of policy and business interest in grassroots innovation. We have seen with our case studies how institutional engagement with the grassroots tends towards a narrow framing. It is important to resist such narrowing, since it overlooks the social basis of innovations and denies the broader transformative aims of grassroots innovation movements.

Most recently, policy and business interest in grassroots initiatives has arisen through international discussion about inclusive innovation. Among the troubling features of an increasingly inequitable world is the exclusion of more and more people from the benefits of innovation and development. An inclusive innovation agenda, linked to ideas about inclusive economic growth, is intended as a response (OECD, 2015; UNDP, 2010; World Bank, 2012). Grassroots innovation activity has attracted interest as both a source of potentially inclusive ideas and practices and a relevant field of experience from which programmes for inclusive innovation might learn. As researchers studying grassroots innovation, we were invited into some inclusive innovation discussions, for example, by speaking at policy events and commenting on draft reports (Smith, 2014a). A recurring theme to the invitations, as in the related field of social innovation, has been an emphasis on scaling up promising initiatives and rolling them out widely.

Typically, scaling up is framed as proceeding through measures to formalize and commercialize the grassroots innovation. The facilities and tools of conventional innovation systems are brought to the service of promising grassroots innovators and their innovations through the provision of research, development and demonstration; assistance with standards procedures; and help in securing intellectual property. Investment and marketing assistance is also offered. The grassroots furnish prototypes for entrepreneurs and investors; and these are then turned into goods and services for scaling up, principally by expanding markets, but also through more conventional development programmes. It is a framing that presumes an obvious risk-taking innovator (analogous to a firm or inventor) to support and reward, and an innovation that can be turned into a proprietary object for marketing.

There is nothing inherently wrong with such a move. Indeed, it can help considerably to improve those innovations that can more readily be marketed. And, given the way that policy and business interest in grassroots innovation is organized towards this end, it is a dynamic that we can expect to have considerable momentum. But while doing that well, it performs badly at supporting the more transformative possibilities in grassroots innovation. As we have seen across the cases in this book, altering a grassroots innovation so that it might 'find' markets neglects the social basis of that innovation. It fails to acknowledge the less-entrepreneurial subjectivities and relationships that originally cultivated the grassroots innovation. And it discounts the socially transformative framings that motivated the grassroots activity. Entrepreneurship alone cannot create and maintain the conditions of grassroots mobilization upon which it relies. The recent fashion for innovation prizes, with the winners taking all, has a similarly myopic notion of grassroots innovation subjects and the social basis of grassroots innovation capabilities. Grassroots innovation movements build additional social relationships, organizational forms and purposes that operate beyond and beneath entrepreneurship, markets and insertion. These relationships build the capacities for people to organize at grassroots level and to contribute and direct innovation along development pathways particular to their contexts. Grassroots innovators tend to want to be involved in the breadth of the relevant decisions, from prioritizing and framing the development issue, to making design choices and decisions about evaluative criteria, as well as evaluating 'success' and undertaking further development and production. This includes deciding how investments are made, having a stake in the way value is realized, captured and distributed into wider community developments and livelihoods.

This is why insertion risks being insufficient, at best, and counterproductive, at worse. It is in this sense that insertion alone needs to be resisted; not necessarily to stop a narrower scaling up of innovations but, rather, to continually point out what is being overlooked and neglected. If people as inventive and empowered as grassroots innovators are unnecessarily straightjacketed by inflexible support structures, then they are likely to ignore or even resist the invitations to insertion anyway.

However, for all the evident potential for grassroots innovation movements to promote plurality and reflexivity in the politics of innovation, it is vitally important not to romanticize it. Questions of inclusion, exclusion, conviviality and injustice are just as pertinent in grassroots innovation spaces as they are in conventional innovation institutions. Grassroots spaces are also prone to exclusions arising through expertise, knowing how and knowing what, skills, tacit knowledge, practices and cultures that variously constrain and enable different social groups to become involved. Initiatives have to be designed and cultivated carefully, through ongoing community development processes that address structural inequalities and exclusions in terms of education, gender, class, ethnicity, age, disability and so forth. People have to be supported in gaining confidence with and within alternative forms of innovation. Nor does everyone want to be involved actively, which raises questions of representation.

In sum, grassroots innovation movements need to be continually in tune with the dynamic contexts in which people live. As such, grassroots spaces are a key locus for confronting and experimenting with some practical challenges in the democratization of innovation. Some of the critical lessons learnt will no doubt point beyond the cultivation of the grassroots spaces themselves and towards changes required in society, over which grassroots innovation movements have only limited agency.

Challenging dominant and unsustainable pathways

Ultimately, making the most of grassroots innovation is a question of challenging power. Through their successions of initiatives, grassroots innovation movements cultivate ideas and practices that contribute important reflexivity, debate and plurality to discussions of innovation in society. They open questions about the social, economic and political causes and consequences of technological change. We see in the movements for socially useful production and for hackerspaces, fablabs and makerspaces, for example, two periods of critical exploration of the rise of computing and digital technologies. These movements have been imagining and anticipating different configurations for the development of digital technologies. Such activity reminds us that, in this case, nothing is automatic about automation. Social choices are involved. Plural possibilities exist between human-centred and human-excluding applications, as tools for liberation or instruments of control. Usually in diverse, emergent and unruly ways, grassroots innovation movements open up important spaces, demonstrations, prototypes, ideas and methods for exploring open-ended, contingent futures.

Yet it would be naïve to claim that those futures are wide open. There are relations of political and economic power that give advantages to the cultivation of some pathways over others. Grassroots innovation is motivated by commitments that imply changes to social and economic relations and that are ambitious in their breadth and depth. However, while incumbent structures of asymmetric agency constitute considerable privileges, the privileged are never fully in control (Stirling, 2015). Vested interests are susceptible to the inventive richness of people and their associational power. We have seen how spaces for grassroots innovation can open up an unruly inventiveness. However, we have also seen that if such spaces are to have greater influence, they have to overcome restrictive political economies, locked-in institutions and overbearing cultures that often characterize dominant pathways.

All the case studies succeeded in creating grassroots power at the grassroots to do innovation. Few, however, were able to build power over wider support structures in society, such as power over the institutions promoting innovation. Here, it is the power of social movements that becomes important. It is through social movement pressure that these institutions can be changed, by contributing momentum and significance to more specific agendas such as scaling down innovation systems, opening up design processes, distributing prototyping capabilities and making a material contribution to the development of more sustainable pathways.

Social movements are one means to challenging power, opening up possibilities and building momentum for alternative pathways. Whether drawing upon support among workers, peasants, environmentalists, pacifists, hackers, community activists or others, we have seen in the case studies how wider social movements have been vital for grassroots innovation initiatives. That support has been both discursive and material, mobilizing around relevant framings as well as providing resources. Support has manifested through direct links and through looser associations. It has arisen when grassroots initiatives were seen as trying to infuse social movement ideals into innovation practice, whether for social justice or environmental sustainability. Indeed, in our case studies it was difficult to understand some of their framings of grassroots innovation in the absence of an appreciation of wider social movements. It is important to recognize how the movement in grassroots innovation links to these wider social movements and their claims for rights, recognition and justice. Social movements provide solidarity, energy, people, skills, strategies, resources and facilities for initiatives, but they also serve as bridges between grassroots innovation movements in different places and across different times.

However, movement pressure works most visibly when it translates into favourable response from business and government. The kinds of institutional changes envisaged in a transformational framing of grassroots innovation require committed partnership. The point is, however, that unless business and government realistically understand grassroots innovation as social movement, with all the social relations and motivations implied, then any partnership will remain fraught with misunderstanding. It is in deeper social movement demands, for socially just and environmentally sustainable development pathways, that grassroots innovation draws its strength and it is these demands that partnerships with business and government need to recognize and understand if they are to engage successfully.

Final remarks

In this book, looking across experiences at different times and places, we have identified recurring features in grassroots innovation movements (e.g. Table 9.4 in Chapter 9). By recognizing these experiences, we hope to have highlighted the real relevance of grassroots innovation movements for the creation of alternative pathways of development. The framing of grassroots innovation variously emphasizes its potential in ingenuity, empowerment or transformation. We have seen how important it is for grassroots innovators to open up and occupy different spaces – physical, institutional and discursive. Here, alternative forms of innovation attract resources but also become subject to reciprocal requirements that affect what can be practised and what is achieved in those spaces. Moving beyond those spaces, and seeking wider roles in development pathways, we identified strategies of insertion and transformation with respect to conventional institutions for innovation. We then discussed the dilemmas that these strategies present to grassroots innovation movements in terms of becoming co-opted, mainstreaming or remaining marginal.

It is important to remember that these insights were abstracted from cases whose messy realities involved hybrid arrangements, compromised positions, contradictory outcomes and some influential achievements. Grassroots innovation will continue to be messy. We intended our analysis to provide some clarity that, while simplified, nevertheless provides some helpful bearings for working through those messy realities. If there is one direction we would particularly emphasize in closing this book, however, it is that the full compass of possibilities will not be realized without a struggle for transformational possibilities.

The stories, struggles, successes, ideas and technologies that we traced in this book are just a glimpse of some of the undercurrents of grassroots innovation. We expect that this book will contribute to extend the understanding of grassroots innovation around the world and, we hope, inspire further research and experimentation. We hope that a new and renewed focus on grassroots innovation will help us to recognize the dormant power of these initiatives to create alternative pathways.

Grassroots innovation movements do not have the map for more sustainable futures. But they are exploring critical points of departure.

REFERENCES

Abrar, P. and Nair, R. (2011) 'When grassroots innovation goes global', *Economic Times*, 15 March, http://economictimes.indiatimes.com/quickiearticleshow/7625954.cms, accessed 21 February 2011.
Abrol, D. (1998) *Technological Transformation of Rural Areas: A Guidebook on Network System of Technology Implementation*, National Institute of Science, Technology and Development Studies, New Delhi.
Abrol, D. (2004) 'Lessons from the design of innovation systems for rural industrial clusters in India', *Asialics, Journal of Technology Innovation*, special issue, vol. 12, no. 2, pp. 67–98.
Abrol, D. (2005) 'Embedding technology in community based production systems through People's Technology Initiatives: Lessons from the Indian experience', *International Journal of Technology Management and Sustainable Development*, vol. 4, no. 1, pp. 1–28.
Abrol, D. (2014a) 'Pro-poor innovation-making, knowledge production and technology implementation for rural areas: Lessons from the Indian experience', in S. V. Ramani (ed.) *Innovation in India*, Cambridge University Press, Cambridge, pp. 337–378.
Abrol, D. (2014b) 'Mobilizing for democratization of science in India: Learning from the PSM experience', *Journal of Scientific Temper*, vol. 2, nos 1–2, pp. 10–32.
Abrol, D. and Gupta, A. (2014), 'Understanding the diffusion modes of grassroots innovations in India: A study of Honey Bee Network supported innovators', *African Journal of Science, Technology, Innovation and Development*, vol. 6, no. 6, pp. 541–546, http://dx.doi.org/10.1080/20421338.2014.976974.
Alier, J. M. (2002) *The Environmentalism of the Poor: A Study of Ecological Conflicts and Valuation*, Edward Elgar, Cheltenham.
Altieri, M. and Yurjevich, A. (1991) 'La agroecología y el desarrollo rural, sostenible en America Latina', *Agroecologia y Desarrollo*, vol. 1, http://www.clades.cl/revistas/1/rev1art3.htm, accessed 14 February 2016.
Altieri, M., Norgaard, R., Hecht, S. B., Farrell, J. G. and Liebman, M. (1987) *Agroecology: The Scientific Basis of Alternative Agriculture*, Westview Press, Boulder, CO.
Alves da Silva, R. M. (2003) 'Entre dois paradigmas: Combate à seca e convivência com o semi-árido', *Sociedade e Estado*, vol. 18, nos 1–2, pp. 361–385, doi.org/10.1590/S0102-69922003000100017.

Alves da Silva, R. M. and Sardá de Faria, M. (2010) 'Tecnologías sociais e Economía solidaría', in RTS, *Tecnología Social e Desenvolvimento Sustentável*, RTS, Brasilia, pp. 65–70.

Amin, S. (1993) 'Social movements at the periphery', in P. Wignaraja (ed.) *New Social Movements in the South: Empowering the People*, Zed Books, London, pp. 76–100.

Anderson, C. (2012) *Makers: The New Industrial Revolution*, Random House, London.

Asaro, P. M. (2000) 'Transforming society by transforming technology: The science and politics of participatory design', *Accounting Management and Information Technologies*, vol. 10, no. 4, pp. 257–290.

Asdal, K., Brenna, B. and Moser, I. (2007) 'The politics of interventions: A history of STS', in K. Asdal, B. Brenna, and I. Moser (eds), *Technoscience: The Politics of Interventions*, Unipub, Oslo, pp. 7–53.

Ashby, J. (2009) 'Fostering farmer first methodological innovation: Organizational learning and change in international agricultural research', in I. Scoones and J. Thompson (eds) *Farmer First Revisited: Innovation for Agricultural Research and Development*, Practical Action Publishing, Rugby, pp. 39–45.

Asquith, P. (1979) 'Workers' control or control of the workers', *Science for People*, vol. 42, pp. 8–12.

Baquedano, M. (1985) '¿Qué son las tecnologías apropiadas?' *Revista Comunidad*, vol. 48/49, n.p.

Barbosa, A. G. (2010) 'A innovação tecnológica a servicio da democratição a do acceso à água: A experiêencia da ASA no Semiárido brasilero', in RTS, *Tecnología Social e Desenvolvimento Sustentável*, RTS, Brasilia, pp. 31–35.

Barratt Brown, M. (1978) 'Profits and losses and the social audit', in K. Coates (ed.), *The Right to Useful Work*, Spokesman, Sheffield, pp. 25–60.

Barros, L. (2009) 'Apresentação: RTS – um olhar para o futuro', in RTS, *Tecnologias Sociais: Caminhos para a Sustentabilidade*, Brasilia, pp. 7–13.

Baumgarten, M. (2006) 'Tecnologias sociais e inovação social', in A. Cattani and L. Holzmann (eds), *Dicionario de Trabalho e Tecnologia*, Universidade Federal do Rio Grande do Sul, Porto Alegre, pp. 410–413.

Bauwens, M. (2006) 'The political economy of peer production', *Post-autistics Economics Review*, vol. 37, no. 3, pp. 33–44.

Bebbington, A. and Kothari, U. (2006) 'Transnational development networks', *Environment and Planning A*, vol. 38, no. 5, pp. 849–866.

Beckett, A. (2010) *When the Lights Went Out: Britain in the Seventies*, Faber and Faber, London.

Benford, R. D. and Snow, D. A. (2000) 'Framing processes and social movements: An overview and assessment', *Annual Review of Sociology*, vol. 26, pp. 611–639.

Benkler, Y. (2006) *The Wealth of Networks: How Social Production Transforms Markets and Freedom*, Yale University Press, New Haven, CT.

Benkler, Y. and Nissenbaum, H. (2006) 'Commons-based peer production and virtue', *Journal of Political Philosophy*, vol. 14, no. 4, pp. 394–419.

Bhaduri, S. and Kumar, H. (2011) 'Extrinsic and intrinsic motivations to innovate: Tracing the motivation of "grassroot" innovators in India', *Mind & Society*, vol. 10, no. 1, pp. 27–55, doi:10.1007/s11299-010-0081-2.

Bijker, W. E. (1995) *Of Bicycles, Bakelites and Bulbs*, MIT Press, Cambridge, MA.

Birtchnell, T. and Hoyle, W. (2014) *3D Printing for Development in the Global South*, Palgrave Macmillan, Basingstoke.

Birtchnell, T. and Urry, J. (2012) 'Fabricating futures and the movement of objects', *Mobilities*, vol. 8, no. 3, pp. 388–405.

Blackburn, P., Green, K. and Liff, S. (1982) 'Science and technology in restructuring', *Capital & Class*, vol. 6, no. 3, pp. 15–38, doi:10.1177/030981688201800102.

Bodington, S., George, M. and Michaelson, J. (1986) *Developing the Socially Useful Economy*, Macmillan, Basingstoke.

Bookchin, M. (1967) 'Towards a liberatory technology', *Anarchy*, vol. 78, no. 7.

Boyle, G. and Harper, P. (1976) *Radical Technology*. London: Wildwood House.

Brachi, P. (1974) 'Sun on the roof', *New Scientist*, (19 September), pp. 712–714.

Bradley, P. (n.d.) 'Simplified hydroponics in urban agriculture', *City Farmer*, http://www.cityfarmer.org/hydroponicsBradley.html, accessed 14 February 2016.

Brandão, F. C. (2001) *Programa de Apoio ás Tecnologías Apropriadas – PTA: Avaliação de um Programa de Desenvolvimento Tecnológico Induzido pelo CNPq*, Brasilia, University of Brasilia.

Braverman, H. (1974) *Labor and Monopoly Capital: The Degradation of Work in the Twentieth Century*, Monthly Review Press, London.

Brito Cruz, C. H. and Chaimovich, H. (2010) 'Brazil', in L. Brito (ed.) *UNESCO Science Report 2015: The Current Status of Science around the World*, UNESCO, Paris, pp. 102–121, http://unesdoc.unesco.org/images/0018/001899/189958e.pdf, accessed 25 February 2016.

Brödner, P. (1990) *The Shape of Future Technology: The Anthropocentric Alternative*, Springer-Verlag, London.

Brödner, P. (2007) 'From Taylorism to competence-based production', *AI & Society*, vol. 21, no. 4, pp. 497–514, doi:10.1007/s00146-007-0087-4.

Buchanan, R. (2001) 'Human dignity and human rights: Thoughts on the principles of human-centered design', *Design Issues*, vol. 17, no. 3, pp. 35–40.

Buechler, S. M. (2000) *Social Movements in Advanced Capitalism*, Oxford University Press, Oxford.

Cardoso, F. H. and Faletto, E. (2003) *Dependencia y desarrollo en América Latina*, Siglo XXI Editores, Buenos Aires.

Carr, M. (1985) *The AT Reader: Theory and Practice in Appropriate Technology*, Intermediate Technology Publications, London.

Carson, R. (1962) *Silent Spring*, Houghton Mifflin, Boston, MA.

Carstensen, T. (2013) 'Gendered FabLabs?', in J. Walter-Herrmann and C. Büching (eds) *FabLab: Of Machines, Makers and Inventors*, transcript Verlag, Bielefeld.

Castilhos Fernandez, R. M. and Suarez Maciel, A. L. (2011) 'Os caminhos das tecnologías sociais: Reflexoes iniciais', *Journal Primeiro Plano*, vol. 20, pp. 40–43.

Cavarozzi, M. (1991) 'Más allá de las transiciones a la democracia en América Latina', *Revista de Estudios Políticos*, 74, pp. 85–112, http://dialnet.unirioja.es/servlet/articulo?codigo=27140&orden=0&info=link, accessed 14 February 2016.

CAITS (1978) *Alternatives to Unemployment: New Approaches to Work in Industry and Community*, Centre for Alternative Industrial and Technological Systems, London.

CET (1985) *Necesidades básicas y tecnología apropiada. Una experiencia de desarrollo*, Centro de Educación Tecnológica, Santiago de Chile.

Chambers, R. (1997) *Whose Reality Counts? Putting the First Last*, ITDG Publishing, Rugby.

Chathukulam, J. and John, M. S. (2002) 'Five years of participatory planning in Kerala: Rhetoric and reality', in *Economic and Political Weekly*, vol. 37, no. 49, December, pp. 4917–4926.

Chattopadhyay, S. and Franke, R. W. (2006) *Striving for Sustainability: Environmental Stress and Democratic Initiatives*, Concept Publishing House, New Delhi.

Cherns, A. (1976) 'The principles of sociotechnical design', *Human Relations*, vol. 29, no. 8, pp. 783–792, doi:10.1177/001872677602900806.

Chesbrough, H., Vanhaverbeke, W. and West, J. (eds) (2006) *Open Innovation: Researching a New Paradigm*, Oxford University Press, New York.

CIAAT (2015) 'Tecnologia social PAIS', Centro de Informaçao e Assessoria Técnica, http://www.ciaatgv.com.br/artigos/tecnologia-social-pais, accessed 18 February 2016.

CIFI (1985) *Tecnologia apropiada: Resumenes de Investigaciones Realizadas en el Departamento de Ingenieria Mecánica de la Universidad de Los Andes*. CIFI, Bogotá.

Clark, P. (1983) 'Working with people', *Radical Science Journal*, vol. 13, pp. 100–104.

Coates, K. (1981) *Work-ins, Sit-ins and Industrial Democracy*, Spokesman, Sheffield.

Collective Design/Project (1985) *Very Nice Work if You Can Get It: The Socially Useful Production Debate*, Spokesman, Sheffield.

Collier, D. (1978) 'Industrial modernization and political change: A Latin American perspective', *World Politics*, vol. 30, no. 4, pp. 593–614.

Community Development Project (1977) *Gilding the Ghetto: The State and the Poverty Experiments*, CDP, London.

Cooke, B. and Kothari, U. (eds) (2001) *Participation: The New Tyranny?* Zed Books, London.

Cooley, M. (1981) 'The Taylorisation of intellectual work', in L. Levidow and B. Young (eds) *Science, Technology and the Labour Process*, Blackrose, London, pp. 46–65.

Cooley, M. (1985) 'After the Lucas Plan', in Collective Design/Project (ed.) *Very Nice Work if You Can Get It: The Socially Useful Production Debate*, Spokesman, Sheffield, pp. 19–26.

Cooley, M. (1987) *Architect or Bee? The Human Price of Technology* (2nd edn), Hogarth Press, London.

Cooley, M. (2007) 'From judgment to calculation', *AI & Society*, vol. 21, no. 4, pp. 395–409, doi:10.1007/s00146-007-0106-5.

Cornwall, A. and Coelho, V. S. (2007) *Spaces for Change? The Politics of Citizen Participation in New Democratic Arenas*, Zed Books, London.

Costa, A. B. and Dias, R. (2013) 'Políticas públicas e tecnologia social: Algunas liçoes das expêriencias em desenvolvimento no Brasil', in A. B. Costa (ed.) *Tecnologia Social e Políticas Públicas*, Fundaçâo Banco do Brasil, Brasilia, pp. 223–246.

Coventry Workshop (1978) *Progress Report 1976–77*, Coventry Workshop, Coventry.

Cox, L. and Flesher Fominaya, C. (2009) 'Movement knowledge: What do we know, how do we create knowledge and what do we do with it?' *Interface: A Journal for and About Social Movements*, vol. 1, no. 1, pp. 1–20.

CSSTD [CMD] and CSIR (1981) *Gaon Ke Karigar Aur Science* (Village Artisans and Science), Council of Scientific and Industrial Research, New Delhi.

Dag Hamaarskjöld Foundation (1975) *What Now? Another Development*, Dag Hamaarskjöld Foundation, Uppsala.

Dagnino, R. (2004) 'A tecnologia social e seus desafios', in A. De Paulo (ed.) *Tecnologia Social: Uma Estratégia para o Desenvolvimento*, Fundação Banco do Brasil, Rio de Janeiro, pp. 187–216.

Dagnino, R., Brandão, F. C. and Tahan Novaes, H. (2004) 'Sobre o marco analítico conceitual da tecnologia social', in A. De Paulo (ed.) *Tecnologia Social: Uma Estratégia para o Desenvolvimento*, Fundação Banco do Brasil, Rio de Janeiro, pp. 15–64.

Darlington, R. and Lyddon, D. (2001) *Glorious Summer: Class Struggle in Britain 1972*, Bookmarks, London.

Darrow, K. and Pam, K. (1978) *Appropriate Technology Sourcebook*, Volunteers in Asia, Stanford, CA.

Davis, J. and Bollard, A. (1986) *As Though People Mattered*, Intermediate Technology Publications, London.

de Beer, J., Kun Fu and Wunsch-Vincent, S. (2013) *The Informal Economy, Innovation and Intellectual Property: Concepts, Metrics and Policy Considerations*, World Intellectual Property Organization, Geneva.

De Keersmaecker, A., Parmar, V., Kandachar, P., Baelus, C. and Vandenbempt, K. (2011) 'Towards scaling up grassroots innovations in India: A preliminary framework', in P. Teirlinck, S. Kelchtermans and F. de Beule, *Proceedings of the 8th European Conference on Innovation and Entrepreneurship*, Academic Conferences and Publishing International, Reading.

De Olivera Pena, J. (2009) 'Tecnologia social e o desenvolvimento rural', in RTS, *Tecnología Social e Desenvolvimento Sustentável*, RTS, Brasilia, pp. 197–201.

De Olivera Pena, J. and Mello, C. J. (2004) 'Tecnologia social: A experiencia da Fundação Banco do Brasil na disseminação e reaplicação de soluções sociais efectivas', in A. De Paulo (ed.) *Tecnologia Social: Uma Estratégia para o Desenvolvimento*, Fundação Banco do Brasil, Rio de Janeiro, pp. 83–87.

De Paulo, J. (2009) 'RTS: Novos desafios', in RTS, *Tecnologias Sociais: Caminhos para a Sustentabilidade*, RTS, Brasilia, pp. 131–138.

Dias, R. (2011) 'O que é a política científica e tecnológica?', *Sociologias*, vol. 13, no. 28, pp. 316–344.

Dias, R. (2012) 'Uma análise sociotécnica do Programa Um Milhão de Cisternas (P1MC)', paper presented at the conference IX Jornadas Latinoamericanas de Estudios Sociales de la Ciencia y la Tecnología – ESOCITE, México DF, 5–6 June 2012.

Dickel, S., Ferdinand, J. and Petschow, U. (2014) 'Shared machine shops as real-life laboratories', *Journal of Peer Production*, vol. 5, pp. 1–9.

Dickson, D. (1974) *Alternative Technology and the Politics of Technical Change*, Fontana/Collins, London.

Diez, T. (2012) 'Personal fabrication: Fab Labs as platforms for citizen-based innovation, from microcontrollers to cities', *Nexus Network Journal*, vol. 14, no. 3, pp. 457–468.

Dougherty, D. (2012) 'The maker movement', *Innovations: Technology, Governance, Globalization*, vol. 7, no. 3, pp. 11–14.

DST (2008) *Technology for Rural Development*, Department of Science and Technology, New Delhi.

DST (2012) All India Coordinated Programme on Bio-Integrated Farming (Bio Farm), Catalyzed and supported by Department of Science and Technology, Science Society Division, www.drcsc.org/biofarm/aicp.html.

Dutfield, G. (2006) 'Promoting local innovation as a development strategy, innovation case discussion: The Honey Bee Network', *Innovations: Technology, Governance, Globalization*, (Summer), pp. 67–77.

Eastall, R. (1989) *Restructuring for Labour? Job Creation by the Greater London Enterprise Board*, Department for Government, Victoria University of Manchester, Manchester.

Eglash, R. and Banks, D. A. (2014) 'Recursive depth in generative spaces: Democratization in three dimensions of technosocial self-organization', *The Information Society*, vol. 30, no. 2, pp. 106–115, doi:10.1080/01972243.2014.875775.

Ehn, P. (1988) *Work-oriented Design of Computer Artifacts*, Arbetslivscentrum, Stockholm.

Ehn, P., Nilsson, E. M. and Topgaard, R. (eds) (2014) *Making Futures: Marginal Notes on Innovation, Design and Democracy*, MIT Press, Cambridge, MA.

Elliott, D. (1975) 'What is to be made?', *Undercurrents*, vol. 13, pp. 17–19.

Ely, A., Smith, A., Stirling, A., Leach, M. and Scoones, I. (2013) 'Innovation politics post-Rio+20: Hybrid pathways to sustainability', *Environment and Planning C: Government and Policy*, vol. 31, no. 6, pp. 1063–1081, http://doi.org/10.1068/c12285j.

Escobar, A. (2004) 'Beyond the Third World: Imperial globality, global coloniality and anti-globalisation social movements', *Third World Quarterly*, vol. 25, no. 1, pp. 207–230.

Escobar, A. and Alvarez, S. E. (1992) *The Making of Social Movements in Latin America: Identity, Strategy, and Democracy*, Westview Press, Boulder, CO.

Eyerman, R. and Jamison, A. (1991) *Social Movements: A Cognitive Approach*, Polity Press, Malden, MA.

Fals Borda, O. (1979) 'Investigating reality in order to transform it: The Colombian experience', *Dialectical Anthropology*, vol. 4, no. 1, pp. 33–55.

Faramelli, N. J. (1972) 'Toying with the environment and the poor: A report on the Stockholm Environmental Conferences', *Boston College Environmental Affairs Law Review*, vol. 2, no. 3, pp. 469–486.

Faria, J., Pavam Serafim, M. and Brito de Jesus, V. (2011) *Tecnologia Social na Area de Alimento*, Internal Report for the IDRC Project 'Technologies for social inclusion and public policies', IDRC, Campinas.

Ferris, P. (1972) *The New Militants: Crisis in the Trade Unions*, Penguin, Harmondsworth.

Field, P. (1985) 'Making people powerful: Coventry Workshop', in Collective Design/ Project (ed.) *Very Nice Work if You Can Get It: The Socially Useful Production Debate*, Spokesman, Sheffield, pp. 53–60.

Finley, K. (2012) 'The military-maker complex: DARPA infiltrates the hackerspace movement', *Technoccult*, http://technoccult.net/archives/2012/02/24/the-military-maker-complex-darpa-infiltrates-the-hackerspace-movement/, accessed 22 January 2016.

Flowers, S. (2008) 'Harnessing the hackers: The emergence and exploitation of Outlaw Innovation', *Research Policy*, vol. 37, no. 2, pp. 177–193.

Flyvbjerg, B. (2006) 'Five mis-understandings about case study research', *Qualitative Inquiry*, vol. 12, no. 2, pp. 219–245.

Fonseca, R. (2011) 'Analise da Rede de Tecnología Social', mimeo, unpublished draft paper, University of Campinas.

Forrester, C. (2012) 'Alternative technology in 1970s Britain', in *AT at 40*, London: Centre for Alternative Technology.

Franke, R. W. and Chasin, B. H. (1997) 'Power to the Malayalee People', *Economic and Political Weekly*, vol. 32, no. 48, pp. 3061–3065, 3067–3068.

Freeman, C. (1992) *The Economics of Hope*, Pinter, London.

Freeman, C. and Soete, L. (1994) *Work for All or Mass Unemployment? Computerised Technical Change in the Twenty-first Century*, Pinter, London.

Freire, P. (1973) *Pedagogía del oprimido*, Siglo XXI Editores, Buenos Aires.

Fressoli, M., Arond, E., Abrol, D., Smith, A., Ely, A. and Dias, R. (2014) 'When grassroots innovation movements encounter mainstream institutions: Implications for models of inclusive innovation', *Innovation and Development*, vol. 4, July, pp. 277–292, doi:10.1080/2157930X.2014.921354.

Fressoli, M., Garrido, S., Picabea, F., Lalouf, A. and Fenoglio, V. (2013) 'Cuando las transferencias tecnológicas fracasan: Aprendizajes y limitaciones en la construcción de Tecnologías para la Inclusión Social', *Universitas Humanitas*, vol. 76, pp. 73–95, http://search.ebscohost.com/login.aspx?direct=true&db=a9h&AN=92589407&lang=es&site=ehost-live.

Frickel, S. (2004) 'Building an interdiscipline: Collective action framing and the rise of genetic toxicology', *Social Problems*, vol. 51, no. 2, pp. 269–287, doi:10.1525/sp.2004.51.2.269.

Frickel, S. and Gross, N. (2005) 'A general theory of scientific/intellectual movements', *American Sociological Review*, vol. 70, no. 2, pp. 204–232, doi:10.1177/000312240507000202.

Frickel, S., Gibbon, S., Howard, J., Kempner, J., Ottinger, G., Hess, D. J. (2010) 'Undone science: Charting social movement and civil society challenges to research agenda setting', *Science, Technology & Human Values*, vol. 35, no. 4, pp. 444–473. doi:10.1177/0162243909345836.

Fukuoka, M. (1978) *One Straw Revolution*, Rodale Press, Emmaus PA 5.
Fundação Banco do Brasil (2013) 'Apresentação', in A. B. Costa (org.) *Tecnologia Social e Políticas Públicas*, Fundação Banco do Brasil, Brasilia, pp. 11–16.
Gadgil, M. and Guha, R. (1994) 'Ecological conflicts and environmental movements in India', *Development and Change*, vol. 25, pp. 101–136, http://wgbis.ces.iisc.ernet.in/biodiversity/pubs/mg/pdfs/mg129.pdf.
Gamser, M., Adjebeng-Asem, S., Basant, R., Fernando, P., Kadappum, J., Massaquoi, J. G. M. et al. (1990) *Tinker, Tiller, Technical Change*, Intermediate Technology Publications, London.
Gárgano, C. (2013) 'La reorganización de las agendas de investigación y extensión del Instituto Nacional de Tecnología Agropecuaria (INTA) durante la última dictadura militar argentina (1976–1983)', *Realidad Económica*, pp. 120–149.
Garretón, M. A. (2002) 'La transformación de la acción colectiva en América Latina', *Revista de La Cepal*, vol. 76, pp. 7–22.
Garud, R. and Gehman, J. (2012) 'Metatheoretical perspectives on sustainability journeys: Evolutionary, relational and durational', *Research Policy*, vol. 41, no. 6, pp. 980–995.
Garud, R., Kumaraswamy, A. and Karnøe, P. (2010) 'Path dependence or path creation?' *Journal of Management Studies*, vol. 47, no. 4, pp. 760–774, doi:10.1111/j.1467-6486.2009.00914.x.
Gauntlett, D. (2013) *Making is Connecting*, Polity Press, Oxford.
Geels, F. W. (2002) 'Technological transitions as evolutionary reconfiguration processes: A multi-level perspective and a case-study', *Research Policy*, vol. 31, no. 8–9, pp. 1257–1274.
Geels, F. W. (2010) 'Ontologies, socio-technical transitions (to sustainability), and the multi-level perspective', *Research Policy*, vol. 39, no. 4, pp. 495–510.
Geels, F. W. and Deuten, J. J. (2006) 'Local and global dynamics in technological development: A socio-cognitive perspective on knowledge flows and lessons from reinforced concrete', *Science and Public Policy*, vol. 33, no. 4, pp. 265–275.
Geels, F. W. and Schot, J. (2007) 'Typology of sociotechnical transition pathways', *Research Policy*, vol. 36, no. 3, pp. 399–417.
George, M. (1978) 'Which future and whose future in manufacturing industry in the UK?' in CAITS, Lucas Aerospace Combine Shop Stewards Committee and NELP, *Alternatives to Unemployment: New Approaches to Work in Industry and the Community*, Centre for Alternative Industrial & Technological Systems, London, pp. 171–185.
Gershenfeld, N. (2005) *FAB: The Coming Revolution on Your Desktop: From Personal Computers to Personal Fabrication*, Basic Books, New York.
Giri, A. K. (2005) *Reflections and Mobilizations: Dialogues with Movements and Voluntary Organizations*, Sage Publications, New Delhi.
Gomez, S. and Echenique, J. (1988) *Agricultura chilena: las dos caras de la modernización*, FLACSO, Santiago de Chile.
Gradl, C. and Knobloch, C. (2010) *Brokering Inclusive Business Models: A Supporting Document to the IMD Handbook*, UNDP Private Sector Division, New York.
Graziano da Silva, J. (2009) 'Zero hunger and territories of citizenship: Promoting food security in Brazil's rural areas', in J. von Braun, R. Vargas Hill and R. Pandya-Lorch (eds) *The Poorest and Hungry: Assessments, Analyses, and Actions: An IFPRI 2020 Book*, IFPRI, Washington DC, pp. 367–374.
Greater London Enterprise Board (1984a) *Corporate Plan 1984–1985*, Greater London Enterprise Board, London.
Greater London Enterprise Board (1984b) *Saving Jobs – Shaping the Future: An Introduction to Enterprise Planning*, Greater London Enterprise Board, London.
Greater London Enterprise Board (1984c) *Technology Networks: Science and Technology Serving London's Needs*, Greater London Enterprise Board, London.

Greenhalgh, C. (2014) 'Perspective on IP systems for emerging and developing economies. These comments draw on several papers presented at 4th Asia Pacific Innovation Network Annual Conference, Taiwan, December 2013', paper presented at OECD Workshop, Paris, 13 January 2014.

Grin, J., Rotmans, J. and Schot, J. (2010) *Transitions to Sustainable Development: New Directions in the Study of Transformative Long-term Change*, Routledge, New York.

Gupta, A. K. (1990) 'Survival under stress in South Asia: Socio ecological perspective on farmers innovation', revised version published in *Capitalism, Nature and Socialism*, vol. 5, (October), pp. 79–96.

Gupta, A. K. (1992) 'Debate on biotechnology and intellectual property rights, Protecting the interests of third world farmers', IIM-A WP 1057, Indian Institute of Management Ahmedabad.

Gupta, A. K. (2000) 'Grassroots Innovations for survival', *LEISA India*, vol. 2, no. 2, pp. 20–21.

Gupta, A. K. (2001a) 'Kho-kho model of innovation: techpedia.in', *Anil K Gupta Blog*, 6 March, http://www.sristi.org/anilg/comments.php?post blog id=213, accessed 22 February 2016.

Gupta. A. K (2001b) 'Will patents preserve the experimental and innovative spirit at grassroots? Traditional knowledge, contemporary grassroots innovation and intellectual property rights', paper presented at UNEP workshop on IPRs, the WTO TRIPS Agreement and the Environment, Geneva, 10 December 2001.

Gupta, A. K. (2003) 'Learning from green grassroots innovators: How does a tail wag the dog?' Keynote lecture presented at the International Conference on Innovations in Technology and Governance, organized by the Ash Institute of Democratic Governance and Innovation and the Science, Technology and Public Policy Program at John F. Kennedy School of Government, Harvard University, Cambridge, 30–31 October 2003, http://ash.harvard.edu/files/learning_fm_green_grassroots.pdf, accessed 22 February 2016.

Gupta, A. K. (2009) 'Managing knowledge, creating networks and triggering innovations for sustainable agriculture', paper invited for National Seminar on Agriculture Extension, Ministry of Agriculture, New Delhi, 27–28 February 2009.

Gupta, A. K. (2014a) 'Innovation, investment, enterprise: Generating sustainable livelihood at grassroots through honey bee philosophy', in D. A. Vazquez-Brust, J. Sarkis and J. J. Cordeiro (eds) *Collaboration for Sustainability and Innovation: A Role for Sustainability Driven by the Global South*, Springer, Dordrecht, Chapter 11.

Gupta, A. K. (2014b) 'Theory of green grassroots frugal innovations', *Anil K Gupta Blog*, 15 August, http://anilg.sristi.org/theory-of-green-grassroots-frugal-innovations, accessed 24 February 2016.

Gupta, A. K., Sinha, R., Koradia, D. et al. (2003) 'Mobilizing grassroots' technological innovations and traditional knowledge, values and institutions: Articulating social and ethical capital', *Futures*, vol. 35, no. 9, pp. 975–987.

Hall, A. (2006) 'From Fome Zero to Bolsa Família: Social policies and poverty alleviation under Lula', *Journal of Latin America Studies*, vol. 38, no. 4, pp. 689–709, http://doi.org/10.1017/S0022216X0600157X.

Hargreaves, T., Hielscher, S., Seyfang, G. et al. (2013) 'Grassroots innovations in community energy: The role of intermediaries in niche development', *Global Environmental Change*, vol. 23, pp. 868–880.

Herrera, A. O. (1973) 'Los determinantes sociales de la política científica en América Latina: Politica cientifica explicita y politica cientifica implicita', *Desarrollo Económico*, vol. 13, no. 49, pp. 113–134.

Hertz, G. (2012) 'Interview with Matt Rato', *Critical Making*.
Hess, D. J. (2005) 'Technology and product-oriented movements: Approximating social movement studies and STS', *Science, Technology, and Human Values*, vol. 30, no. 4, pp. 515–535, doi:10.1177/0162243905276499.
Hess, D. J. (2007) *Alternative Pathways in Science and Industry: Activism, Innovation and the Environment in an Era of Globalization*, MIT Press, Cambridge, MA.
Hickey, S. and Mohan, G. (2004) *Participation – from Tyranny to Transformation? Exploring New Approaches to Participation in Development*, Zed Books, London.
Hielscher, S. (2015) *FabLab Amersfoort, De War: An Innovation History*, Centre for Innovation and Energy Demand, Brighton.
Hielscher, S. and Smith, A. (2014) *Community-based Digital Fabrication Workshops: A Review of the Research Literature*, Working Paper, University of Sussex, Brighton.
Hirschmann, A. O. (1984) *Getting Ahead Collectively: Grassroots Experiences in Latin America*, Pergamon Press, New York.
Hirschmann, A. O. (1986) *The Political Economy of Latin American Development: Seven Exercises in Retrospection*, Working Paper for the Centre for US–Mexican Studies, University of California, San Diego and Helen Kellogg Insitute San Diego, https://kellogg.nd.edu/publications/workingpapers/WPS/088.pdf, accessed 14 February 2016.
Hochstetler, K. (2004) *Civil Society in Lula's Brazil*, CBS 57-04, Centre for Brazilian Studies, University of Oxford, Oxford.
Holman, W. (2015) 'Makerspace: Towards a new civic infrastructure', *Places*, November, https://placesjournal.org/article/makerspace-towards-a-new-civic-infrastructure/#, accessed 20 February 2016.
Howard, R. (1985) 'UTOPIA: Where workers craft new technology', *Technology Review*, vol. 8, no. 3, pp. 43–49.
Huws, U. (1985) 'Challenging commoditisation: Producing usefulness outside the factory, in Collective Design/Project (ed.) *Very Nice Work if You Can Get It: The Socially Useful Production Debate*, Spokesman, Sheffield, pp. 149–167.
Illich, I. (1973) *Tools for Conviviality*, Harper & Row, London.
Instituto de Tecnología Social (2004) 'Reflexões sobre a construção do conceito de tecnología social', in A. De Paulo (ed.) *Tecnologia Social: Uma Estratégia para o Desenvolvimento*, Fundação Banco do Brasil, Rio de Janeiro, pp. 117–113.
Instituto de Tecnología Social (2007) *Declaração das ONGs: Ciência e Tecnologia com Inclusão Social*, Instituto de Tecnología Social, Rio de Janeiro.
IRTC (1993) *Annual report 1992–93*, Integrated Rural Technology Centre, Mundar, Palakkad.
IRTC (2001) *Annual report 2000–2001*, Integrated Rural Technology Centre, Mundar, Palakkad.
Jacobs, M. (1999) 'Sustainable development as a contested concept', in A. Dobson (ed.) *Fairness and futurity*, Oxford University Press, Oxford, pp. 21–45.
Jamison, A. (2001) *The Making of Green Knowledge: Environmental Politics and Cultural Transformation*, Cambridge University Press, Cambridge.
Jamison, A. (2003) 'The making of green knowledge: The contribution of activism', *Futures*, vol. 35, pp. 703–716.
Jasanoff, S. (2004) *States of Knowledge: The Co-production of Science and the Social Order*, Routledge, London.
Jenkins, J. C. (1983) 'Resource mobilization theory and the study of social movements', *Annual Review of Sociology*, vol. 9, no. 1, pp. 527–553.
Jéquier, N. (1982) *The World of Appropriate Technology: A Quantitative Analysis*, OECD, Paris.
Jordan, T. (2008) *Hacking*, Polity, Cambridge.

Kaimowitz, D. (1993) 'The role of nongovernmental organizations in agricultural research and technology transfer in Latin America', *World Development*, vol. 21, no. 7, pp. 1139–1150, doi.org/10.1016/0305-750X(93)90004-S 4.

Kannan, K. P. (1979) *Towards a People's Science Movement*, KSSP, Calicut.

Kaplinsky, R. (1984) *Automation*, Longman, Harlow.

Kaplinksy, R. (1990) *The Economies of Small: Appropriate Technology in a Changing World*, Intermediate Technology Publications, London.

Kaplinsky, R. (2011) 'Schumacher meets Schumpeter: Appropriate technology below the radar', *Research Policy*, vol. 40, no. 2, pp. 193–203, doi:10.1016/j.respol.2010.10.003.

Keck, M. E. and Sikkink, K. (1998) *Activists Beyond Borders: Advocacy Networks in International Politics*, Cornell University Press, Ithaca, NY.

Kemp, R., Loorbach, D. and Rotmans, J. (2007) 'Transition management as a model for managing processes of co-evolution towards sustainable development', *International Journal of Sustainable Development and World Ecology*, vol. 14, no. 1, pp. 78–91.

Kemp, R., Schot, J. and Hoogma, R. (1998) 'Regime shifts to sustainability through processes of niche formation: The approach of strategic niche management', *Technology Analysis & Strategic Management*, vol. 10, no. 2, pp. 175–198.

Kostakis, V. and Bauwens, M. (2015) *Network Society and Future Scenarios for a Collaborative Economy*, Palgrave Macmillan, Basingstoke.

Kraft, P. and Bansler, J. (1994) 'The collective resource approach: The Scandinavian experience', *Scandinavian Journal of Information Systems*, vol. 61, pp. 71–84.

Lassance Jr, A. E. and Pedreira, J. S. (2004) 'Tecnología sociais e políticas públicas', in A. De Paulo (ed.) *Tecnologia Social: Uma Estratégia para o Desenvolvimento*, Fundação Banco do Brasil, Rio de Janeiro, pp. 65–82.

Latour, B. (1993) *We Have Never Been Modern*, Harvard University Press, Cambridge, MA.

Leach, M. and Scoones, I. (2007) *Mobilising Citizens: Social Movements and the Politics of Knowledge*, IDS Working Paper 37, Institute of Development Studies, Brighton.

Leach, M., Scoones, I. and Stirling, A. (2010) *Dynamic Sustainabilities: Technology, Environment, Social Justice*, Earthscan, London.

Leach, M., Scoones, I. and Wynne, B. (2005) *Science and Citizens*, Zed Books, London.

Leppe, A. Z. and Velasco, B. V. (1985) 'Tecnologías apropiadas: Soluciones de necesidades humanas?' *Communidade*, vol. 50.

Letty, B., Shezi, Z. and Mudhara, M. (2012) *An Exploration of Agricultural Grassroots Innovation in South Africa and Implications for Innovation Indicator Development*, Maastricht Economic and Social Research Institute on Innovation and Technology (UNU_MERIT), Maastricht.

Levidow, L. (1983) 'We won't be fooled again? Economic planning and left strategies', *Radical Science Journal*, vol. 13, pp. 28–38.

Levy, D. (1981) 'Comparing authoritarian regimes in Latin America: Insights from higher education policy', *Comparative Politics*, vol. 14, no. 1, pp. 31–52.

Lew, A. (2008) 'It's a bus. It's a train. It's both', *Wired*, 27 May, http://www.wired.com/autopia/2008/05/half-bus-half-t, accessed 11 February 2016.

Liff, S. (1985) 'Women factory workers: What could socially useful production mean for them?', in Collective Design/Project (ed.) *Very Nice Work if You Can Get It: The Socially Useful Production Debate*, Spokesman, Sheffield, pp. 178–186.

Linn, P. (1987) 'Socially useful production', *Science as Culture*, vol. 1, no. 1, pp. 105–138, doi:10.1080/09505438709526191.

Loboguerrero, J. (2008) 'Tecnología apropiada: Sus inicios en la Universidad de los Andes', *Revista de Ingeniería Universidad de Los Andes*, vol. 25, pp. 132–138.

Loney, M. (1983) *Community Against Government: The British Community Development Project 1968–78*, Heinemann, London.
Loorbach, D. (2007) *Transition Management: New Mode of Governance for Sustainable Development*, International Publishing, Utrecht.
Lowe, B. (1985) 'A report from the Unit for the Development of Alternative Products', in Collective Design/Project (ed.) *Very Nice Work if You Can Get It: The Socially Useful Production Debate*, Spokesman, Sheffield, pp. 61–69.
Lucas Aerospace Combine Shop Stewards Committee (1978) 'The Lucas Plan', in K. Coates (ed.) *The Right to Useful Work*, Spokesman, Nottingham, pp. 212–232.
Lucas Aerospace Combine Shop Stewards Committee (1979) *Democracy Versus the Circumlocution Office*, Institute for Workers' Control, London.
McCarthy, J. D. and Zald, M. N. (1977) 'Resource mobilization and social movements: A partial theory', *American Journal of Sociology*, vol. 82, no. 6, pp. 1212–1241.
Mackintosh, M. and Wainwright, H. (1987) *A Taste of Power: The Politics of Local Economics*, Verso, London.
McRobie, G. (1981) *Small is Possible*, Abacus, London.
Mathie, A. and Gaventa, J. (eds) (2015) *Citizen-led Innovation for a New Economy*, Practical Action, Rugby.
Maxigas (2012) 'Hacklabs and hackerspaces: Tracing two genealogies', *Journal of Peer Production*, 2 (June), pp. 1–10.
Maxigas and Troxler, P. (2014) 'We now have the means of production, but where is my revolution?' *Journal of Peer Production*, vol. 5, pp. 1–5.
Ministério da Ciência e Tecnologia (2002) *Livro Branco: Ciência, Tecnologia e Inovação*, Ministério da Ciência e Tecnologia, Brasília, http://www.cgee.org.br/arquivos/livro_branco_cti.pdf, accessed 25 February 2016.
Ministério do Desenvolvimento Social e Combate à Fome (2015) 'Dados SIG Cisternas', http://aplicacoes.mds.gov.br/sagi/simulacao/cisterna/lista.php, accessed 20 February 2016.
Miranda, I., Lopez, M. and Couto Soares, M. C. (2011) 'Social technology network: Paths for sustainability', *Innovation and Development*, vol. 1, no. 1, pp. 151–152.
Mole, V. and Elliott, D. (1987) *Enterprising Innovation: An Alternative Approach*, Pinter, London.
Moore, K. (2006) 'Powered by the people: Scientific authority in participatory science', in S. Frickel and K. Moore (eds) *The New Political Sociology of Science: Institutions, Networks and Powers*, University of Wisconsin Press, Madison, WI, pp. 299–325.
Moore, K., Kleinman, D. L., Hess, D. and Frickel, S. (2011) 'Science and neoliberal globalization: A political sociological approach', *Theory and Society*, vol. 40, no. 5, pp. 505–532.
Morozov, E. (2014) 'A critica at large: Making it', *The New Yorker*, 13 January.
Mota, C. (2011) 'The rise of personal fabrication', in *Proceedings of the 8th ACM Conference on Creativity and Cognition*, New York, ACM, pp. 279–288.
Murray, R. (1985a) 'Benetton Britain: The new economic order', *Marxism Today*, (November), pp. 28–32.
Murray, R. (1985b) 'London and the Greater London Council: Restructuring the capital of capital', *IDS Bulletin*, vol. 16, no. 1, pp. 47–55.
National Innovation Foundation (2013) *Annual Report 2012–13*, NIF, Ahmedabad.
National Innovation Foundation (n.d.) 'MVIF', NIF, http://nif.org.in/bd_mvif, accessed 25 February 2016.
Noble, D. (1979) *America by Design: Science, Technology and the Rise of Corporate Capitalism*, Knopf, New York.
Noble, D. (1984) *Forces of Production: A Social History of Industrial Automation*, Knopf, New York.

North East Trade Union Studies Information Unit (1980) *A Farewell to Arms? The Future Facing Vickers Elswick on Tyneside*, North East Trade Union Studies Information Unit, Newcastle.

O'Malley, J. (1977) *The Politics of Community Action*, Spokesman, Sheffield.

Oberschall, A. (1973) *Social Conflict and Social Movements*, Prentice-Hall, Englewood Cliffs, NJ.

OECD (2015) *Innovation Policies for Inclusive Development: Scaling up Inclusive Innovations*, Organisation for Economic Co-operation and Development, Paris.

Paes de Barros, R. and Carvalho, M. de (2003) *Desafios para a Política Social Brasileira*, Textos para Discussão no 985, IPEA, Brasilia.

Palmer, J. (1986) 'Municipal enterprise and popular planning', *New Left Review*, vol. 159 (February), pp. 117–124.

Pansera, M. and Owen, R. (2014) 'Eco-innovation at the "bottom of the pyramid"', in D. A. Vazquez-Brust, J. Sarkis and J. J. Cordeiro (eds) *Collaboration for Sustainability and Innovation*, Springer, Dordrecht, pp. 293–314.

Parayil, G. (1992) 'Social movements, technology and development: A query and an instructive case from the third world', in *Dialectical Anthropology*, vol. 17, no. 3, pp. 339–352, http://www.jstor.org/stable/29790513, accessed 14 February 2016.

Passos, N. (2011) 'Na "guerra das cisternas", 15 mil protestam no sertão contra governo', *Carta Maior*, pp. 13–16, http://www.cartamaior.com.br/?/Editoria/Movimentos-Sociais/Na-guerra-das-cisternas-15-mil-protestam-no-sertao-contra-governo/2/18388, accessed 20 February 2016.

Pattnaik, B. K. and Sahoo, S. (2006) 'Science popularization movement in the Indian state of Orissa', *International Journal of Contemporary Sociology*, vol. 43, no. 2, pp. 211–244.

Paucar Santana, R. and Zambrano, G. M. (1991) 'Reinforcing campesino wisdom', *Development Communication Report*, vol. 77, pp. 57–59.

Pelly, D. (1985) 'Arms conversion and the labour movement', in Collective Design/Project (ed.) *Very Nice Work if You Can Get It: The Socially Useful Production Debate*, Spokesman, Sheffield, pp. 104–115.

Perez, C. (1983) 'Structural change and assimilations of new technologies in the economic and social systems', *Futures*, vol. 15, no. 5, pp. 357–375.

Pieterse, J. N. (1998) 'My paradigm or yours? Alternative development, post-development, reflexive development', *Development and Change*, vol. 29, pp. 343–373.

Piore, M. J. and Sabel, C. F. (1984) *The Second Industrial Divide*, Basic Books, New York.

Prahalad, C. K. (2009) *The Fortune at the Bottom of the Pyramid*, Pearson FT Press, London.

Prasad, C. S. (2001) 'Towards an understanding of Gandhi's views on science', *Economic and Political Weekly*, vol. 36, no. 39, pp. 3721–3732.

Pursell, C. (1993) 'Address presidential: The rise and fall of the appropriate technology movement in the United States, 1965–1985', *Technology and Culture*, vol. 256, no. 3, pp. 629–637.

Raina, V. (1997) 'The Idea behind IADEA', in D. Quesada and N. N. Kyanpēn Iinkai (eds) *Integrating Alternative Development Efforts in Asia (IADEA), Report on the Workshop at Palakkad, Kerala, 1–4 March 1996*, JCNC, PP21 RUA and KSSP, Tokyo.

Rasmussen, L. B. (2007) 'From human-centred to human-context centred approach: Looking back over "the hills", what has been gained and lost?' *AI & Society*, vol. 21, no. 4, pp. 471–495, doi:10.1007/s00146-007-0088-3.

Ratto, M. and Boler, M. (2014) *DIY Citizenship: Critical Making and Social Media*, MIT Press, Cambridge, MA.

Rauner, F., Rasmussen, L. and Corbett, J. M. (1988) 'The social shaping of technology and work: Human-centred computer integrated manufacturing systems', *AI & Society*, vol. 2, no. 1, pp. 47–61.

Reddy, A. K. N. (1979) 'National and regional technology groups and institutions: An assessment', in A. S. Bhalla (ed.), *Towards Global Action for Appropriate Technology, Technology and Employment Branch*, Pergamon, Oxford, pp. 63–136.
Reilly, T. (1976) 'Trade unions and technology', *Science for People*, vol. 32, pp. 13–15.
Rip, A. and Kemp, R. (1998) 'Technological change', in S. Rayner and E. L. Malone (eds) *Human Choices and Climate Change. Volume 2: Resources and Technology*, Bateller, Columbus, OH.
Rist, G. (2011) *The History of Development: From Western Origins to Global Faith*, 3rd edn, Zed Books, London.
Romero, S. (2009) 'An isolated village finds the energy to keep going', *New York Times*, 15 October.
Rosenbrock, H. H. (ed.) (1989) *Designing Human-centred Technology*, Springer-Verlag, London.
Rowthorn, B. (1981) 'The politics of the alternative economic strategy', *Marxism Today*, January, pp. 4–10.
RTS (2005) 'Histórico e elementos conceituais', Rede Tecnologia Social,www.rts.br.or.
RTS (2009a) *Exhibition of Social Technologies*, Rede Tecnologia Social, Rio de Janeiro.
RTS (2009b) 'Propostas da plenária final para a RTS', *Relatorio de 2º Fórum Nacional da Rede de Tecnologia Social e 2ª Conferência Internacional de Tecnologia Social,* http://rts.ibict.br/publicacoes/arquivos/relatorio_2_forum_nacional_da_rts_e_2_conferencia_de_TS.pdf, accessed 20 February 2016.
RTS (2010) *Relatório dos 5 anos da RTS*, Rede Tecnologia Social, Rio de Janeiro.
RTS (2011) *Relatório dos 6 anos da RTS*, Rede Tecnologia Social, Rio de Janeiro, http://rts.ibict.br/bibliotecarts/publicacoes/relatorio_6anos_jul14.pdf, accessed 20 February 2016.
RTS (2014) 'Rede Tecnologia Social', http://www.rts.org.br/english?set_language=en&cl=en, accessed 15 March 2014.
Rustin, M. (1986) 'Lessons of the London industrial strategy', *New Left Review*, vol. 155 (January–February), pp. 75–84.
Rybczynski, W. (1980) *Paper Heroes: A Review of Appropriate Technology*, Prism Press, Dorchester.
Samuels, D. (2004) 'From democracy to socialism: Party organization and the transformation of the Worker's Party in Brazil', *Comparative Political Studies*, vol. 37, no. 9, pp. 999–1024.
Sandbrook, D. (2012) *Seasons in the Sun: The Battle for Britain, 1974–1979*, Penguin, London.
Schamis, H. E. (2009) 'Reconceptualizing Latin American authoritarianism in the 1970s: From bureaucratic-authoritarianism to neoconservatism', *Comparative Politics*, vol. 23, no. 2, pp. 201–220.
Scholz, T. (ed.) (2013) *Digital Labour: The Internet as Playground and Factory*, Routledge, New York.
Schor, J. B. (2010) *Plenitude: The New Economics of True Wealth*, Penguin Press, New York.
Schot, J. and Geels, F. W. (2008) 'Strategic niche management and sustainable innovation journeys: Theory, findings, research agenda, and policy', *Technology Analysis & Strategic Management*, vol. 20, no. 5, pp. 537–554, doi:10.1080/09537320802292651.
Schumacher, F. W. (1973) *Small is Beautiful*, Blond and Briggs, London.
Scoones, I., Leach, M. and Newell, P. (2015) *The Politics of Green Transformations*, Earthscan Routledge, London.
Scott, J. C. (1999) *Seeing like a State*, Yale University Press, New Haven, CT.
SEBRAE Agronegocios (2007) 'Entrevista: Joe Valle, Secretário de Inclusão Social do Ministério da Ciência e Tecnologia', *SEBRAE Agronegocios*, vol. 7, pp. 34–35.
Senker, P. (1986) *Toward the Automatic Factory? The Need for Training*, Springer-Verlag, Berlin.
Serrano, P. B. (1985) 'Función de las tecnologias apropiadas en el medio ambiente', *Ambiente y Desarrollo*, vol. 1, no. 2, pp. 61–80.

Seyfang, G. and Smith, A. (2007) 'Grassroots innovations for sustainable development: Towards a new research and policy agenda', *Environmental Politics*, vol. 16, no. 4, pp. 584–603.

Shivarajan, S. and Srinivasan, A. (2013) 'The poor as suppliers of intellectual property: A social network approach to sustainable poverty alleviation', *Business Ethics Quarterly*, vol. 23, no. 3, pp. 381–406, doi:10.5840/beq2013233268.

Sleigh, A., Stewart, H. and Stokes, K. (2015) *Open Dataset of UK Makerspaces*, NESTA, London.

Smith, A. (2005) 'The alternative technology movement: An analysis of its framing and negotiation of technology development', *Human Ecology Review*, vol. 12, no. 2, pp. 106–119.

Smith, A. (2007) 'Translating sustainabilities between green niches and socio-technical regimes', *Technology Analysis Strategic Management*, vol. 19, no. 4, pp. 427–450.

Smith, A. (2013) 'What the new Ahmedabad declaration means for grassroots innovation', *STEPS Centre Blog*, 31 January, http://steps-centre.org/2013/blog/what-the-new-ahmedabad-declaration-means-for-grassroots-innovation/, accessed 20 February 2016.

Smith, A. (2014a) 'Scaling-up inclusive innovation: Asking the right questions?' *STEPS Centre*, 20 March, http://steps-centre.org/2014/blog/scaling-up-inclusive-innovation/, accessed 20 February 2016.

Smith, A. (2014b) 'Technology networks for socially useful production', *Journal of Peer Production*, vol. 5, pp. 1–9.

Smith, A., Fressoli, M. and Thomas, H. (2014) 'Grassroots innovation movements: Challenges and contributions', *Journal of Cleaner Production*, vol. 63, pp. 114–124.

Smith, A., Hargreaves, T., Hielscher, S., Martiskainen, M. and Seyfang, G. (2015) 'Making the most of community energies: Three perspectives on grassroots innovation', *Environment and Planning A*, doi:10.1177/0308518X15597908.

Smith, A., Hielscher, S., Dickel, S., Söderberg, J. and van Oost, E. (2013) *Grassroots Digital Fabrication: Reconfiguring, Relocating and Recalibrating Production and Consumption?* Working Papers SWPS 2013-02, SPRU, University of Sussex, Brighton.

Smith, A. and Raven, R. (2012) 'What is protective space? Reconsidering niches in transitions to sustainability', *Research Policy*, vol. 41, no. 6, pp. 1025–1036.

Smith, A. and Stirling, A. (2007) 'Moving outside or inside? Objectification and reflexivity in the governance of socio-technical systems', *Journal of Environmental Policy & Planning*, vol. 9, no. 3–4, pp. 351–373.

Smith, A., Stirling, A. and Berkhout, F. (2005) 'The governance of sustainable socio-technical transitions', *Research Policy*, vol. 34, no. 10, pp. 1491–1510.

Smith, A., Voß, J.-P. and Grin, J. (2010) 'Innovation studies and sustainability transitions: The allure of the multi-level perspective and its challenges', *Research Policy*, vol. 39, no. 4, pp. 435–448.

Snow, D. A., Rochford, E. B., Worden, S. K. and Benford, R. D. (1986) 'Frame alignment processes, micromobilization, and movement participation', *American Sociological Review*, vol. 51, no. 4, pp. 464–481.

Söderberg, J. (2012) 'The unmaking of the working class and the rise of the maker', *Re-public: Re-imagining Democracy*, 15 October.

Söderberg, J. (2013) 'Automating amateurs in the 3D printing community', *Work Organisation Labour and Globalisation*, vol. 7, no. 1, pp. 124–139.

Soete, L. (2013) 'Is innovation always good?' in J. Fagerberg, B. Martin and E. S. Anderson (eds) *Innovation Studies: Evolution and Future Challenges*, Oxford University Press, Oxford, chapter 6.

Souza Costa, J., Grainger Ribeiro Maia, A. B., Pinheiros de Freitas, A. R., Lázaro da Silva Filho, J. C., Cavalcanti Sá Abreu, M. and Correia Teixeira Filho, M. (2013) 'Social technology as a sustainable public policy: The Mandalla Project in Ceará', *Journal of Technology Management and Innovation*, vol. 8, special issue, pp. 177–187.

Speke Joint Shops Stewards Committee (1979) *Dunlop: Jobs for Merseyside*, Speke Joint Shops Stewards Committee, Merseyside.

Stangler, D. and Maxwell, K. (2012) 'DIY Producer Society', *Innovations: Technology, Governance, Globalization*, vol. 7, no. 3, pp. 3–10.

Stirling, A. (2015) 'Emancipating transformations: From controlling "the transition" to culturing plural radical processes', in P. Newell, M. Leach and I. Scoones (eds) *The Politics of Green Transformations*, Routledge, London, pp. 54–67.

Suarez Maciel, A. L. and Castilhos Fernandez, R. M. (2011) 'Tecnologias sociais: Interfase con as politicas públicas e o servicio social', *Serviço Social & Sociedade*, vol. 105, pp. 146–165.

Tarrow, S. (2004) *Power in Movement. Social Movements and Contentious Politics*, Cambridge University Press, New York.

Tekhne (1990) *Tecnología y desarrollo rural. Una experiencia en zonas áridas*, Tekhne, Santiago de Chile.

Thackara, J. (2015) *How to Thrive in the Next Economy*, Thames & Hudson, London.

Thomas, H. (2012) 'Tecnologías para la inclusión social en América Latina: De las tecnologías apropiadas a los sistemas tecnológicos sociales. Problemas conceptuales y soluciones estratégicas', in *Tecnología, Desarrollo y Democracia. Nueve estudios sobre dinámicas socio-técnicas de exclusión/inclusión social*, Ministerio de Ciencia, Tecnología e Innovación Productiva, Buenos Aires, pp. 25–78.

Thomas, H., Davyt, A. and Dagnino, R. (2000) 'Inculacionismo-neovinculacionismo. Racionalidades de la interaccion universidad-empresa en América Latina', in R. Casas and G. Valenti (eds) *Dos Ejes en la Vinculación de las Universidades a la Producción*, IIS-UNAM/UAM-Xochimilco/Plaza y Valdés Ed., México DF, pp. 25–48.

Thompson, L. and Tapscott, C. (2010) *Citizenship and Social Movements: Perspectives from the Global South*, Zed Books, London.

Thompson, P. (1989) *The Nature of Work*, 2nd edn, Macmillan, Basingstoke.

Thompson, P. and Bannon, E. (1985) *Working the System: The Shop Floor and New Technology*, Pluto Press, London.

Thorpe, A. (2012) *Architecture and Design Versus Consumerism: How Design Activism Confronts Growth*, Earthscan, Abingdon.

Thrissur Declaration (2014) 'Time for a new vision on alternative technologies and organisational forms for social transformation', statement of participants at the workshop on Alternative Technologies and Organisational Forms for Social Transformation, Thrissur, India 13–16 October 2014, http://www.southsolidarity.org/wp-content/uploads/sites/2/2014/11/Thrissur-Declaration.pdf, accessed 14 February 2016.

Tilly, C. (2008) *Contentious Performances*, Cambridge University Press, New York.

Tratado de Cooperación Amazonica (n.d.) *Tecnologias Apropiadas y Saneamiento Basico y Energias Alternativas: Experiencias Amazónicas como Base para la Creación de la Red de Tecnologías Apropiadas de la Amazonia*, Tratado de Cooperación Amazonica, Secretaria Pro Tempore, Caracas.

Troxler, P. (2014) 'Fab Labs forked: A grassroots insurgency inside the next industrial revolution', *Journal of Peer Production*, vol. 5, pp. 1–3.

Tuckman, A. (2011) 'Workers' control and the politics of factory occupation', in I. Ness and D. Azzellini (eds) *Ours to Master and to Own: Workers' Councils from the Commune to the Present*, Haymarket, Chicago, pp. 284–301.

UNDP (2010) *Brokering Inclusive Business Models*, United Nations Development Programme, New York.

UNEP (1979) *Directory of Institutions and Individuals Active in Environmentally-Sound and Appropriate Technologies*, United Nations Environment Programme Reference Series 1, Pergamon Press, Oxford.

Ustyuzhantseva, O. V. (2014) 'From policy statements to real policy', *Current Science*, vol. 106, no. 11, pp. 1472–1474.

Ustyuzhantseva, O. V. (2015) 'Institutionalization of grassroots innovation in India', *Current Science*, vol. 108, no. 8, pp. 1476–1482.

Vidal, C. M. and Mari, M. (2002) 'La Escuela Latinoamericana de Pensamiento en Ciencia, Tecnología y Desarrollo Notas de un Proyecto de Investigación', *Revista iIeroamericana de Ciencia Tecnología y Sociedad*, 4, www.oei.es/revistactsi/numero4/escuelalatinoamericana.htm, accessed 25 February 2016.

Voss, J.-P., Smith, A. and Grin, J. (2009) 'Designing long-term policy: Rethinking transition management', *Policy Sciences*, vol. 42, no. 4, pp. 275–302.

Wainwright, H. and Elliott, D. (1982) *The Lucas Plan. A New Trade Unionism in the Making?* Allison & Busby, London.

Weisman, A. (1998) *Gaviotas: A Village to Reinvent the World*, Chelsea Green Publishing, White River Junction, VT.

Weisman, A. (2008) *Gaviotas: A Village to Reinvent the World*, 2nd edn, Chelsea Green Publishing, White River Junction, VT.

Wezel, A., Bellon, S., Doré, T., Francis, C., Vallod, D. and David, C. (2009) 'Agroecology as a science, a movement and a practice: A review', *Agronomy for Sustainable Agriculture*, vol. 29, no. 4, pp. 2503–515.

Whitecombe, R. and Carr, M. (1982) *Appropriate Technology Institutions: A Review*, ITDG Publishing, London.

Willoughby, K. W. (1990) *Technology Choice: Critique of the Appropriate Technology Movement*, ITDG Publishing, London.

Winner, L. (1977) *Autonomous Technology: Technics out of Control*, MIT Press, Cambridge, MA.

Wolf, P., Troxler, P., Kocher, P-Y., Harboe, J. and Gaudenz, U. (2014) 'Sharing is sparing: Open knowledge sharing in FabLabs', *Journal of Peer Production*, special issue, Shared machine workshops, vol. 3, no. 5.

World Bank (2012) *Inclusive Green Growth: The Pathway to a Sustainable World*, World Bank, Washington DC.

World Commission on Environment and Development (1987) *Our Common Future*, Oxford University Press, Oxford.

Zachariah, M. and Sooryamoorthy, R. (1994) *Science for Social Revolution: Achievements and Dilemmas of a Development Movement: The Kerala Sastra Sahitya Parishad*, New Delhi: Vistaar Publications.

Zapp, J. (1991) *Cultivos Sin Tierra: La Hidroponía Popular, una Opción para la Superación de la Pobreza*, PNUD, Bogotá.

Zijp, H. (2013) 'How to start a Fab Lab in 7 days with 4 people and about 5000 Euros @ Fabfuse 2012', video, http://vimeo.com/48702977, accessed 15 February 2016.

INDEX

activism 2, 3, 53, 184–185; appropriate technology 63, 75–76, 78n5, 167, 169; Barcelona 118; hackerspaces, fablabs and makerspaces 105; movement for socially useful production 12, 33, 35–36, 38, 40, 47, 50–51, 54, 175–176, 182; POC21 1, 191; repertoires of action 26; Social Technology Network 123; South America 60
actors 188, 189, 193
agency 4, 27, 196
agriculture 3; alternative technology 87; appropriate technology 61, 65–66, 67, 69; Honey Bee Network 150–151; People's Science Movements 82, 84, 92, 93
agroecology 7; appropriate technology 61–62, 66, 67, 69, 70, 72–73, 74–75, 169; People's Science Movements 81, 84, 94; Powwow 2; Social Technology Network 124, 126, 132, 133, 134–135, 170
All India Peoples Science Network (AIPSN) 83, 86, 91, 95, 99n2
alliances 121, 187–188, 189
alternative technology 101; intellectual property rights 145; People's Science Movements 86–87, 89, 90, 91, 93, 96–97, 98
Altieri, Miguel 65, 68
Altman, Mitch 112
Alvares, Claude 149, 153
Alvarez, S. E. 21

Amersfoort FabLab 111, 113–115, 120
Appropriate Technologies Transfer Programme (PTTA) 68
appropriate technology (AT) 3, 12–13, 22, 56–79, 101, 176; development intervention 60–63; framings 60–66, 167, 169–170; historical background 57–60; illustrative examples 70–73; India 82–83, 86, 88–89, 96; pathways 73–76, 186; spaces and strategies 66–70, 179, 185
appropriation of technologies 130
Argentina: appropriate technology 59–61, 67, 71, 74–75, 79n6; Las Barracas Hacklab 102; Mercosur 144n9; Social Technology Network 132, 138
arms conversion 37
artefacts 187, 188–189, 192
Ateneus de Fabricació Digital 111, 115–118, 120
automation 38–39, 53, 196

Bajaj, Rahul 156
Bank of Brazil Foundation (BBF) 123, 126, 131, 133, 134, 135, 140
Baquedano, Manuel 64, 79n9
Barcelona 110, 111, 115–118, 120
Barros, Larissa 132, 140
Baumgarten, M. 143n5
Benford, R. D. 23
Benkler, Y. 106
Benn, Tony 32–33
Bijker, W. E. 23

biodiversity 148, 149–150, 151–152, 160, 161, 163n8
biotechnology 4, 7, 82, 163n9, 163n11
Bolivia 62, 71
Bookchin, Murray 101
boomerang effect 22
bottom-of-the-pyramid (BoP) innovation 145, 157, 162n1
Boyle, Godfrey 101
Bramachari, Samir 90
Brand, Stewart 101
Brazil: appropriate technology 59–60, 68, 69–70, 71, 74, 77; Mercosur 144n9; Social Technology Network 2–3, 13–14, 75–76, 77, 123–144, 168, 170–171, 180
Bremen Innovation and Technology Centre 49
Build Brighton 111–113, 119

Can Batlló 117
capabilities 188, 189, 193
capitalism 89, 107, 122, 175
Carson, Rachel 2
Castilhos Fernandez, R. M. 141
Centre for Alternative Industrial and Technological Systems (CAITS) 36, 41, 42, 44, 55n4
Centre for Ecology and Rural Development (CERD) 83, 90, 96
Centre for Social Research, Tripura 83
Centre for Studies in Science, Technology and Development (CSSTD) 84
Centre for Technology and Development (CTD) 83, 85, 90, 92, 94, 96
Centro Científico Tecnológico Barrancas (CECITEB) 61
Centro de capacitación y experimentación en Technología Apropriada (Tekhne) 61, 63, 67, 70, 74
Centro de Educación Tecnológica (CET) 63, 67, 69, 72–73
Centro de Estudios sobre Tecnología Apropiada para América Latina (CETAL) 61, 63–64, 67, 70, 71, 72–73, 75
Centro de Estudios sobre Tecnologías Apropiadas de Argentina (CETAAR) 61, 67, 74
Centro de Tecnología Apropiada, Catholic University (CTA) 62
Centro Experimental Gaviotas 62, 67–68, 69, 70, 73, 74
Centro Internacional para la Agricultura Tropical (CIAT) 62

Centro para la Gestión Tecnología Popular 62
Centro Uruguayo de Tecnología Apropiada (CEUTA) 61, 67, 74
Chevron 110
Chile 59, 60, 61, 63–64, 67–69, 73–75
cities 101
citizenship: appropriate technology 75–76; Ateneus programme 117, 118; technological 107, 119, 193
Ciutat Invisible cooperative 118
Ciutat Meridiana 117
civil society 17, 18, 21; appropriate technology 63; framings 24; Social Technology Network 123, 124, 126, 131, 132, 143; South America 59, 60; see also social movements
climate change 1, 152, 191
cognitive justice 5, 150, 151, 153
Colau, Ada 118
collaboration 18, 53, 193; appropriate technology 59; hackerspaces, fablabs and makerspaces 104–105, 106, 108–109, 115, 117, 119–120, 168, 174
collective action 17, 18, 21, 23
collective production 87–88
Colombia: alternative technology 61–62, 67–70, 72–74, 77, 78n5; political unrest 58; Social Technology Network 132, 138; universities 181
commercialization 11, 25, 194; grassroots ingenuity framing 177; Grassroots Innovation Augmentation Network 147; hackerspaces, fablabs and makerspaces 103, 105, 111, 120, 121–122; Honey Bee Network 153, 156, 157, 158, 160, 168, 172; movement for socially useful production 47, 51, 54
community activism 35–36, 38, 53, 105; see also activism
community development 63
community health 7
competition 150, 152, 161
concepts and ideas 193
Conference of the Parties to the UN Framework Convention on Climate Change (COP21) 1, 191
construction 81, 93
constructive technology assessment 53, 55
consumption practices 101, 107, 108–109, 121, 174
contexts 20–22, 27, 30, 165, 167–168, 189
convivial tools 101

cooking: People's Science Movements 80, 84, 85, 93; solar cookers 70, 74; witch cooker 70–71
Cooley, Mike 33, 40, 43, 55n1, 55n3, 101
co-option 11, 30, 53, 122, 186, 187–188, 193–194
Corporación de Investigación en Agricultura Alternativa (CIAL) 69
corporations 10
Costa, A. B. 141
Council of Scientific and Industrial Research (CSIR) 82, 83–84
Cox, L. 17
creativity 4, 101, 146, 148, 153, 173
crowd-funding 106, 115, 122, 191, 193
crowd-sourcing 9
Cryer, Bob 35
cultural nationalism 150, 153
culture 64

Dag Hamaarskjöld Foundation 59
Danish Technical University 49
De Paulo, J. 138
De War collective 113–114, 115
decentralized production 100, 174, 187
Defense Advance Research Projects Agency (DARPA) 111
Delhi Science Forum (DSF) 83–84, 87–88, 92
democracy, industrial 37, 39–40
democratization 21, 125, 193; hackerspaces, fablabs and makerspaces 105, 106, 107, 121, 174; of innovation 196; manufacturing 187; Social Technology Network 124, 129, 140, 142, 143, 168; technology commons 53
dependency theory 57, 58, 78n3
development 3; appropriate technology 56, 59, 60–63, 65–66, 76, 78; hackerspaces, fablabs and makerspaces 121; pathways 185, 189, 197; Social Technology Network 13–14, 123, 127–128, 138; *see also* sustainable development
Dias, R. 141
Dickel, S. 108
Diez, Tomas 119
diffusion of innovation 146, 149, 157–158, 159, 162, 171, 189
digital design and fabrication 10, 102–105, 106–109, 116–118, 119, 121
disruptive innovation 9
diversity 28
drones 10

eco-hackers 1
economic crisis 22, 59, 75
economic development: dependency theory 58; framings 166; Honey Bee Network 160–161; India 162n6; movement for socially useful production 176; People's Science Movements 182; Social Technology Network 130
economic growth 4, 6, 7, 25; Brazil 126; hackerspaces, fablabs and makerspaces 101; inclusive 194; South America 58
economic strategy 40–41, 51
Ecuador 62
education 3; hackerspaces, fablabs and makerspaces 104, 110, 175; lack of investment 99; People's Science Movements 81, 89; Social Technology Network 126, 138
Ehn, Pelle 42
Eklavya 83
elites 8, 17, 35, 185; appropriate technology 56; Brazil 137, 140, 143
Elliott, Dave 34, 47
empowerment: appropriate technology 57, 60, 64, 75–76, 77, 79n6, 170; grassroots empowerment framing 177, 178, 186, 190; Honey Bee Network 162; movement for socially useful production 52; Social Technology Network 10–11, 123, 128, 129–130, 135–137, 140, 141–142
energy 3; alternative technology 86; appropriate technology 60, 62, 70; hackerspaces, fablabs and makerspaces 108; India 82; People's Science Movements 81, 84; Powwow 2; Social Technology Network 126; *see also* renewable energy; solar energy
entrepreneurship 4, 9, 195; hackerspaces, fablabs and makerspaces 101, 105, 106–107, 117, 120, 121, 168, 174, 175; Honey Bee Network 152, 159, 161, 172; movement for socially useful production 51; People's Science Movements 94, 95
Environmental Development Action in the Third World (ENDA) 61, 70
environmentalism 2, 3, 9, 18; alternative technology 86–87; appropriate technology 65–66; hackerspaces, fablabs and makerspaces 101, 114–115; Honey Bee Network 150, 151–152; movement for socially useful production 12, 35–36, 37–38, 51, 167; *see also* sustainability

Escobar, A. 18, 21
Espinosa, Nicolas 72
European Strategic Programme on Research in Information Technology (ESPRIT) 49
evolutionary economics 20, 21
exclusion 195
Eyerman, R. 17

Fab Academy 109, 110
Fab Foundation 104, 109, 110, 184
FabLab Amersfoort 111, 113–115, 120
FabLab Flotante 103–104
fablabs 3, 10, 13, 53, 100–122, 172, 196; Ateneus de Fabricació Digital 115–118; background 102–105; FabLab Amersfoort 111, 113–115, 120; framings 106–109, 168, 173–175; pathways 118–121, 186–187; POC21 191; spaces and strategies 109–111, 180, 184
Fals Borda, Orlando 63, 77, 79n8
feminism 12, 18, 36, 38, 40
Flesher Fominaya, C. 17
Fletcher, Richard 34, 44
Fonseca, R. 130
food production 3, 8; alternative technology 60, 61, 66, 72; Social Technology Network 126, 128, 134, 138
Forum of Scientists, Engineers and Technologists, West Bengal 83
framings 22–24, 27–28, 30, 165, 166–178, 182, 190, 194; ambiguity over 187; appropriate technology 60–66, 167, 169–170; hackerspaces, fablabs and makerspaces 106–109, 119, 168, 173–175; Honey Bee Network 149–154, 168, 172–173; movement for socially useful production 36–41, 54, 167, 175–176; People's Science Movements 86–90, 167, 171–172; Social Technology Network 126–131, 168, 170–171
free hardware 106
free software 103, 104, 106, 168, 193
Free Software Foundation 86
Freire, Paulo 63, 77, 79n8, 126
Frickel, Scott 18
Fukuoka, Masanobu 86
Fundação Centro Tecnológico de Minas Gerais (CETEC) 68
Fundación Ecuatoriana de Tecnología Apropiada (FEDETA) 62
funding: appropriate technology 64, 69, 72, 74, 77; Ateneus programme 116; crowd-funding 106, 115, 122, 191, 193; hackerspaces, fablabs and makerspaces 110, 113, 119; Honey Bee Network 155–156; Social Technology Network 134, 138, 140, 141; see also investment
Future Group 156, 162n3

Gadgil, M. 84
Gamser, M. 63
Gandhi, Mohandas 86
Garretón, M. A. 58, 59
Gauntlett, D. 107
gender: movement for socially useful production 38, 45, 51, 176; People's Science Movements 94
geo-engineering 7
George, Mike 36–37
Germany 42
global South 2–3, 21
governments 110–111, 148, 197
Grassroots Innovation Augmentation Network (GIAN) 147, 155–156, 160
Greater London Council (GLC) 36, 43, 47, 49, 175, 188
Greater London Enterprise Board (GLEB) 43, 45, 46, 48
green economy 185
Gross, N. 18
Grupo Talpuy 65, 75
Guallart, Vicente 116
Guha, Ramchander 84, 149
Gui, Bonsiepe 68
Gupta, Anil Kumar 9, 11, 145, 146, 149–153, 159, 162–163, 172
Gushiken, Luiz 131

hackerspaces 3, 10, 13, 53, 100–122, 172, 196; Ateneus de Fabricació Digital 115–118; background 102–105; Build Brighton 111–113; framings 106–109, 168, 173–175; pathways 118–121, 186–187; POC21 191; spaces and strategies 109–111, 180, 184
hardware: free 106; open 102, 104, 105, 109, 174, 193
Harper, Peter 101
healthcare 60, 81, 89, 99, 126
Herrera, Amílcar 58, 68
Hess, David 9, 20, 26
Hirschmann, A. O. 79n7
Hochstetler, K. 125
Honey Bee Network (HBN) 3, 9, 11, 14, 145–164, 176; framings 149–154, 168, 172–173; future challenges 158–161;

origins and background 146–149; pathways 156–158, 186; spaces and strategies 154–156, 180, 182, 184
horticulture 92, 93
housing 3, 7, 121; appropriate technology 60, 61, 70, 71, 74; hackerspaces, fablabs and makerspaces 120; Powwow 2; Social Technology Network 124, 126, 133, 138
human-centred technology 37, 38–39, 49, 52

identity 17, 23, 26, 108, 119
Illich, Ivan 59, 101
inclusion 4, 24, 195; Brazil 125; framings 166; Honey Bee Network 161; movement for socially useful production 48; open software 128; pathways 28; Social Technology Network 13–14, 124, 128, 137, 141–142
incubation: hackerspaces, fablabs and makerspaces 100, 105, 107, 108, 121; Honey Bee Network 152, 159, 173; innovation incubation centres 181; People's Science Movements 90; Social Technology Network 133
India: Honey Bee Network 3, 14, 145–164, 168, 172–173, 176, 180; People's Science Movements 2, 3, 13, 80–99, 167, 171–172, 176, 179, 185
indigenous knowledge 4, 6; appropriate technology 61, 64–65, 66, 73, 77; Honey Bee Network 14, 149, 150, 172; People's Science Movements 88; Social Technology Network 129
industrial democracy 37, 39–40
industrial restructuring 32, 33–34, 167
industrialization 56, 58, 59, 66, 81, 169, 171
inequality 22, 195; appropriate technology 76; Brazil 126, 127, 128, 136; dependency theory 58; movement for socially useful production 52; South America 60
information and communications technologies (ICTs) 4, 45, 107, 116, 147
infrastructures 188, 193
ingenuity framing 11, 177, 178, 182, 183, 186, 190
innovation 4, 5, 11; alternative forms of 192–194, 195, 197; bottom-of-the-pyramid 145, 157, 162n1; contexts 20–21; conventional 129; democratization of 196; disruptive 9; hackerspaces, fablabs and makerspaces 105, 108, 121; Honey Bee Network 14, 146, 154–155, 157, 158, 159; inclusive 7–8, 22, 53, 95, 162, 177, 194; movement for socially useful production 48; open 8, 10; pathways 24; People's Science Movements 97–98; social 8, 108, 116, 194; social movements 18; Social Technology Network 129, 130; transformational 192, 194
insertion strategies 182–183, 184, 185, 186, 192, 195, 197
Institute of Advanced Architecture Catalunya (IAAC) 116
Institute of Social Technology (ITS) 126
institutions 6–7, 9, 10, 178; access to 171; appropriate technology 60, 66–67, 69; engagement with 11, 18, 121, 194; hackerspaces, fablabs and makerspaces 104, 109, 120; Honey Bee Network 145, 152, 154, 158–159, 160; insertion strategies 183; mobilization strategies 183–184; pathways 28, 29, 185; power relations 196; Social Technology Network 127, 131, 132–133, 140, 142, 187; spaces 26, 181
Instituto de Transferencia de Technologías Apropriadas para Sectores Marginales (ITACAB) 61, 74
Integrated Rural Technology Centre (IRTC) 85, 89, 90, 93, 96
intellectual property 7, 8, 11, 19, 105, 162n5, 177; Gupta on 163n9, 163n11, 163n13; hackerspaces, fablabs and makerspaces 103; Honey Bee Network 145, 147, 149–150, 151–152, 154, 163n8, 168, 172–173, 184; NWPGL 163n10; People's Science Movements 90–91, 171; prior informed consent 163n14
Inter-American Development Bank 59
intermediaries 25, 29; Honey Bee Network 158; People's Science Movements 90, 96
Intermediate Technology Development Group (ITDG) 59, 67, 68, 78n4
International Development Bank 67
International Labour Organization 22
investment 11, 34, 171; Honey Bee Network 155; India 99; movement for socially useful production 41, 50; Social Technology Network 135; *see also* funding

Jagani, Mansukhbhai 155
Jamison, Andrew 9, 17, 23

Jan Vigyan Vedika 83
Jodo Gyan 86, 90, 96

Kannan, K. P. 88
Kemp, R. 29
Kerala Sasthra Sahithya Parishad (KSSP) 2, 80, 83, 84–85, 87, 88–89, 93, 97, 98
knowledge 4, 6, 7, 11; appropriate technology 60–63, 64–66, 68–69, 73–74, 77–78, 167; development pathways 187; free and open 105; hackerspaces, fablabs and makerspaces 102; Honey Bee Network 14, 147, 148–149, 150–153, 158, 168, 173; movement for socially useful production 52; production of 17, 18–19, 20, 23, 24, 52; sharing 25, 45; Social Technology Network 129, 130, 140, 142
Kothari, Ashish 149
Kothari, Smitu 149

Las Barracas Hacklab 102
Lassance Jr, A. E. 128
Latin America Consortium of Agroecology and Development (CLADE) 67, 74–75
Leach, M. 18, 21
leadership: Honey Bee Network 159–160, 162; People's Science Movements 88, 90
the Left 34, 54, 79n7
Linn, P. 48
literacy 81
livelihoods: appropriate technology 60, 61; hackerspaces, fablabs and makerspaces 105; Honey Bee Network 153; People's Science Movements 91
Local Agenda 21 7
local authorities 40, 43
local development 181; appropriate technology 59; movement for socially useful production 176; People's Science Movements 13, 172; Social Technology Network 129
Lok Vigyan Sangthana 83
London Energy and Employment Network (LEEN) 43, 47, 52
London Innovation Network (LIN) 43
London New Technology Network (LNTN) 43, 45
Lowe, Brian 39–40, 44
Lucas Aerospace 32, 34, 41, 42, 43
Lucas Plan 32–33, 34–36, 37–38, 42, 44–45, 49, 55n1
Lugari, Paolo 67–68
Lula da Silva, Luiz Inácio 123, 124, 136, 170

Mackintosh, Maureen 45, 47–48
Madhya Pradesh Vigyan Sabha (MPVS) 83, 90, 96
MadLab 113
Make magazine 109, 111
maker movement 9–10
Makerbot 103
makerspaces 3, 10, 13, 53, 100–122, 172, 196; Ateneus de Fabricació Digital 115–118; background 102–105; Build Brighton 111–113; framings 106–109, 168, 173–175; pathways 118–121, 186–187; POC21 191; spaces and strategies 109–111, 180, 184
MAKLab 113
market economy 89–90, 150
Marxism 37; ecological 84
Massachusetts Institute of Technology (MIT) 103, 104, 110, 115, 155
materiality 29
Mathur, Kuldeep 149, 160
medicine 7
Mercosur 138, 144n9
methodologies 49–50, 53, 188, 193
Micro Venture Innovation Fund (MVIF) 147, 155
Miró, Ivan 118
mobilization 19–20, 21, 181, 192; appropriate technology 60, 75, 77, 78, 79n6; Honey Bee Network 146, 149, 158; People's Science Movements 81; resources 25, 26; Social Technology Network 127, 131, 137, 139, 142, 184–185; strategies for 182–184, 186, 197
Mondal, Joydeep 160
Moore, Kelly 18
Moore, Mary 45, 48
motivation 193, 194; framings 24; hackerspaces, fablabs and makerspaces 100, 115; Honey Bee Network 173
movement for socially useful production 3, 12, 32–55, 196; background 33–36; framings 36–41, 54, 167, 175–176; illustrative examples 44–50; methodologies 49–50; objects 44–45; pathways 50–53, 186; spaces and strategies 41–43, 50, 51, 53, 54, 179, 182, 185; Technology Networks 45–49, 53
Munjal, Sunil 156

Nandy, Ashis 149, 153
nanotechnology 4, 7

National Council of Science and Technology Development (CNPq) 68, 70, 125
National Innovation Foundation (NIF) 147, 148, 154, 156, 157–158, 160, 161, 163n15, 164n16, 173
National Working Group on Patent Laws (NWGPL) 151, 163n10, 163n12
Nav Nirmati 86, 96
neoconservatism 58
neoliberalism 21, 185; appropriate technology 60; India 86, 168, 171, 172; South America 73, 74, 77, 124; United Kingdom 33, 36, 50, 167, 175
Netherlands 113–115
networks 25, 181; appropriate technology 66–68, 74–75, 77, 78; hackerspaces, fablabs and makerspaces 100, 108, 109, 115, 120; international 22; People's Science Movements 86, 97; Social Technology Network 131, 132, 138–139; Technology Networks 45–49, 53, 175, 188
niches 27, 29
Noisebridge 111, 112
non-governmental organizations (NGOs) 8, 18, 143n5; appropriate technology 56, 67, 68, 69, 75–76, 77, 79n6; Brazil 125; Honey Bee Network 146; People's Science Movements 82; Social Technology Network 13, 123–124, 126, 127, 129, 131–132, 139, 142–143
North East London Polytechnic (NELP) 42, 44
nutrition 60, 70, 81

Obama, Barack 101
Ohlig, Jens 112
One Million Cisterns Programme (P1MC) 133, 135–137, 139–140, 141, 142, 184–185
open software 128
open source networks 1, 10, 105
Open Toko 114
openness 119, 120, 168
Organisation for Economic Co-operation and Development (OECD) 22
outreach 110

Paraguay 62, 144n9
Parekh, Sunil 156
Parsons, Susie 47
participation 19, 25; appropriate technology 63, 64, 71–78, 167, 169, 170; Brazil 125; hackerspaces, fablabs and makerspaces 122; movement for socially useful production 39, 40, 53; Social Technology Network 123, 129–130, 131, 136, 138, 141–142
partnerships 4, 129–130, 197
Paschim Bengal Vigyan Manch 83
patents 147, 151, 157, 163n13, 172; *see also* intellectual property
pathways 24, 27–30, 31, 185–189, 197, 198; appropriate technology 73–76, 186; challenging dominant and unsustainable 196–197; hackerspaces, fablabs and makerspaces 118–121, 186–187; Honey Bee Network 156–158, 186; mobilization for alternative 192; movement for socially useful production 50–53, 186; People's Science Movements 95–99, 186; Social Technology Network 137–142, 186, 187–188
Patriotic and People-oriented Science and Technology Group (PPST) 150, 162n7
Paucar Santana, R. 65
peace movement 35–36, 37, 167
Pedreira, J. S. 128
peer production 171, 187; hackerspaces, fablabs and makerspaces 105, 106, 107, 109, 115; POC21 1–2, 193
Pelly, D. 33
People's Science Movements (PSMs) 2, 3, 13, 80–99, 149, 176; framings 86–90, 167, 171–172; origins and background 82–86; pathways 95–99, 186; spaces and strategies 90–94, 179, 182, 185
People's Summit 2–3
Peru: appropriate technology 61, 64–65, 72, 74; Social Technology Network 132
planning 81, 89, 93
POC21 1–2, 6, 191–192, 193
policy 4, 7, 8, 194; Brazil 124–125; industrial 33; Social Technology Network 130–131, 133–134, 137, 138, 139–140
politics 19–20, 28; appropriate technology 63, 76; Ateneus programme 118; Brazil 124–125; political power 17–18; South America 57, 58–59, 78n5
poverty 126, 127, 128, 141, 171–172
power 28, 196–197
Powwow 2, 3
Prahalad, C. K. 145, 157
prior informed consent (PIC) 163n14

production 101, 107, 108–109, 121; collective 87–88; decentralized 100, 174, 187; *see also* peer production; socially useful production
prototyping 8, 181, 182, 196; hackerspaces, fablabs and makerspaces 100, 103–105, 108, 111, 114, 116, 119–120, 174, 187; movement for socially useful production 40–42, 44–46, 48–49, 51–52, 54, 175, 179, 188; People's Science Movements 96; POC21 1, 191; repertoires of action 26; scaling up 194
Public Laboratory 10

radical science movement 54
Rasmussen, L. B. 49
reapplication 127, 129, 130–133, 135, 139, 143
recycling: appropriate technology 61; Social Technology Network 124, 128, 133, 135
Red Colombiana de Tecnología Apropiada 62
Reddy, A. K. N. 86
redundancies 32, 34, 39
reflexivity 6, 11, 17, 195, 196
renewable energy 7; alternative technology 86; People's Science Movements 81, 93; Social Technology Network 128; *see also* solar energy
repertoires of action 25, 26
RepRap 3D printer 102–103
research and development (R&D) 4, 7; appropriate technology 65, 66, 70; Delhi Science Forum 83; dependency theory 58; movement for socially useful production 40; People's Science Movements 85, 89, 91, 96; Social Technology Network 141
resistance: appropriate technology 64; movement for socially useful production 50, 176; *see also* activism
Resistor hackerspace 103, 111
resources 7, 30, 171, 181; mobilization 25, 26; social movements 17–18; Social Technology Network 127, 130
Restart Project 107, 122
the Right 34
Right to Warmth campaign 47, 52
Rio+20 Summit 2–3
rural development 65–66, 69–70

Sachs, Ignacy 65, 68
Sahai, Suman 149, 151
sanitation 3, 8; appropriate technology 60, 70, 71–72, 74; People's Science Movements 81; Social Technology Network 124, 126, 133
São Paulo 116
scaling up 8, 11, 29, 188–189, 194–195; insertion strategies 183; People's Science Movements 97, 99; Social Technology Network 130, 141–142
Schumacher, Fritz 8–9, 59, 86, 101
science: appropriate technology 68–69; People's Science Movements 2, 13, 80–99; radical science movement 36, 37, 54; social movements 18
science and technology (S&T) 154; access to 26; appropriate technology 74; dependency theory 58; Honey Bee Network 145, 152–153, 154, 158–159, 160; institutions 6–7; People's Science Movements 2, 82–83, 84–85, 88, 90–91, 93–94, 95–99; Social Technology Network 13, 128–129, 130–131, 141, 142; *see also* technology
Scoones, I. 21
scouting 11, 14, 147, 153–154, 160, 168
self-governance 81
Semi-Arid Association 136, 137
Serrano, Pedro 63–64, 69, 71–72
Servicios Múltiples de Tecnologías Apropiadas (SEMTA) 62
Sheffield Centre for Product Development and Technological Resources (SCEPTRE) 43
Shiva, Vandana 149, 151, 153
Shodh Yatras 146–147, 148–149, 153, 157
Singh, Navjyoti 150, 162n7
Smart Citizen initiative 115
Snow, D. A. 23
Social, Technological and Environmental Pathways to Sustainability (STEPS) 12, 28
social audit 37, 40
social change 9, 10, 20, 121; appropriate technology 56, 169; framings 24; grassroots ingenuity framing 177; hackerspaces, fablabs and makerspaces 104, 119, 120; Lucas Plan 35
social diffusion of innovation 146, 149, 157, 158, 159, 162
social engagement 63–64
social entrepreneurship 120
social innovation 8, 108, 116, 194
social justice 3, 5, 8, 9, 18, 197; appropriate technology 59; hackerspaces, fablabs and

makerspaces 122; Honey Bee Network 153; pathways 28; People's Science Movements 96, 97
social media 10, 53, 104, 106, 111, 181
social movements 9, 17–20, 26, 181, 197; appropriate technology 169; Brazil 125; contexts 20–21; framings 22–23, 24; grassroots ingenuity framing 177; movement for socially useful production 12, 35–36; People's Science Movements 97, 98, 99, 167; repertoires of action 26; Social Technology Network 123–124, 126, 127, 131, 132, 139, 140, 142–143; South America 59; *see also* civil society
social relationships 195
social technology (ST) 124, 125–133, 137–142, 143, 168, 170–171
Social Technology Network (STN) 2–3, 10–11, 13–14, 75–76, 77, 123–144; framings 126–131, 168, 170–171; illustrative examples 134–137; origins and background 124–126; pathways 137–142, 186, 187–188; spaces and strategies 131–134, 180, 184–185
socially useful production 3, 12, 32–55, 196; background 33–36; framings 36–41, 54, 167, 175–176; illustrative examples 44–50; methodologies 49–50; objects 44–45; pathways 50–53, 186; spaces and strategies 41–43, 50, 51, 53, 54, 179, 182, 185; Technology Networks 45–49, 53
Society for Promoting Participatory Ecosystem Management (SOPPECOM) 83, 86, 90, 96
Society for Research and Initiatives for Sustainable Technologies and Institutions (SRISTI) 147, 148, 151, 156, 160
Society for Technology and Development (STD) 83, 90, 94, 96, 98
socio-technical landscapes 21–22, 52
Soete, Luc 162n1
software: free 103, 104, 106, 168, 193; open 128
solar energy 5, 191; appropriate technology 61, 62, 70–71, 73, 74; hackerspaces, fablabs and makerspaces 108; People's Science Movements 93; *see also* renewable energy
solidarity 17, 26; appropriate technology 63, 64, 70, 71, 77, 167; social movements 22–23, 197; solidarity economy 123, 126, 128, 132, 143n3
Solidarity Economy Secretariat (SENAES) 125
Solidworks 110
Soluciones Prácticas 61
South America 21; appropriate technology 12–13, 22, 56–79, 167, 169–170, 176, 179, 185; Mercosur 138, 144n9; Social Technology Network 10
spaces 24–27, 30, 166, 178–185, 186, 190, 194, 197; ambiguity over 187; appropriate technology 66–70, 179, 185; hackerspaces, fablabs and makerspaces 109–111, 112, 180; Honey Bee Network 154–156, 180, 182, 184; movement for socially useful production 41–43, 50, 51, 53, 54, 179, 182, 185; People's Science Movements 90–94, 179, 182, 185; Social Technology Network 131–134, 180
Stockholm summit (1982) 2
strategies 24–27, 30, 166, 178–185, 186, 190, 194, 197; ambiguity over 187; appropriate technology 66–70, 179, 185; hackerspaces, fablabs and makerspaces 180; Honey Bee Network 154–156, 180, 182, 184; movement for socially useful production 41–43, 44, 179, 182, 185; People's Science Movements 90–94, 179, 182, 185; Social Technology Network 180
Suarez Maciel, A. L. 141
sustainability 9, 18, 197; framings 166; hackerspaces, fablabs and makerspaces 101, 108–109, 114–115, 121, 122; Social Technology Network 128; socio-technical landscapes 21–22; transitions 29
Sustainable and Integrated Agro-Ecological Production (PAIS) 133, 134–135, 140, 144n7
sustainable development 1, 2, 3, 6, 187, 192; appropriate technology 66, 68; definition of 4–5; hackerspaces, fablabs and makerspaces 101, 108–109, 174, 175; Honey Bee Network 153, 161; pathways 28, 197; Social Technology Network 10, 123, 128; *see also* development
Sustainable Development Goals 6, 8
sustainable livelihoods 153

Tarrow, S. 23
teaching aids 81
technology 4; access to 26; frames 23; hackerspaces, fablabs and makerspaces 102, 104, 107, 122; human-centred 37, 38–39, 49–50, 52; knowledge

production 19; movement for socially useful production 37–39, 45–49, 53, 54, 55; pathways 29; People's Science Movements 2, 88–89, 91, 92–99; social 124, 125–133, 137–142, 143, 168, 170–171; social movements 18; social shaping of 53, 54–55; sustainable development 5; technological change 19; technology transfer 46, 59, 60, 64, 71–72, 96, 147, 156; *see also* appropriate technology; information and communications technologies; science and technology
Technology Networks 45–49, 53, 175, 188
Thackara, John 9
Thatcher, Margaret 36, 50
Thatcherism 33
Thorpe, Ann 109
Thring, Meredith 34
trade unions 181; movement for socially useful production 35, 37, 39, 41–42, 54, 167, 175, 179; Social Technology Network 123
Trade-Related Aspects of Intellectual Property Rights (TRIPS) 151, 162n5
training: appropriate technology 67, 69, 72; hackerspaces, fablabs and makerspaces 103, 104, 108, 109, 112, 113, 175; movement for socially useful production 35, 45, 46, 49, 51; People's Science Movements 81, 88, 92, 95
transformation framing 177–178, 183, 185, 186, 190, 195
Transnet 43
Trias, Xavier 116, 118
Troxler, Peter 115

unemployment 33, 43, 117
Unit for the Development of Alternative Products (UDAP) 43, 44
United Kingdom: Build Brighton 111–113, 119; movement for socially useful production 12, 32–55, 167, 175–176; political economy of production 188
United Nations (UN): Stockholm summit 2; Sustainable Development Goals 6, 8
United Nations Development Programme (UNDP) 22, 68, 94
United Nations Educational, Scientific, and Cultural Organization (UNESCO) 68

United Nations Environment Programme (UNEP) 22, 59
United States 73, 110–111
Universidad de Los Andes 62, 69, 70, 79n10
universities 7, 26, 181; appropriate technology 57, 65, 66; hackerspaces, fablabs and makerspaces 109; movement for socially useful production 42; Social Technology Network 123, 128, 131, 132, 138, 140, 142
University of Manchester Institute of Science and Technology (UMIST) 49
Uruguay: appropriate technology 60, 61, 67, 71, 74, 75, 79n6; Mercosur 144n9; Social Technology Network 132, 138
Ustyuzhantseva, O. V. 162n4

values 17, 26, 29, 186, 193; framings 24, 166; hackerspaces, fablabs and makerspaces 102, 106
Varsavsky, Oscar 58
Venezuela: alternative technology 62, 71; Social Technology Network 132, 138
Visvanathan, Shiv 149, 153

Wainwright, Hilary 45, 47–48
waste management 89, 93, 124
water 3, 8; appropriate technology 60, 61, 62, 70; People's Science Movements 81; Social Technology Network 124, 126, 133, 135–137, 138, 170; *see also* sanitation
Weiler, Lars 112
Whole Earth project 101
Wildschut, Diana 113–114
Willoughby, K. W. 76
women: Honey Bee Network 148; movement for socially useful production 35–36, 38, 45, 48, 167; People's Science Movements 80, 81, 92
World Bank 22, 59, 73, 110–111
World Commission on Environment and Development 4–5
World Intellectual Property Organization (WIPO) 151

Zambrano, G. M. 65
Zijp, Harmen 113–114